D0804287

Protestants & Catholics

Do They Now Agree?

John Ankerberg & John Weldon

HARVEST HOUSE PUBLISHERS
Eugene, Oregon 97402

PROTESTANTS AND CATHOLICS: DO THEY NOW AGREE?

Copyright © 1995 by The Ankerberg Theological Research Institute
Published by Harvest House Publishers
Eugene, Oregon 97402

Library of Congress Cataloging-in-Publication Data

Ankerberg, John, 1945–
    Protestants & Catholics : do they now agree? / John Ankerberg, John Weldon.
      p.   cm.
    Includes bibliographical references.
    ISBN 1-56507-314-2
    1. Catholic Church—Doctrines—Controversial literature.   2. Catholic Church—Relations—Evangelicalism.   3. Evangelicalism—Relations—Catholic Church.   I. Weldon, John.   II. Title.   III. Title: Protestants and Catholics.
BX1765.2.A53   1995   94-45446
280'.042—dc20   CIP

Printed in the United States of America.

95   96   97   98   99   00   01   02 – 10   9   8   7   6   5   4   3   2   1

Dedication

For Mike Charbonet, Paul Dekker,
Mike Dosh, and Russell Karaviotis.

Acknowledgments

The authors extend their special gratitude to Don and Louise Ebner, Lynda Moore, and Ruth Wilson for their very kind assistance in the production of this work.

A personal statement from Dr. Ankerberg about events transpiring *after* the writing of this book

On January 19, 1995, four days before this book went to press, I participated in a private meeting with ten Evangelical Christian leaders. Among those at the meeting were individuals who had signed the *Evangelicals and Catholics Together* (ECT) statement in 1994, which declared that "Evangelicals and Catholics are brothers and sisters in Christ." It also stated, "We promise one another that we will work to deepen, build upon, and expand this pattern of convergence and cooperation."

In light of these and other proclamations made in the ECT statement (which caused the concerns discussed in this book), I and some other Evangelical leaders believed it was necessary to meet with some of the signers for clarification.

During our meeting, God graciously brought us all to agreement and reconciliation on the definition and nature of the gospel, as well as a full commitment to justification by faith alone in Jesus Christ as central to the gospel.

At the conclusion, we agreed to issue the following news release, which supplies the background for the important doctrinal statement on the next page. The doctrinal statement clarifies the intent of the Protestant leaders who signed the *Evangelicals and Catholics Together* document.

News Release

At Chuck Colson's request, a group of Evangelical leaders and theologians met on January 19, 1995 to discuss a number of issues relating to the ECT statement that was released last spring (March 1994). It was the second such meeting called by Colson. The intent of both Colson and those in attendance was to achieve a measure of understanding, clarification and harmony around the truth as recognized by historic orthodoxy.

This meeting included two signers of the ECT document in addition to Chuck Colson; they were J.I. Packer and Bill Bright. Also participating were John Ankerberg, Michael Horton, John MacArthur, R.C. Sproul, Joseph Stowell, John Woodbridge and D. James Kennedy, who hosted the meeting at Coral Ridge Presbyterian Church in Ft. Lauderdale, Florida.

Discussion focused on Evangelical distinctives, particularly the definition and nature of the gospel. The group, without reservation, affirmed its commitment to justification by faith alone in Jesus Christ as central to the gospel.

Out of this meeting has come the following statement, initially drafted by J.I. Packer, that will carry the signatures of Packer, Bright, and Colson. It is being circulated among the other Protestant signers of ECT for their signatures as well.

The doctrinal statement mentioned in the news release reads as follows:

Doctrinal Statement

We Protestants, who signed ECT, took this action to advance Christian fellowship, cooperation, and mutual trust among true Christians in the North American cultural crisis and in the worldwide task of evangelism. The same concern leads us now to elucidate our ECT commitment by stating:

1. Our para-church cooperation with evangelically committed Roman Catholics for the pursuit of agreed objectives does not imply acceptance of Roman Catholic doctrinal distinctives or endorsement of the Roman Catholic Church system.

2. We understand the statement that "we are justified by grace through faith because of Christ," in terms of the substitutionary atonement and imputed righteousness of Christ, leading to full assurance of eternal salvation; we seek to testify in all circumstances and contexts to this, the historic Protestant understanding of salvation by faith alone *(sola fide)*.

3. While we view all who profess to be Christian—Protestant and Catholic and Orthodox—with charity and hope, our confidence that anyone is truly a brother or sister in Christ depends not only on the content of his or her confession, but on our perceiving signs of regeneration in his or her life.

4. Though we reject proselytizing as ECT defines it (that is, "sheep-stealing" for denominational aggrandizement), we hold that evangelism and church planting are always legitimate, whatever forms of church life are present already.

5. We think that the further theological discussions that ECT promised should begin as soon as possible.

We make these applicatory clarifications of our commitment as supporters of ECT in order to prevent divisive misunderstandings of our beliefs and purposes.

Where We Stand Now

As a result of our meeting and this new addendum to the ECT document, where do we stand now? My own personal thoughts are:

First, this new doctrinal statement correctly recognizes *sola fide* as being essential to the gospel of Jesus Christ—the heart of our concerns.

Second, this statement rectifies what we believed to be ambiguity in the original ECT document in regard to the content of the gospel message.

Third, this statement does not extend carte blanche acceptance to any person professing Christianity in either the Catholic or Protestant communities; rather, it defines the content of the true gospel message which saves—justification through grace alone, by faith alone, in Christ alone, nothing else being necessary.

Fourth, I and the others look forward to participating in the clarification of other theological issues of concern in the days ahead.

Finally, I am thankful for our brothers who listened patiently to our concerns and were willing to affix their names to this new statement that reaffirms and clarifies the gospel, which is the life of the church.

—Dr. John F. Ankerberg
The Ankerberg Theological
Research Institute

A Personal Word

The Protestant Reformation of the sixteenth century witnessed the fragmentation of the visible church into literally hundreds of individual pieces. The unity for which Christ prayed seemed to be torn asunder, perhaps for ages to come. Repeated efforts toward reconciliation and dialogue have been attempted in order to heal the schism.

In our day of philosophical relativism and theological pluralism a climate of rapprochement between Rome and Evangelicalism has dawned. Professed Evangelicals such as Charles Colson, Bill Bright, J.I. Packer, Os Guinness, and others have closed ranks with professing Catholics to declare a new unity of faith and mission in order to work as cobelligerents against the threat of secularism. The 1994 document "Evangelicals and Catholics Together" struck a chord of harmony to this end.

What has become blurred in the new irenicism is the critical issues raised during the Reformation regarding essential points of the gospel. Is the new "peace" a godly peace or what Luther once declared a "carnal peace," the kind of peace the false prophet of Israel declared that healed the wounds of the daughter of Zion but slightly? Those prophets cried "Peace! Peace! when there was no peace" and truth was slain in the streets.

What is obscured is the reality of the past 4½ centuries of theological debate. What divided Protestants from Rome in the sixteenth century was seen by both sides as a matter of eternal significance. Luther's conviction that *sola fide* was the article upon which the Church stands or falls was countered by the Tridentine conclusion that the Reformation doctrine of justification was worthy of the anathema of the church. Both sides were playing for keeps. Both sides were convinced that the very essence of the gospel was at stake.

The issue and division was real and lasting. The ensuing years brought only further division. In one sense the issues that divided Rome and Protestantism during the Reformation have only been exacerbated since then. The decree of papal infallibility did not occur until 1870. It is in the nineteenth and twentieth centuries that the crucial dogmas of Mariology have been defined *de fide* by Rome. Though the atmosphere and tone of the debate have changed, the essential issues remain. At Vatican I Protestants were called "schismatics and heretics." At Vatican II Protestants were addressed as "separated brethren." The move away from harsh polemical language has led many people mistakenly to believe that substantive agreement on the crucial issues has been reached.

Another factor that blurs the landscape is the widespread internal fomentation that currently exists within the Roman Catholic community. In recent decades Rome has struggled with critical disputes that are rivaled in history only by the sixteenth-century struggle.

Just as Protestantism has been torn apart by the conflict between liberalism and orthodoxy, so Rome has been assailed from within. The use of the so-called *theologie nouvelle* has manifested this struggle. There is conflict between the magisterium of the Church and the Church's theologians. Hans Kung has been censured for his views. A rift is clear between the Latin wing of the Church (which dominates Catholic thinking in such nations as Italy, Spain, Portugal, and Latin America) and the Western wing of more "progressive" Catholicism (which dominates Catholic expression in Germany, Switzerland, Holland, and the United States).

At the grass roots Rome is not as monolithic as she claims to be. Polls indicate, for example, that the majority of American Roman Catholic constituents disagree with the pope's ruling on artificial birth control. Individual clerics may be found, especially in the West, who unabashedly proffer belief in justification by faith alone.

But the Roman Catholic Church remains *Roman*, both in rule and in doctrinal definition. Those who look for an official source for official teaching of Roman Catholicism still look to the Vatican for authoritative definitions. Those of us who do that may be dismissed as "Denzinger Theologians" who miss the "living faith of the church" by being locked into formal documents such as papal encyclicals and/or conciliar decrees.

But where else can we look to find the real teaching of the Roman communion save in the official declarations of their institution? An amorphous "living church" is a vagary that turns the doctrine of Rome into a waxed nose that may be formed or molded into anyone's personal preference.

This book offered by John Ankerberg and John Weldon is an attempt to set forth the crucial issues that have divided and continue to divide Roman Catholicism from historic Evangelicalism. My hope is that it will stimulate debate—the kind of debate that forces real discussion of substantive issues, issues that dare not be ignored or glossed over. Controversy, though at times odious and bloody, often has the salutary effect of bringing clarity to our understanding of the truth of God. Our times demand a clear and unambiguous understanding, definition, and confession of the biblical gospel, now more than ever.

—R.C. Sproul
President, Ligonier
Ministries
Orlando, Florida

A Personal Word

from *John MacArthur, Jr.*

The past decade has brought evangelicals and Catholics together on an unprecedented scale. The main catalyst for this movement has been our common opposition to abortion, homosexuality, and moral relativism. As political solidarity between the two groups has developed, more and more leaders on both sides are calling for spiritual union as well.

Should evangelicals now view Roman Catholicism as true Christianity? Should we presume our Catholic friends are actually spiritual brothers and sisters who love and worship the same Lord we do? Have the doctrinal differences that sparked the Protestant Reformation five hundred years ago now become moot? Is unity among professing Christians more important than sound doctrine?

The spiritual ignorance of our age has left many evangelicals ill-equipped to answer those questions. Too many on both sides have no real understanding of the historic differences between Rome and the Reformers. They don't realize that the doctrinal differences that divide us are far more important than the moral convictions we share. After all, the central issue we differ on is the gospel itself—the very thing that distinguishes true Christianity from damning heresy (Galatians 1:8,9). We dare not gloss over this matter of eternal significance.

John Ankerberg and John Weldon have done a superb job of explaining how Catholicism and evangelicalism differ with regard to the gospel. Presenting both sides evenhandedly, they call readers to judge the issues biblically. I'm very grateful for this clarion answer to the rampant confusion of our day.

—John MacArthur, Jr.
Pastor-Teacher
Grace Community Church
Sun Valley, California

A Personal Word

from D. James Kennedy

Justification by faith alone! This is that doctrine which broke the shackles from the soul of Martin Luther and set him free, exulting in his God and glorying in the mercy of Jesus Christ. This is that doctrine which he took upon his tongue and with flaming eloquence proclaimed all over Europe. This is that doctrine which became the very heartbeat of the Protestant Reformation. This is that doctrine without which there would be no Protestantism. John Calvin said, "This is the foremost pillar of religion." The great Gerhardus Vos said, "It is the pivotal point around which all else turns." The immortal Bavinck said, "This is the article of the creed by which the church either stands or falls."

The doctrine of justification is the gospel of our Lord Jesus Christ. Here the full-orbed mercy and grace of God comes into its own. But, alas, we live in a time almost like that of Luther's. The darkness of spiritual ignorance has so pervaded the minds of men that vast numbers of people in this so-called Christian America live in abject ignorance of this central teaching of the Christian faith; this central doctrine of the Bible. I think it can be safely said that without at least a rudimentary knowledge of the basic principle involved in this doctrine, no person will ever see heaven. Truly by this the church stands or falls and our souls stand or fall with it. If this be the case then, indeed, most of the church is sadly fallen in our day. And how great is that fall! From that time, only 450 years ago, when this was the clarion call—the trumpet blast—that woke countless hundreds of thousands from their death in sin unto life eternal, we have come to our time when in myriads of churches across our land the question, "What is justification?" would meet merely with a raised eyebrow and a quizzical look. "The just shall live by faith" was the watch-word of the Protestant Reformation.

This new book by John Ankerberg and John Weldon examines the meaning of this crucial doctrine at a time when current confusion and controversy are crying out for a reclarification of this great truth.

13

In this doctrine lies the truth that answers the greatest need that man has: How can man be rightly related to God? In the book of Job, probably the oldest book of the Bible, Job cries out from the depths of his heart, asking how a sinful man can ever stand in the presence of a holy God. This is the cry that has been wrung from the blanched lips of countless millions of penitent sinners down through the centuries.

This book gives the biblical answer to that age-long cry.

—D. James Kennedy, Ph.D.
Senior Minister, Coral Ridge
Presbyterian Church
Fort Lauderdale, Florida

Contents

I am astonished that you are so quickly deserting the one who called you by the grace of Christ and are turning to a different gospel— which is really no gospel at all. Evidently some people are throwing you into confusion and are trying to pervert the gospel of Christ. But even if we or an angel from heaven should preach a gospel other than the one we preached to you, let him be eternally condemned!

As we have already said, so now I say again: If anybody is preaching to you a gospel other than what you accepted, let him be eternally condemned!

Am I now trying to win the approval of men, or of God? Or am I trying to please men?

—*Galatians 1:6-10*

.1.

The Winds of Change

On March 29, 1994, wire services around the world broadcast the conclusions of an unofficial declaration that was signed by 40 leading Evangelicals and Roman Catholics titled "Evangelicals and Catholics Together: The Christian Mission in the Third Millennium." This report begins by stating, "We are Evangelical Protestants and Roman Catholics who have been led through prayer, study, and discussion to common convictions about Christian faith and mission."[1]

It continues:

> Evangelicals and Catholics are brothers and sisters in Christian.... We recognize that we are called by God to a fuller realization of our unity in the body of Christ.[2]

This new unity is said to lead to joint action:

> We are called and we are therefore resolved to explore patterns of working and witnessing together in order to advance the one mission of Christ. We promise one another that we will work to deepen, build upon, and expand this pattern of convergence and cooperation.[3]

And:

> We are bound together in contending against all that opposes Christ and his cause.[4]

Finally:

The mission that we embrace together is the necessary consequence of the faith that we affirm together.[5]

Evangelicals and Catholics Together?

Anyone knowledgeable about history realizes that for 450 years Protestants and Catholics have been divided. Hearing that an agreement has now been reached between these two groups, one would expect those claiming agreement to provide clear explanations of how past differences have been resolved.

Specifically, one would be looking for an explanation of the differences over the nature of salvation, which centers on the doctrine of justification. Martin Luther believed that justification by faith was the watershed doctrine upon which the church stands or falls.

Did the two sides accomplish this? At first glance there seems to be hope that they did. The statement declares that the Catholics and Protestants who signed this agreement have reached "common convictions about Christian faith and mission," enough so that they are ready to recognize each other as "brothers and sisters in Christ."

This being the case, all Roman Catholics will want to read this document to learn how past issues have been resolved. After all, they have been taught from childhood that "the Catholic Church is the one true Church founded by Jesus Christ for the salvation of all mankind."[6] Therefore, Catholics will assume that it is the Evangelical community which has finally seen the light and changed its mind.

On the other hand, Evangelicals will want to find out on what points the Catholics finally have realized they were wrong. After all, Evangelicals assume their leaders would never compromise the truth which they have publicly taught.

Which side, then, finally admitted it has been wrong all these years? You will learn the answer in the chapters that follow.

Have the Basic Roman Doctrines Changed?

One might be tempted to think the basic Roman Catholic doctrines have changed. If agreement has actually been reached between Catholics and Evangelicals, one could assume it is probably because the basic doctrines of Rome were altered due to the internal change taking place within Catholicism or because of the different kinds of scholarship employed in the Church. For example, there are scholars who are liberal, those who are conservative and traditional, and even those who are mystical. It would be easy to conclude that this diverse mixture of scholarship impacted official doctrine.

But the truth is that most of the influential segments of Catholicism and its scholarship are still bound by the decrees of the Church councils. Neither internal doctrines (see Appendix E) nor modern scholarship have changed. The basic doctrines have not changed because the official documents of the Church have not changed official Catholic theology.

Anyone who attempts to evaluate modern Roman Catholicism can do so only by evaluating what is on the books—the Council of Trent, Vatican I and II, papal decrees, authoritative texts, etc. These tell us what Roman Catholicism officially believes and teaches.

Issues of a New Era

But make no mistake, the recent "Evangelicals and Catholics Together" statement is an important document for many reasons. It has not only been circulated among top Vatican officials, but it has also received the apparent blessing of leading Evangelical figures on the world scene, in addition to those who signed the document itself.[7]

Are we truly entering into a new era in which Catholics and Evangelicals can agree that they share a common faith? Are the barriers of the past now torn down, so that Catholics and Protestants can freely worship together in the same churches, no longer questioning one another's faith? Are Protestants really part of the body of Christ and heirs of full salvation apart from Rome? Are Catholics really brothers and sisters in Christ whom Evangelicals have neglected for far too long?

In this book we will show you how the agreement answered these questions. We will also examine the document's conclusions in light of the Bible. Since both conservative Catholics and conservative Protestants believe the Bible to be the Word of God, both can welcome an investigation into what the Bible says about all of these matters. Rome, of course, declares that all its doctrines are biblical and that therefore all Catholics must believe them.

As Catholic apologist Karl Keating correctly points out in *What Catholics Really Believe—Setting the Record Straight*, "Catholics are required to hold and believe all the declared doctrines of the Church."[8]

So is the new alliance between Evangelicals and Catholics a blessing that will help unite the churches? Or is the new alliance something else? In his book *Crossing the Threshold of Hope,* Pope John Paul II stated, "Although the Catholic Church knows it has received *the fullness of the means of salvation,* it rejoices when other Christian communities join her in preaching the Gospel.... The Church wants to preach the Gospel *together with all who believe in Christ.*"[9] But is this possible?

The end result of the sixteenth-century Reformation determined the future of the church. Likewise, the final outcome of the current alliance may dictate not only the nature of the church that is to be, but its overall spiritual health as well. It may dictate the kinds of churches our children grow up in.

Join us as we examine the new alliance and learn the answers to the important questions it raises.

.2.

The Dividing Issues

If any man stands before God, he'd better have a good lawyer.
—Peter Marshall

*N*early every murderer on death row, approaching his final days, asks his lawyer to appeal to the governor of the state for a pardon. The governor has the authority to officially issue a pardon to any condemned man if he believes there is reason to do so. The concept of a legal pardon leads us into the idea and meaning of the joyous biblical term "justification."

Biblically, to be "justified" means a sinner is pardoned or declared legally acquitted by God from any and all punishment due him because of the sins he has committed. If you would like to know how the Bible says God will issue an official pardon for you, then you should be interested in the information that follows.

The apostle Paul believed justification by faith was the heart of the gospel itself (Romans 1:17). Martin Luther called justification the doctrine on which the church stands or falls. It can be truthfully stated that this doctrine makes Christianity unique from all the other religions in the world.

This doctrine also caused the split between Catholics and Protestants in the Reformation of the sixteenth century and has been the central dividing point ever since. If there is to be a biblical agreement as to unity between Catholics and Protestants, they must reconcile their differences over this crucial doctrine of justification.

To know whether the leaders who drafted the "Evangelicals and Catholics Together" statement actually have reconciled their differences surrounding the doctrine, we will look at the issues which have divided Catholics and Protestants for 450 years.

The doctrine of justification deals with the question, "How can a sinful person be accepted by a holy and righteous God?" Both Roman Catholics and Protestants agree that a correct interpretation of this doctrine is vital, because if people seek to be forgiven by God in a way in which God says they cannot be forgiven, then, of course, they won't be forgiven.

Both Catholics and Protestants also agree that the benefits of Christ's death on the cross are necessary for a sinner to receive justification. These benefits involve what God intended for Christ to accomplish on the cross, such as the forgiveness of sins. God judged Christ in our place so that through faith in Him we could be forgiven. His death atoned for or paid the price of our sins. Where Catholics and Protestants disagree concerns the question, "How do the benefits of Christ become personally applied?"

The Source of Justification

According to the Protestant view, when God declares or pronounces that a sinful person is fully pardoned because of Christ's atoning death, that person is, in fact, legally acquitted and now viewed as standing justified or declared righteous before God.

This view is based on the Scripture passage of Romans 4:3. Here the apostle Paul states that "Abraham believed God" when God made certain promises to him. And because Abraham believed God, the Bible says God "reckoned," "imputed," or "credited" righteousness to him. That is, God declared Abraham's status was that of one who was now completely righteous in His sight.

For Luther and the Protestant Reformers, then, the basis of Abraham's justification is found in God's declaration—that He fully justified Abraham the moment he believed. This is known as "forensic justification." "Forensic" comes from the Latin word for "forum." In the ancient Roman forum, a court could meet and make judicial declarations; public issues were spoken and debated. So "forensics" has to do with speech, as well as legal declarations or official pronouncements made in court.

The reason why Protestants label their position "forensic justification" is because for them the ultimate basis of justification or pardon is the "spoken declaration"—actually the "verdict" or the "legal pronouncement" which God makes concerning the sinner. Forensic justification is, therefore, an act that God does outside of man. It is the judicial pronouncement of God about a sinful man that, as a result of placing faith in Christ, he now stands before God having been given the status of justness.

Now the Roman Catholic Church considers this type of justification a *legal fiction* because it involves God calling a person "just" who in and of himself is not just. The question Catholicism raises is, "How can God declare a man to be just when, in fact, he remains a sinner?"

This issue has its roots in the dispute stemming from Luther's famous slogan: "at the same time just and a sinner" *(simul justus et peccator)*. What Luther meant was that when God sees that a man truly believes in Christ, he then declares that man justified legally in His sight. But at the same time, the pardoned sinner is still a sinner in and of himself (see Romans 7:19,23,25; James 3:2; 1 John 1:8).

Catholicism, on the other hand, believes that God only declares a man to be just after a man works in cooperation with God's grace and has actually *become* just *in and of himself*. In other words, God will not declare a "smelly ashtray" to be a "beautiful rose."

So Catholicism believes that the Protestant concept of justification involves a very serious problem for the character of God—that of calling someone *just* who in and of himself really is not just.

How Is a Person Declared Righteous?

To understand why the Protestant Reformers did not believe forensic justification maligned God's character we must more closely examine their view of God calling unjust people just.

According to the Bible, when a man believes, he becomes united with Christ. Philippians 3:8,9 states, "That I may gain Christ and be found *in him*, not having a righteousness of my own that comes from the law, but that which is through faith in Christ" (emphasis added). Because God sees the sinner standing with or "in Christ," Christ's righteousness becomes his—that is, it is added to the sinner's account (see also 2 Corinthians 5:21).

To the Protestant Reformers this meant there is a "synthesis," a combining or adding of something to the sinner as he stands before God. Namely, the sinner appears before God in union with Christ.

The biblical imagery depicts the believer clothed in the righteousness provided by God (Isaiah 61:10). The righteousness and merits of Christ cover him and are given to him.

When God declares a sinner just, He does so because He sees him standing with or in Christ. God does not declare a person just because He looks at the person's character and good deeds; this has nothing to do with it. Rather, it is the unlimited merits of Christ freely given to the believer which constitutes a man's righteousness—not the merits of the man himself.

As Paul preached, "Through Jesus the forgiveness of sins is proclaimed to you. Through him everyone who believes is justified [declared by God legally acquitted] from everything you could not be justified from by the law of Moses" (Acts 13:38,39). Justification, then, is not a legal fiction, but a legal fact. This is why God can be both "just and the justifier of the one who has faith in Jesus" (Romans 3:26 NASB).

How does Catholicism respond to this? The Catholic Church believes God declares a person just only *after* He analyzes the person and finds real righteousness and real justness *within the person*.

From the Catholic viewpoint, because of His righteous character, God cannot declare an ashtray to be a rose, but He will call a true rose a rose. In other words, God only calls a person righteous when that person really is righteous.

Is Righteousness Imputed or Infused?

Protestants believe that the merits of Christ are credited or transferred from the account of Jesus, so to speak, and placed into the account of the believer. The moment a person believes in Christ, God sees him standing "with or in Christ," where all the riches and merits of Christ are added (or *imputed*) to the sinner's account, thus overwhelming and canceling out any of the sinner's debts.

A synthesis has taken place: Christ and His merits have been added to the account of the believer. The believer pleads nothing of his own before God; rather, he pleads everything of Christ—that is, Christ's righteous life and atoning death. Therefore, it is on the basis of the merits of Christ alone, which are imputed to the sinner, that God declares him justified—that is, officially pardoned (forgiven) of his sins.

To illustrate, imagine that you are somehow overdrawn 10,000 dollars in your bank account. You know you are in trouble. But before your banker has time to notify you, Ross Perot calls your banker. Ross Perot is a billionaire, and he tells your banker he wants to join his account to yours. What belongs to him, now belongs to you. When his account is transferred or credited to your account, what happens to your debt? It is covered by Ross Perot's immeasurable riches. What happens to your status? You are now treated as a billionaire—even though you never earned a penny of it.

In justification, God "deposits" the righteousness of Jesus Christ to the believer's account. That is, God imputes, credits, or transfers to the believer the moral righteousness of His own Son.

What does Catholicism believe at this point? Something entirely different: Catholicism teaches that first, there is the grace of God that assists the will to have faith, known as *prevenient* grace. This is *infused* or placed into the sinner. Then, when this grace or power is given and the sinner cooperates with it, Catholicism teaches that the sinner can, by effort, arrive at a state of justness within. Only then will God declare that person to be just because he has, in fact, become just.

Catholicism is not teaching a crass view of justification—that a person in and of himself can live a holy life and earn justification entirely in his own strength. But Catholicism is teaching that by using the power of Christ, a person can arrive at a point where he will become just enough within that God will declare him justified.

To summarize, Catholicism believes the basis of a man's justification is the righteousness which God finds within him as a result of a man's cooperating with God's power. For Protestantism, the basis of justification is Christ's righteousness alone, which is judicially imputed or given to the sinner apart from anything the sinner does.

According to the Protestant view, when a man places his faith in Christ, at that moment, God, the righteous Judge, passes judgment on his sin problem. That is, He justifies him. God's justification takes place at the point of time at which a man believes. It is a once-for-all divine act, God's final judgment, brought into the present.

Once passed, God's justifying sentence about the sinner is irrevocable. To say God justifies is to say God has issued a verdict of acquittal concerning the sinner. It is a legal pronouncement that forever excludes the sinner from receiving any punishment for the sins he has committed during his life.

If justification settles the legal status of the person who has broken God's law, what is the ground or basis for God justifying the ungodly (Romans 4:5)? After all, isn't God righteous in all His ways (Psalm 145:17)? Isn't He "a God . . . without iniquity" (Deuteronomy 32:4 KJV)? How can God be righteous when He declares sinful men to now be righteous?

The answer is that He justifies sinners on a just basis, namely, by Jesus Christ acting as the sinner's substitute. God's law is not altered, suspended, or flouted for any sinner's justification because Jesus Christ perfectly kept the law during His life. When He died on the cross, He bore the penalty of the law in men's place (Galatians 3:13) to make propitiation for their sins (Romans 3:25).

This explains why Scripture declares God's righteousness is actually vindicated by the atonement, "that He might be just and the justifier of the one who has faith in Jesus" (Romans 3:26 NASB).

What Christ has purchased for us by His death is applied to us the moment that God declares us justified.

The transfer of righteousness from Christ to the sinner is expressed by the classical Protestant phrase, "the imputation of Christ's righteousness." God reckons or imputes righteousness to sinners not because He accounts them to have kept His law personally (which would be a false judgment), but because God reckons sinners to be united to the One who actually did keep it, namely, Christ (and that is a true judgment). Once God has uttered the verdict of justification concerning the sinner, He is then able to set apart or sanctify that person to serve Him from that moment on.

In Protestantism, spiritual transformation within a person by the Holy Spirit comes as a *result* of justification.[1] Sanctification or spiritual growth never is the means by which a man *attains* justification. In Catholicism, however, sanctification, or the inner transformation of the person to live a righteous life is that process by which a man eventually *gains* justification.

According to this view, God puts His sanctifying grace into man by infusion, whereupon the man starts to be disposed toward God. Catholicism teaches that by using the power of Christ that has been infused into him, a man can arrive at a state of justness where it is "congruous" or "fitting" for God to declare that he is just.

But Catholicism says that this process of sanctification has only led to the beginning or *initial* state of justification, not to the *final* state of justification. (We will look at these two states of justification shortly.)

Throughout life, the faithful Catholic is to continue in his sanctification—cooperating with the power of Christ within and participating in the different Church sacraments so that his works of merit and his faith in Christ join together to hopefully attain God's *final* justification.

What Is God's Basis for Judgment?

This next related point is very important. Protestants believe that man has no merit of his own whatsoever that can dispose God to justify him. Justification is not God's judgment based on the personal righteousness within the sinner or any kind of good works a man can do.

Rather, justification is God's judgment based on the work of Christ at the cross in whom the sinner believes. The Bible says, "But now a righteousness from God, *apart* from the law, has been made known. . . . This righteousness *from* God *comes through faith in Jesus Christ to all who believe*" (Romans 3:21,22, emphasis added).

Elsewhere the apostle Paul emphatically states, "He saved us, not on the basis of deeds which we have done in righteousness, [either those deeds done in the power of Christ or those deeds done in our own power] but according to his mercy" (Titus 3:5). Thus the status of true righteousness before God is attained only on the basis of faith in Christ. This is the essence of the Christian gospel.

As noted earlier, in contrast to this, Catholicism teaches that working in cooperation with the infused power of Christ within a person, the sinner can live a life that is not absolutely perfect, but a life that is meritorious enough that it makes it "fitting" for God to grant justification. Catholics term this "congruous merit."

This whole issue is very important in Catholicism because a person's good works done in the power of Christ are *necessary* for salvation and must be present *before* justification takes place. These good works are a condition for receiving God's justification; without them the prospect of attaining heaven cannot be had. As Pope John Paul II states, "a good life is the *condition* of salvation."[2]

Can Justification Be Lost?

Historically, the Protestant Reformers argued that since a man's justification depended solely on God's never-ending favor and Christ's meritorious life and atoning death—and not upon anything which a man can do—a person could not lose his justification before God.

Since Christ has already successfully lived a perfect life and died to pay for all of man's sins, nothing will ever change this fact. Christ is the unchanging basis of a man's justification.

Therefore, once a person believed in Christ, he was entirely and eternally secure. In essence, because salvation was a *gift* from God based solely on Christ's atoning death, the number of good or bad deeds in a person's life would never change a person's perfect standing before God.[3]

Across from the Protestant position declaring that a person "can't lose justification" is the Roman Catholic position emphasizing that a person "can lose justification."

Catholicism believes that the justifying grace within a man *can* be obliterated by his committing "mortal" sin. Roman Catholicism distinguishes between venial sins (sins that are not so serious that they involve the destruction of justifying grace) and mortal sins (sins so serious that the grace of justification can be destroyed within a man).

If a man commits a mortal sin and destroys his justification, in order for him to regain it Catholicism teaches he must come to the Church via the sacrament of penance, which involves confession, absolution, and satisfaction. (We discuss these later.)

Catholics who believe in Christ are constantly reminded that their justification depends on their works *cooperating* with Christ. Catholics are taught that a man cannot know his own heart. Because he is subject to so many temptations, he may commit a variety of mortal sins, any one of which could destroy his justification.

That is why in the sixteenth century the Council of Trent warned, "Each one, when he considers himself and his own weakness and indisposition, may have fear and apprehension concerning his own grace; since no one can know with the certainty of faith, which cannot be subject to error, that he has obtained the grace of God."[4] So for Catholicism a man *can lose* his justification, which means he *can never be certain* he will someday be in heaven.

"Faith Alone" or "Faith and Works"?

The sixth major point representing the views of Protestants concerning justification is the famous words of the Reformation: "by faith alone."

For Protestants, faith is not merely an intellectual assent to certain facts about Christ's salvation; rather, faith is a knowledge of the facts plus a total trust and resting of one's eternal destiny in Jesus Christ, who is the sole reason and grounds upon which God justifies us.

For Protestants, justification is an act that takes place in a single moment—the moment when the sinner *through faith* trusts Christ completely. At that moment, the benefits of Christ are applied or imputed to the sinner's life and he is officially judged and declared by God to stand in His sight as completely and finally justified.

Faith is an instrument by which a man is saved, but it is also an act not deserving of merit. Picture a burning building with a man trapped on the third floor. As the flames approach him, he is urged to jump and to have faith in the firemen below that they will catch him in their net.

Now if he jumps, his faith will be that which leads him to trust in the firemen's ability to catch him. But his faith will not be that which actually saves him. It is only the instrument which leads him to trust the firemen. It will be the firemen holding the net who actually save him.

For Protestants, it is not the instrument of faith which saves us; rather, it is Christ in whom we believe who saves us. Faith merely reaches out to Christ who does the rescuing. Faith leads us to place ourselves into Christ's hands (see John 10:28).

Consider once again the man jumping off the burning building. Do you think the man's "faith" would save him if he discovered after jumping off the third floor that the firemen were only standing in a circle and were not holding any net? At that point, it would be very clear that his faith could not save him. What the man needs is a real net with real firemen holding it. The same is true spiritually.

It is not a man's faith that provides his salvation; rather, it is Christ alone who provides salvation. Only Christ has the strength to do all the saving. Believing faith is confidence in *Christ's* power to save and forgive, and our total reliance on Him to do so.

Why should anyone think that if he reaches out to Christ by faith and asks Christ to save him that his request helps Christ provide salvation and is deserving of meritorious credit? That's why Protestants believe that faith is only an instrument and that salvation is by faith alone, involving no works on our part.

In contrast to the Protestant words "faith alone" is the Catholic concept of "faith plus works." For Catholicism, faith is required, but Catholicism strongly objects to saying that faith alone is all that God requires for Him to justify a person. In addition to faith, Catholicism also requires works.

Catholics and Protestants completely split on this issue. Their dispute centers on some key passages in the New Testament, most notably the third and fourth chapters of Romans and the second chapter of the epistle of James. We will examine the argument of both sides in our next chapter.

For now, the chart below summarizes the entirely opposite views that Catholics and Protestants have believed and taught concerning justification.

Protestant	Catholic
1. Forensic	1. Legal fiction
2. Synthetic	2. Analytic
3. Imputation	3. Infusion

4. No human merit	4. Congruous merit
5. Can't lose it	5. Can lose it
6. Faith alone	6. Faith and works are necessary

Knowing these points of disagreement, are you a bit curious to learn how the leaders who signed the "Evangelicals and Catholics Together" statement were able to work out these differences? After all, they have said they now agree on enough issues to recognize each other as brothers and sisters in Christ. To see if they actually worked things out, and to discover which side changed its mind or compromised on what has historically been believed, we have examined their statement in chapters 12 and 13 of this book. But until we arrive there, we have carefully sought to document exactly what the Roman Catholic Church believes and teaches. With this background you will be able to reach your own conclusions.

▪3▪

The Apostle James

We maintain that a man is justified by faith apart from works of the Law.

—Romans 3:28 NASB

You see that a man is justified by works, and not by faith alone.

—James 2:24 NASB

*I*n a legal case, it is easy for a jury to be confused over particular points of evidence when experts on both sides offer seemingly conflicting testimony. But in court, initially conflicting testimony can often be resolved by tougher cross-examination and/or the introduction of new and better evidence.

In the historic battle over the doctrine of justification, the Catholic Church claims that a man is ultimately justified by works and not by faith alone. On the other hand, the Protestant church says the Bible supports their view of justification by faith alone. Who is right?

To answer these questions, we will examine the evidence closely by presenting what Protestants believe the apostle Paul is teaching in the book of Romans and then evaluate what the Catholic Church claims is taught in the book of James.

An Apparent Contradiction

At first glance, a seeming contradiction exists. The apostle Paul states, "For we maintain that a man is justified by faith apart from works of the Law" (Romans 3:28 NASB). On the other hand, the apostle James states, "You see that a man is justified by works, and not by faith alone" (James 2:24 NASB). Do the apostles contradict each other in their teachings on justification? Let's examine what each apostle says.

Romans chapter 3 beginning at verse 28 (NASB) says: "For we maintain that a man is justified by faith apart from works of the Law." Protestants believe that since Paul says that a man is justified by faith *apart* from the works of the law, then one can only conclude that justification must be by faith alone. There are no other options.

Then Paul builds his case for justification by faith without works by giving a historical example, where he appeals to the case of Abraham. He writes, "For what does the Scripture say? 'And Abraham believed God, and it was reckoned to him as righteousness'" (Romans 4:3 NASB). Once again the word "reckoned" means "counted," or "imputed" (i.e., "placed to the account" of Abraham).

After citing Abraham, Paul argues, "Now to the one who works, his wage is not reckoned as a favor, but as what is due. But to the one who does not work, but believes in Him who justifies the ungodly"—notice he says God justifies "the ungodly," not those righteous within—"his faith is reckoned [or imputed] as righteousness" (verses 4,5 NASB).

Now, what Paul is very clearly saying is that when Abraham believed God, *that* was the time he was justified. In other words, "Abraham believed God, and it was right *then* counted to him as righteousness."

So, the apostle Paul links his statement from chapter 3, "We are justified by faith apart from works of the law," with the historical situation of Abraham to prove his case that a man is declared justified by God the moment he believes.

Paul labors this point in Romans 5:1. Here he says that the basis of God's justifying a man is by faith alone in Christ and has nothing to do with a man's works. "Therefore, since we *have been* justified [officially declared righteous] through faith, we *have peace* with God through our Lord Jesus Christ, through whom we have gained access by faith into this grace in which we now stand" (emphasis added).

The Roman Catholic Church counters this teaching of justification by faith alone with an appeal to the passage in James: "You see that a man is justified by works, and not by faith alone."

Roman Catholics say, "Can the Bible make it any clearer? Here you are going around teaching that justification is by faith alone and yet we have a statement from the apostle James that says, 'You see that justification is by works, and *not* by faith alone.' And what's more, James appeals to Abraham, the very historical figure to which the apostle Paul appealed, to prove his point."

Catholics believe this verse in James refers not to the *initial* phase of justification, which they accept is by grace, but to the progressive phase of justification which leads to final and ultimate salvation by faith and *works of merit* (see chapters 4 and 6).

Start with Definitions

Are the two apostles teaching different doctrines?

No, and here is why. First, we need to realize that the word "justified" is not defined the same way in Romans as it is in James. The error that many people make is to assume that "justified" has only one meaning in the Bible. But Jesus Himself used the word "justified" in a different sense than the apostle Paul. In Romans, Paul uses the word "justified" (Gk. *dikaioō*) to mean "fully acquitted" or "brought into right standing." In Luke 7:35 (KJV) Jesus uses the same word but gives it a different meaning. He says, "Wisdom is justified of all her children." Catholics would agree that here Jesus is not saying that wisdom is brought into right standing or pardon with God *through* or *because of* her children. Rather it means simply that wisdom is proved right or vindicated by the fruit it produces.

We hope you can see that the sense of the word "justified" here in Luke is not the same use of the term by Paul in the book of Romans.* If you see the difference here, you may see how it is also possible for James to use the word "justify" in a different sense than Paul.

In examining a given use of the word "justify," we must be careful to ascertain the overall context of the passage. In other words, in comparing Scripture with Scripture, the overall context should clearly indicate what meaning of a word is meant. The question is, "What meaning of 'justify' is found in James?"

In chapter 2 the apostle James is answering the question, "How can someone tell whether or not a person has a true faith?" He

---

* The Greek word used in Luke 7:35 is *dikaioō*, but it obviously has a different application than in Paul's writings. This is why in Luke 7:35 the NASB translates the KJV "justify" as "vindicated" and the NIV translates it as "proved right." Thus, James uses the same meaning Jesus assigned to "justify" in His proverb given in Luke. It means "to vindicate." To vindicate means "to justify by evidence or results; to prove (a thing) to be valid." James is declaring that works vindicate faith and prove it genuine.

introduces this topic with the following question: "What use is it, my brethren, if a man says he has faith, but he has no works? Can that faith save him?" (James 2:14 NASB).

Notice, James does not say, "What use is it if a man has faith?"

Rather, James says, "What use is it, my brethren, if a man *says* he has faith?" (emphasis added). James is pointing out that there is a difference between people who only *profess* faith and those who actually *possess* real faith. The difference is that one person merely claims he has faith, but the other person actually has works that prove his faith is genuine. Thus, James is asking the question, "Can the mere profession of faith save anyone?" His answer is clearly, "No."

Works from Living Faith

Luther and the Reformers agreed. They believed that a living faith will always result in obedience and works. Works do not bring justification, but they do flow from it. Works are the results that show that a man has a true and genuine faith. So a faith that has no works is a dead faith. It is not genuine.

This is the very point James makes as he continues his argument: "If a brother or sister is without clothing and in need of daily food, and one of you says to them, 'Go in peace, be warmed and be filled,' and yet you do not give them what is necessary for their body, what use is that? Even so faith, if it has no works, is dead, being by itself (James 2:15-17 NASB).

Here, James is pointing out an obvious truth: If a brother or sister in Christ needs clothing and food, then for a Christian to merely say to them, "Go in peace, be warmed and be filled," but to do nothing for their needs, is sheer hypocrisy. In other words, the professing Christian who gives no assistance at all to a real Christian in need—other than lip service—cannot have been sincere in his claim to have real faith. If he really meant what he said, then he would have done something to help.

This is why Luther said, "Justification is by faith alone, but not by the faith that *is* alone." By this he meant, first, justification is secured solely on the basis of Christ and what He did at the cross, not by our works. Second, genuine faith will always result in good works flowing from it (Ephesians 2:8-10).

James continues: "But someone will say, 'You have faith; I have deeds.' Show me your faith without deeds, and I will show you my faith by what I do" (James 2:18).

James argues here that it is wrong to assume there are "faith" Christians and "deeds" Christians, as if there were two separate categories of Christian believers. In other words, it is false and wrong to claim that faith and works can exist independent of one another. James' irony is evident when he next asks, "Show me your faith without deeds"—something that is impossible for any person to do. In essence, James is driving home the point that anyone who says he has faith should prove it is real by showing the good works that vindicate his faith.

Faith Is Not Mere Knowledge

Then, in James' day, apparently some people equated faith with knowledge. For example, all orthodox Jews said they believed in the well-known Jewish creed, the Shema, that "God is One." But James shows that mere acceptance of a creed, or even a great intellectual knowledge, is not the kind of faith which saves a person. With sarcasm dripping from his pen, he writes, "You believe that God is one. You do well; the demons also believe, and shudder" (James 2:19 NASB).

Intellectual belief alone only puts one on an equal basis with the demons who also believe, but obviously they are not saved. Paradoxically, one of the Catholic definitions of faith is mere intellectual assent to the doctrines of the Church—the very point which James illustrates to show what faith is *not*. Such a faith, James says, cannot be genuine faith. Why?

Because, as James argues, the mere intellectual acceptance of certain truths without genuine trust in Christ as Savior is demonic (verse 19), useless (verse 20), and dead (verse 26).

Of course, faith includes knowing facts about Christ and how He died for our sins, and then believing those facts are true. But most importantly, a true faith is a *committing* of oneself to Christ.

It is like the man on a tightrope who wheeled a wheelbarrow six times over Niagara Falls. When he asked the crowd, "How many of you think I can do it again?" they all thought that he could. But when he said, "Well, then, which one of you wants to jump into the wheelbarrow and let me take you across?" of course, there were no volunteers. The people believed in the man intellectually, but they were not willing to commit themselves to him.

Faith is a committing of oneself to Christ totally and completely— really trusting and relying on Christ for your eternal destiny. This kind of real faith in Christ always results in works and obedience.

That is why James continues by saying, "But are you willing to recognize, you foolish fellow, that faith without works is useless?" (James 2:20 NASB).

The word "foolish" here means "empty" and refers to a deficiency in thought that is not only intellectual but also errant in theological and moral content. James describes the person who does not have the right view of faith as lacking comprehension of spiritual truth. The person does not see that faith without deeds is useless.

In the next verse James gives two Old Testament examples to illustrate what he has been saying. He first points to Abraham and then to Rahab. "Was not Abraham our father justified by works, when he offered up Isaac his son on the altar?" (James 2:21 NASB).

Here James cites Abraham as an example of one who proves what real faith is. James uses the word "justified" in the same sense Jesus did in Luke 7:35—that Abraham's works *vindicated* his faith.

Again, the Reformers agreed. They believed that the result, the inevitable fruit of a true faith, would always be works and obedience. And one's good works would vindicate or show that the person had a real faith.

Faith Consummated by Works

James continues, "You see that faith was working with his works, and as a result of the works, faith was perfected" (James 2:22 NASB).

When James says Abraham's faith was perfected, he means it was consummated, completed, or realized—it fulfilled itself through the works that it produced. He does not mean that Abraham's faith was previously defective and was made perfect by works as a kind of addition from without, for the works themselves were inspired by faith, and faith cooperated with them. Rather, James is saying faith is strengthened and matured by works that exercise it.

In verse 23 he says, "And the Scripture was fulfilled which says, 'And Abraham believed God, and it was reckoned to him as righteousness,' and he was called the friend of God" (NASB).

These words show James *agrees* with Paul that in Genesis 15 (the words just quoted above) Abraham's belief in God was a genuine and real faith because God imputed to him righteousness and he was called the friend of God. But *in addition*, to prove his point that a genuine faith will always produce good works, he cites Genesis 22, where God puts Abraham to the test with Isaac. For James' purposes of illustration, it is here that Abraham demonstrates or shows the reality of his faith. Notice that Paul and James refer to the life of Abraham in a different context here. Paul cites Genesis 15 where Abraham *first* believed God and was declared righteous. James refers to Genesis 22, Abraham's sacrifice of Isaac, which occurred *30 years later*. Obviously, James could not have been teaching that Abraham was "justified" in the sense of being declared righteous in Genesis 22 when Paul clearly teaches Abraham was justified by God in Genesis 15—30 years earlier. But in Genesis 22 Abraham's faith *is* clearly vindicated because no one could do what Abraham did with Isaac unless his faith were genuine.

Thus, James says, "Abraham is justified by his works," not in the sense of being brought into right relationship with God (the sense used in Romans), but in the sense that his faith is justified (vindicated) by his works. Again, his works prove he had a real faith.

James concludes this argument with verse 24 (NASB): "You see that a man is justified by works and not by faith alone." Again, all this means is that a man is never justified by the faith that is entirely alone and has no works.

This is the very reason Paul appeals to Abraham in Genesis 15, stating that Abraham was justified the moment he believed in God. His faith was real. It was authentic. And because only God can see the heart, He knew Abraham's faith was real and, therefore, justified him apart from any works.

In essence, Paul is writing about a person being justified *before God*, while James is writing about a man being justified *before men*. Men cannot see another person's heart as God can. The only way men can tell that someone has a genuine faith is by seeing his changed life—in other words, by the person's works.

Thus, justification before *God* is by faith alone; justification (or vindication) before *men* is by works.

Both Apostles Agree

Paul and James are in agreement doctrinally. Based on how Jesus used the term "justified," both apostles agree that a man is justified by faith alone before God. They also agree that a genuine faith will always result in a changed life, in works of obedience. But the works of obedience do not bring justification before God; rather, works flow from true justification and demonstrate that a man's faith is real.

We would agree with Dr. R.C. Sproul who comments as follows:

James' concept is not contrary to Paul's. But once you assume the Roman Catholic interpretation, there is no conceivable manner under the sun that James can be harmonized with Paul. Unfortunately, the manner in which the Roman Catholic Church has dealt with this is to avoid Paul like the plague. They have made serious attempts at harmonization, but I believe it has been a miserable failure every time it is tried.[1]

Standard Greek and English commentaries on James 2:21 and 2:24, many of which can be found in Catholic seminaries, agree that James is not teaching "justification by works," as Catholics maintain:

St. James never says that a man is not justified by faith.[2]

"...justified, and not by faith" only [means]—i.e., by faith *severed from works*, its proper fruits.... Faith... alone is the ground of justification.[3]

...*dikaioutai* here, as in v. 21, does not refer to justification by faith before God but to *the proof of faith* before men.[4]

The wholly false deduction... that there is a radical contradiction between [James and Paul]... is due to a failure to see that James is not using the word *justified* with reference to that occasion alluded to by Paul (Romans 4:3...).... James is here speaking not of this original imputation of righteousness to Abraham by virtue of his faith, but of the infallible proof [in Genesis 22]... that the faith that resulted in that imputation was real faith.... The inevitable conclusion is that, while it is faith that justifies, for James never denies this fundamental truth, faith is never static.... In other words, the life of sanctification dates from the moment a man is justified by faith [alone].... The life of sanctification is not a life of faith only; it is a life of what might be called faith-obedience.[5]

In conclusion, James does not ever contradict Paul; if he did, it would not be possible for us to trust anything God has said. James only emphasizes that faith and works are inseparable—not for salvation, but for proof of a genuine faith before men—as the entire context of James reveals.[6]

.4.

The Official
Catholic Standard

*Although some Catholics . . . have adopted the "gospel" of faith
plus good works equals salvation, this view does not represent
Catholic theology.*[1]

—Keith A. Fournier

On the one hand, the Roman Catholic Church claims it *does
not* teach salvation by works. But on the other hand, it also
claims that final justification and salvation *are* accomplished by
works. Which claim is correct? Has Rome's position on justification
really changed, or has it been consistently maintained for hundreds
and hundreds of years?

Works Upheld

No one denies that Rome officially rejects salvation solely by
works. After all, it agreed with the condemnation of Pelagius (a
monk who taught that man could lead a sin-free life without God's
help) at the Synod of Carthage in 418 and ratified this position at the
Council of Trent. (The Council of Trent was the major Catholic gathering [1545–1564] which reaffirmed and decreed official Catholic
doctrine in response to the Protestant Reformation.)

But Rome's official condemnation of salvation by works only confuses the issue of justification. Rome may have officially condemned
salvation by works alone, but it has also officially endorsed salvation by grace *and* works. As Trent decreed, "By his good works the

justified man really acquires a claim to supernatural reward from God."[2] And, "It is both possible and necessary to keep the law of God."[3]

The practical effect of this waffling has been to uphold a doctrine of works salvation in the lives of its people, irrespective of its claim to truly honor the grace of God. In essence, throughout Catholic history "grace" has been so subjugated to Church teaching, it has been institutionalized into a system of works. Indeed, the Catholic Church is known for its stress upon works salvation—that eternal life simply cannot be had without meritorious works.

Thus, official condemnations of salvation by works alone mean little when they are entirely undermined by other official declarations and the basic practices and beliefs of the Catholic Church as a whole.

It must be emphasized once again that the Catholic Church has always claimed that justification occurs by an act of God's grace. This claim is what confuses many Protestants, as well as Roman Catholics. But where Rome's doctrine contradicts and destroys the biblical doctrine of justification by grace through faith alone is where it wrongly teaches that there are two aspects or phases to justification—one by an act of grace, the other necessitating works.

The Endorsement by Pope John Paul II

In 1994 the *Catechism of the Catholic Church*, the first official statement of Catholic teachings issued since the catechism of 1566, was published. It contains a foreword by Pope John Paul II, who noted that it was the product of "over six years of intense work."[4] In his introduction, John Paul II made it clear that this catechism accurately reflects the true teachings of the Roman Catholic Church:

> Guarding the deposit of faith is the mission which the Lord entrusted to His Church, and which she fulfills in every age. . . . The *Catechism of the Catholic Church*, which I approved June 25th last . . . is a statement of the Church's faith and of catholic doctrine, attested to or illumined by Sacred Scripture, the Apostolic Tradition, and the Church's Magisterium. I declare it to be a *sure norm* for teaching the faith and thus a valid and legitimate instrument for ecclesial communion. . . .
>
> This catechism is given to them [Catholic leaders and laity] that it may be a sure and authentic reference text for

teaching *catholic doctrine* and particularly for preparing local catechisms. It is also offered to all the faithful who wish to deepen their knowledge of the unfathomable riches of salvation. . . . [It] is offered to every individual who wants to know what the Catholic Church believes.[5]

Therefore, whenever we cite this catechism, Catholics will agree that we are citing official Catholic doctrine. In fact, our citations of Catholic doctrine are always from texts which carry the two signatures or seals designating that a book is free of doctrinal error (the *nihil obstat* and *imprimatur*).

Concerning the new *Catechism of the Catholic Church*, the pope also invoked the assistance of the Virgin Mary to support the fruit of this catechism. "I beseech the Blessed Virgin Mary, Mother of the Incarnate Word and Mother of the Church, to support with her powerful intercession the catechetical work of the entire Church on every level, at this time when she is called to a new effort of evangelization."[6]

Rome's Twofold Nature of Justification

In the new *Catechism of the Catholic Church*, two aspects of justification are clearly seen. The first aspect of justification occurs when man is moved by God to turn from sin; the second aspect of justification occurs as man progresses in good works and merits for himself the graces needed to attain eternal life:

Like conversion, justification has two aspects. Moved by grace, man turns toward God and away from sin [first aspect of justification], and so accepts forgiveness and righteousness from on high. No one can merit the initial grace which is at the origin of conversion. [But once] moved by the Holy Spirit [first aspect] we can merit for ourselves [second aspect] and for others all the graces needed to attain eternal life.[7]

This two-aspect definition of "justification" allows Roman Catholic theologians to sound perfectly biblical about justification when they are only talking about phase one. The problem is they are not talking about the Catholic concept of justification in its entirety. Consider this answer given to the question, "How is the sinner justified?" by Stephen Keenan's *Doctrinal Catechism*:

> He [the sinner] is justified gratuitously by the pure mercy of God, not on account of his own or any human merit, but purely through the merits of Jesus Christ; for Jesus Christ is our only mediator of redemption, who alone, by his passion and death, has reconciled us to his Father.[8]

If this statement was all that Rome believed concerning justification, Protestants would gladly agree. But sadly, this is not the case. In statements on justification in their second phase, Catholicism teaches man must also cooperate with God's grace, thereby meriting the attainment of eternal life:

> Since the initiative belongs to God in the order of grace, no one can merit the initial grace of forgiveness and justification at the beginning of conversion. Moved by the Holy Spirit and by charity, we can then merit for ourselves . . . the graces needed for our sanctification, for the increase of grace and charity, and for the attainment of eternal life.[9]

This two-phase concept of justification disagrees with the biblical concept which declares justification to be a legal verdict of acquittal, a once-for-all completed act that takes place the moment a person, through faith, trusts Christ completely. At that instant, the Bible teaches, the benefits of Christ's life and righteousness are applied to the believer's life and he is officially judged and declared by God to stand as fully pardoned in His sight (Romans 5:1; 3:24).

On the other hand, in phase one of the Catholic concept of justification, the infusion of sanctifying grace disposes a person to cooperate with God's grace so that the sinner may arrive (phase two) at a state of progressive justification.

As we will see in chapter 6, baptism begins the first phase of justification where justifying grace is infused; in the second phase, the Eucharist and penance increase justification which, when maintained, lead to "final" justification at death. (Purgatorial suffering is also needed to complete justification. See chapter 9.)

In essence, the converted person must sustain his new relationship with God using the power of Christ until death or else his justification will not stand. In brief, Catholicism teaches that the initial infusion of grace only gives a person the opportunity to "begin" cooperating with the power of Christ and to attempt to merit and gain full and final justification.

Because this infusion (phase one) is not merited by anyone, Rome always argues justification is a free gift of God's grace. But is this even technically correct?

Not Entirely Free

Can Rome say Christ's gift is entirely free as a result of their further definition of justification in phase two? How can justification be a free gift when a person can actually increase both his grace and justification throughout life by further cooperating with God's grace and through performance of individual works of merit? And how can the Church say justification is free when adding that the soul becomes good and holy through the infusion of grace, and these are consistently increased throughout life by works so that a person (hopefully) will die in a "state of grace." And how can justification be God's free gift if the converted person must, at the end of his life, do even more to merit salvation?

At death the Catholic believer must then enter the hellish suffering of purgatory in order to pay the final temporal penalty for his sins and to await his eventual heavenly reward (see chapter 9).

Consider what has been said here. In a very real sense, then, isn't Catholic "justification" largely God's recognition of divinely empowered human merit and goodness?

If we examine the Catholic concept of justification further, we see that Catholicism has confused justification with sanctification.[10] For example, Catholic P. Gregory Stevens writes in *The Life of Grace*, "First of all, justification is a real and profound transformation of man, a genuine gift of sanctification to him."[11] But this is wrong because justification (Romans 3:28–4:6; Philippians 3:9) and sanctification (Ephesians 2:10; 2 Peter 3:18) are *distinct* and separate biblical doctrines. To confuse them is to distort the very essence of biblical salvation. (We will discuss this later.)

Stevens quotes the Council of Trent to show that Trent repudiated the Reformation idea of imputed righteousness:

> Catholic thought has always been that [justification] . . .
> actually transforms man into a person pleasing God. . . .
> In a clear, religiously profound statement, the Council
> [of Trent] defines the inner nature and structure of justi-
> fication. It does so in direct opposition to the extrinsecist
> position of Reformation theology.

> The heart of Catholic teaching is contained in this pas-
> sage. First of all comes the assertion that "justification is
> not only the remission of sins, but sanctification and
> renovation of the interior man through the voluntary
> reception of grace and the gifts, whereby man becomes
> just instead of unjust."[12]

But biblically, justification is not God's work of grace in man to actually make him righteous, which is sanctification. It is God's judicial declaration of acquittal that because of a man's faith in Christ, God has now declared his status to be as one perfectly righteous—irrespective of his personal righteousness or sanctification.

Catholicism denies justification by teaching that justification is brought about by sanctification instead of flowing from it. As a result it opposes the very heart of the Christian gospel which teaches that salvation is by grace alone, in Christ alone, through faith alone. This will become even more evident in the pages ahead.

Only Minor Issues?

Many Catholics and Protestants would have us believe that there are really only relatively minor differences between the doctrine of justification as taught by the Reformers and that taught by the Council of Trent and modern Roman Catholics.

A good illustration of this can be seen in the 1964 text by Roman Catholic theologian Hans Kung, *Justification: The Doctrine of Karl Barth and a Catholic Reflection.*

Karl Barth, an eminent Swiss Protestant theologian, had argued for a Protestant view of justification. Kung, however, believed that there were really no serious differences between Catholic and Protestant theology on the subject. His book cover highlighted his ideas: "If, then, there is so much that is 'Protestant' in Catholic teachings, are Catholics really divided in their faith from Evangelical tradition?"

Barth responded to Kung's question in "A Letter to the Author," which was included in Kung's book. He wondered how Kung could explain the fact that this alleged compatibility "could remain hidden so long, and from so many, both outside and inside the Church?" Barth made the following perceptive comments that went to the heart of the matter:

> Of course, the problem is whether what you have pre-
> sented here really represents the teaching of your Church.

This you will have to take up and fight out with biblical, historical, and dogmatic experts among your co-religionists. I don't have to assure you that I am keenly interested in discovering what reception your book will find among them.[13]

Barth was right. Hans Kung was later censored by his own Church for his views. And why not? Logically, if Rome and the Reformers were all along saying the same thing about justification, why didn't Trent just say that? Why all the papal bulls (official papal documents) against what the Reformers were teaching? Why the many anathemas (divine curses) against them? Why were the anathemas repeated in word or spirit by Vatican I and II?

How is it that even former "Evangelicals" who have been in Catholicism for more than 25 years freely comment that "nine out of ten Catholics" don't understand the basic *Catholic* doctrine of salvation by grace, let alone the biblical concept? Rather, they believe their good works alone will take them to heaven and accept "a whole other religion" than found in biblical Christianity (see p. 205).

Reformation Heroes

Anyone who thinks Rome has changed her mind on the doctrine of justification in recent years is mistaken. The Church's position has not changed since the middle part of the sixteenth century when the Council of Trent (1545–64) met to establish Church doctrine on several key issues. This council was called by Pope Paul III in direct response to the success of the Protestant movement. Its voting members consisted of bishops, abbots, and the leaders of religious orders from countries including Italy, Spain, France, and Germany. The decrees this council made concerning justification have never been modified, altered, or rescinded by Rome. They remain the stand of Roman Catholic theology today. The Catholic Church continues to uphold the resolutions of the Council of Trent and cites them repeatedly in defense of its teaching. Contemporary Catholic defender Karl Keating maintains that these decrees are not only true Catholic doctrine, but true biblical doctrine as well. He argues that at Trent and today "the Catholic Church teaches the true biblical doctrine of justification."[14]

Keep in mind that the purpose of the Council of Trent was not principally to restate Catholic doctrine but to reply to the alleged "heresies" of the Reformation begun by the great Protestant Reformer, Martin Luther.

After meditating on Romans 1:16,17, this works-tormented Catholic monk realized the true nature of biblical justification: "Thereupon I felt myself to be reborn and to have gone through open doors to paradise. The whole of Scripture took on new meaning, and whereas before the 'justice of God' had filled me with hate, now it became to me inexpressibly sweet in great love."[15]

What kind of ideas did Luther now embrace? He embraced justification by faith alone. Yet as we read the official pronouncements from the Council of Trent on justification, we see that, as a whole, Rome's decrees were obviously contrary to Luther's beliefs—beliefs which were clearly based in Scripture and not Church tradition.

The Council of Trent began its decrees with the following repudiation of the principles of the Reformation. On January 13, 1547, the council declared that Luther's doctrine of justification was causing many souls to be damned:

> Since there is being disseminated at this time, not without the loss of many souls and grievous detriment to the unity of the Church, a certain erroneous doctrine concerning justification, the holy, ecumenical and general Council of Trent, lawfully assembled in the Holy Ghost ... [will now] expound to all the faithful of Christ the true and salutary doctrine of justification... which the Catholic Church under the inspiration of the Holy Ghost has always retained; strictly forbidding that anyone henceforth presume to believe, preach or teach otherwise than is defined and declared in the present decree.[16]

The council decreed that whoever does not "faithfully and firmly accept, this Catholic doctrine on justification... cannot be justified."[17]

Key Points of the Council

An "anathema" or curse of God is pronounced on all who would reject the decrees of the council. In brief fashion we are now going to summarize some of the key points from that session, citing excerpts from the council documents themselves.

1. *Justification is a process that may be increased.*

> If anyone says that the justice received [i.e., justification] is not preserved and also not increased before God through good works, but that those works are merely the fruits and signs of justification obtained, but not the cause of its increase, let him be anathema.[18]

Luther taught the opposite based on Galatians, chapters 2 and 3, Romans 5:1-10, and Ephesians 2:8,9. Luther did refer to justification in a progressive sense, but by this he meant the whole of justification, sanctification, and glorification—and thus he did not teach justification occurs by works or was increased in the Catholic sense.[19] However, the Council of Trent declared the Catholic believer was:

> . . . . advancing from virtue to virtue . . . faith cooperating with good works, [believers do thereby] increase in that justice [justification] received through the grace of Christ and are further justified. . . .[20]

2. *Justification is an infusion of righteousness.*

> . . . [the justice] of God . . . is infused into us by God through the merit of Christ.[21]

But in Romans 4:3-5 Luther discovered the *imputation* of God's righteousness apart from works, a legal declaration provided (imputed) by God. However, Trent decreed the following—

> If anyone says that men are justified either by the sole imputation of the justice of Christ or by the sole remission of sins, to the exclusion of the grace and the charity which is poured forth in their hearts by the Holy Ghost and remains in them [i.e., the Catholic view of infused justification], or also that the grace by which we are justified is only the good will of God, let him be anathema.[22]

3. *Justification does not occur by faith alone.*

> If anyone says that the sinner is justified by faith alone, meaning that nothing else is required to cooperate in order to obtain the grace of justification let him be anathema.[23]

Luther found justification by faith alone in Romans 3:24, but Trent decreed:

> Wherefore, no one ought to flatter himself with faith alone, thinking that by faith alone he is made an heir and will obtain the inheritance. . . .[24]

> If anyone says that man is absolved from his sins and justified because he firmly believes that he is absolved and justified . . . and that by this faith alone absolution and justification are effected, let him be anathema.[25]

Luther could not help but believe that Acts 13:38,39 stated exactly what was condemned by Rome.

4. *The one justified must keep the commandments of God and the Church.*

> If anyone says that a man who is justified and however perfect is not bound to observe the commandments of God and the Church, but only to believe, as if the Gospel were a bare and absolute promise of eternal life without the condition of observing the commandments, let him be anathema.[26]

Luther found in John 3:16; 5:24; 6:29,47 and Galatians chapters 2 and 3 that the believer did not have to keep the commandments of God and the Church in order to acquire salvation. But Trent declared in its canon on baptism and elsewhere:

> If anyone says that those baptized are by baptism made debtors only to faith alone, but not to the observance of the whole law of Christ, let him be anathema.[27]

And

> But no one, however much justified, should consider himself exempt from the observance of the commandments.[28]

5. *Justification does not offer the confidence of divine mercy.*

> If anyone says that justifying faith is nothing more than confidence in divine mercy, which remits sins for Christ's

sake, or that it is this confidence alone that justifies us, let him be anathema.[29] (But Luther found that Trent was wrong in Romans 5:1.)

6. *Justification can be lost; therefore penance is required to regain the justification lost.*

> Those who through sin have forfeited the received grace of justification can again be justified when, moved by God, they exert themselves to obtain through the sacrament of penance the recovery, by the merits of Christ, of the grace lost.[30]

> If anyone says that he who has fallen after baptism . . . can indeed recover again the lost justice [justification] but by faith alone without the sacrament of penance . . . let him be anathema.[31]

7. *Justification does not cancel out the necessity for indulgences.*

> If anyone says that after the reception of the grace of justification the guilt is so remitted and the debt of eternal punishment so blotted out to every repentant sinner, that no debt of temporal punishment remains to be discharged [through indulgences] either in this world or in purgatory before the gates of heaven can be opened, let him be anathema.[32]

8. *Justification is a genuine merit of the Catholic believer.*

> If anyone says that the good works of the one justified . . . are not also the good merits of him justified; or that the one justified . . . does not truly merit an increase of grace, eternal life, and in case he dies in grace, the attainment of eternal life itself and also an increase of glory, let him be anathema.[33]

The council closed by reinforcing all the above declarations with the following observation:

> If anyone says that the Catholic doctrine of justification as set forth by the Holy Council in the present decree,

derogates in some respect from the glory of God or the
merits of our Lord Jesus Christ . . . let him be anathema.[34]

In other words, what the Catholic Church then taught in opposition to the Protestant Reformation—and *continues* to teach as official
doctrine today—is that God Himself is opposed to all who reject the
Catholic Church's own unique teaching on justification. In fact, in
the decrees of Trent, Rome pronounced scores of anathemas against
Evangelical belief.

Rome further claims that its decrees on justification do not detract from the glory of God or the merits of Christ. But the great
Lutheran authority on the decrees of the Council of Trent, Martin
Chemnitz, a contemporary of the age, was outraged at what the
council had done:

> They [the members of the council] deny that the justifica-
> tion of a sinner is solely the remission of sins. And they
> pronounce many anathemas if anyone says that men are
> righteous before God through the righteousness of Christ,
> or that men are justified solely through imputation of the
> righteousness of Christ. . . . They affirm that the justi-
> fication of the ungodly before God to life eternal is not
> solely the remission of sins but also the sanctification of
> the inner man.[35]

Chemnitz correctly observed the consistent teaching of the Scripture concerning justification "is condemned with many dreadful
curses by the Council of Trent,"[36] and he proceeded to note the
semantic and hermeneutical subterfuge often employed by Rome's
theologians: "The craftiness with which the architects of these
decrees have disguised the matter itself with a certain show of right,
in order that they might not at once be detected by the more inex-
perienced, is worthy of observation."[37]

We agree with Chemnitz that Trent changed the definitions of
"grace" and "justification" into one of the most subtle forms of
salvation by works ever devised. Rome's teachings on salvation may
appear to the uninstructed to be both spiritual and biblical and even
seem to uphold salvation by grace. But they do not.

This subtlety may explain why some Catholics encourage Evangelicals to read the decrees of Trent to "prove" to Protestants that
Catholicism does not actually teach a form of salvation by works.

But if Catholics think that Trent teaches what the Reformation taught on justification, they aren't reading very carefully.

Protestants should open their Bibles and then read these decrees carefully and determine for themselves whether or not the gospel of grace and justification by faith alone have been rejected.

Justification, Mortal Sin, and Insecurity

Because Roman Catholic teaching denies that justification is the final verdict declared by God, the Judge, in which He pronounces a sinner pardoned forever, it thoroughly undermines a believer's certainty of salvation.

If "to justify" means to *make* a person righteous, a person is left to his own inadequate works and subjective feelings as the basis of his acceptance before God. This explains why Catholic justification can fluctuate in the life of a believer from having it to not having it at all. Catholicism's justification is not a completed act of God. Rather, it is entirely based on the grace-empowered works of sinful people for its maintenance. Thus, it can hardly provide any sense of security of salvation.

Since the Catholic Church teaches that justification can be lost by mortal sin, a person can only know he retains his justification if he is certain he has not committed mortal sin. But in Catholic teaching, such knowledge is problematic. Mortal sin is not always clearly defined[38] and so certain knowledge of having committed such a sin is not possible. Further, mortal sins are quite common and include such things as sexual immorality, drunkenness, envy, and failure to attend Mass each Sunday. Here is what Keating says:

> Mortal sin is much more prevalent than we suspect. . . . For a sin to be mortal three requirements must be met. First, it must involve a serious matter. Second, there must be sufficient reflection on its seriousness. And third, there must be full consent in the committing of it. What is a serious matter? Many sins listed in the Ten Commandments or contrary to Scripture or the moral teachings of the Church could qualify: murder, envy, abortion, artificial birth control, thievery, adultery, sodomy, fornication—to list only some of the serious sins. . . .[39]

But to die in a state of mortal sin is to go straight to hell. The punishment for mortal sin is eternal separation from God:

What is the difference between mortal and venial sins? Mortal sins are the sins of great offense that can send the soul directly to hell. If you die in a state of unconfessed mortal sin, according to Roman Catholic theology, you go immediately to hell, since you have not confessed that sin, received absolution, or said an act of contrition prior to your death. . . . According to the Roman Catholic doctrine, you must assume that one has passed from spiritual death to life and back again to death if one commits a mortal sin. Even if you admit (as Catholics will not) that you can be "saved" right now, they maintain that should you commit sin, you could be lost; that is, if you died in a state of mortal sin.[40]

This is why Rome teaches that it is not possible for a person's faith to give confidence that one's sins are forgiven. "As far as the content of justifying faith is concerned, the so-called fiducial faith [the faith, as personal trust in Christ, that gives confidence one's sins are forgiven] does not suffice."[41]

All of this is to say that Catholic theological texts continue to cite Trent as authoritative and continue to reject the biblical teaching on justification by faith alone. Therefore, to say agreement now exists between Evangelicals on the one hand and Catholics on the other is premature, to say the least.

Fundamentals of Catholic Dogma asserts, "It would be incompatible with the veracity and the sanctity of God that he should declare the sinner to be justified, if he remains in reality sinful."[42] But how can Catholic theologians say this when it is the very essence of what the Bible teaches: It is the sinner himself (the one who remains sinful—1 John 1:8-10)—who is declared righteous (Romans 5:6-11). How can anyone misunderstand the apostle Paul when he argues, "But to the one who does not work, but believes in Him who justifies *the ungodly*, his faith is reckoned as righteousness" (Romans 4:5 NASB, emphasis added)?

In conclusion, we have seen that both the sixteenth-century Council of Trent and the most recent 1994 *Catechism* endorsed by Pope John Paul II himself agree that final justification is something earned by the Catholic believers by their good deeds and merits in cooperation with the power of Christ—it is not solely a free gift of God's grace and mercy. Because justification depends on what the believer does, no individual Roman Catholic can ever have any true assurance in this life of his or her final standing before God.

On the other hand, those who accept what the Bible teaches concerning justification have infinitely more spiritual blessings. It is to these infinite spiritual riches that we now turn our attention.

▪5▪

The Bible and Justification

*I*n one of the episodes of the popular "Star Trek: The Next Genera-tion" series, a godlike being named "Q"—an entity who is enigmatic, endearing, and infuriating all at once—places the entire human race on trial for its endless and sundry crimes. Captain Jean-Luc Picard does his best to justify humanity and rationalize its behavior. Not surprisingly, given the track record in human history, "Q" isn't impressed and the trial proceeds.

If ever the entire human race were placed on trial by an omnipo-tent and omniscient being, what do you think the outcome would be? Would humanity be acquitted? On a more practical level, how would you and I fare individually before the searching gaze of God's holiness? Would any person on earth be found entirely guiltless?

As unimaginable as it seems to the average secular person, the Bible emphatically declares this scenario of divine judgment will one day be played out—in fact, Jesus Himself declared He would be the eternal Judge (Matthew 25:31-46; John 5:28,29; Revela-tion 20:11-15).

Think of what it would be like to stand before a holy God and give an account for everything we ever did. What excuse would we give to a holy God? If God requires a perfect record in order to enter heaven, what possible hope would any of us have?

No doctrine is more important, nor, unfortunately, more misun-derstood and neglected (even by Protestants) than justification by faith alone. In earlier chapters we discussed particular points con-cerning this subject, but we have not yet given the bigger picture. Having reconciled the apparent differences between the apostles James and Paul, we will now provide a broader view of what the Bible teaches about justification by faith alone. For this concept is not found in one or two isolated sections, but is woven into the fabric of Scripture itself.

Cleared in One Moment

The Bible teaches that any person who simply and truly believes in Jesus Christ as his or her personal Savior from sin is at that moment irrevocably and eternally justified. Justification is the final verdict of God whereby He not only forgives and pardons the sins of the believer, but He also declares him perfectly righteous by imputing the obedience and righteousness of Christ Himself to him through faith. It is on the basis of Christ's life and atonement that God "pronounces believers to have fulfilled all the requirements of the law which pertain to them."[1]

Because justification is an eternal verdict pronounced of God, it is made final the moment a person believes on Christ. As a result, justification is not a lifelong process such as is personal sanctification or individual growth in holy living.

Both the Old and New Testaments teach the Protestant view of legal (forensic) justification. Consider the following evidence for the Old Testament view of justification:

> Concerning the Old Testament word *hitsdiq*, usually rendered "justified," more often than not it is ". . . used in a forensic or legal sense, as meaning, not 'to make just or righteous,' but 'to declare judicially that one is in harmony with the law.' . . . In the Old Testament, the concept of righteousness frequently appears in a forensic or juridical context. A righteous man is one who has been declared by a judge to be free from guilt."[2]

In his book *Justification*, Catholic theologian Hans Kung argues for this view when he says, "According to the original biblical usage of the term, 'justification' must be defined as a declaring just by court order."[3] Other Catholic theologians have agreed with Kung.[4]

The New Testament Scriptures agree with the Old, clearly showing that justification is 1) a crediting of righteousness on the basis of a person's faith, 2) a completed act of God, and 3) something that occurs wholly apart from personal merit or good works:

> 1. ". . . to the man who. . . trusts God who justifies the wicked, *his faith is credited* as righteousness. . . . [How

blessed is] the man to whom God *credits righteousness* apart from works" (Romans 4:5,6, emphasis added).

2. "Therefore *having been* justified by faith, we have peace with God through our Lord Jesus Christ" (Romans 5:1 NASB, emphasis added).

3. "For we maintain that a man is justified by faith *apart from works of the Law*" (Romans 3:28 NASB, emphasis added).

Please also read Luke 18:1-14; Acts 13:38,39; 15:10,11; Galatians 2:16.

The weight of these Scriptures is formidable; it is indeed impossible to deny the biblical teaching of justification by faith alone. For someone to say that the Bible teaches that sinners "are justified by Christ and by good works"[5] is simply wrong.

Scripture clearly rules out all forms of salvation by works. And if Scripture is equally clear that salvation comes by grace through faith, then salvation must be by faith alone.

To make salvation an achievement of "faith plus works" is to destroy Christ's gospel. No true Christian would ever wish to destroy Christ's gospel, especially realizing the infinite price paid by Christ so that salvation could be offered solely as His free gift. Read the following Scriptures carefully:

Therefore no one will be declared righteous in his sight by observing the law; rather, through the law we become conscious of sin (Romans 3:20).

But now a righteousness from God, apart from law, has been made known, to which the Law and the Prophets testify (Romans 3:21).

This righteousness from God comes through faith in Jesus Christ to all who believe.... [They] are justified freely by his grace through the redemption that came by Christ Jesus (Romans 3:22,24).

God presented him [Jesus] as a sacrifice of atonement, through faith in his blood. He did this to demonstrate his justice ... at the present time, so as to be just and the one who justifies those who have faith in Jesus (Romans 3:25,26).

He saved us, not because of righteous things we had done, but because of his mercy (Titus 3:5).

Having been justified [God's legal verdict pronouncing one pardoned forever] by his grace, we might become heirs having the hope of eternal life (Titus 3:7).

I write these things to you who believe in the name of the Son of God so that you may know that you have eternal life (1 John 5:13).

Since we have now been justified by his blood, how much more shall we be saved from God's wrath through him! (Romans 5:9).

And if by grace, then it is no longer by works; if it were, grace would no longer be grace (Romans 11:6).

Blessed is the man whose sin the Lord will never count against him (Romans 4:8).

These verses indisputably teach that justification is an eternal final verdict by God (not a lifelong process), and that a person is justified by *faith alone*. There is no hint of any additional requirement or works for salvation that would make justification by "faith plus works" (see also Romans 8:30; 10:3,4; 1 Corinthians 6:11; Galatians 3:8-13,21-25).

A Lifelong Process?

Now let's briefly return to the Catholic viewpoint. Catholic theologians claim that justification is a lifelong process in which an individual increases in personal righteousness. If righteousness is something that is initially infused by God and then increases when the believer cooperates by specific works, such as participation in the sacraments (penance, etc.), then Catholicism is correct in claiming that justification is really the end result of sanctification—a process of personal growth in righteousness.

On the other hand, if justification is a legal declaration by God who declares the sinner pardoned and then credits him a perfectly righteous standing simply through faith in Christ, then it is a past action completed at the moment someone places his faith in Christ. Not surprisingly, Catholic theologians claim that Paul's use of the Greek word for justification (*dikaioo*) does not refer to *imputed* or legally declared righteousness. But where did they get this understanding? Not from standard Greek dictionaries. All of these dictionaries define the principal New Testament word for justification in a Protestant and not a Catholic sense—that is, as a legal declaration of righteousness, not an infusing of actual righteousness.

As the premier Greek lexicon puts it, "In Paul, the legal usage is plain and indisputable. . . . [It] does not suggest the infusion of moral qualities [but] the justification of the ungodly who believe the result of a judicial pronouncement."[6]

This is why Bruce Metzger, perhaps the foremost Greek scholar in America, emphasizes that it is "past comprehension" how someone can deny "the unmistakable evidence" of the Pauline meaning of this word. "The fact is that Paul simply does not use this verb to mean 'to be made upright or righteous.' Indeed, it is extremely doubtful whether it ever bore this meaning in the Greek of any period or author. It means 'to be pronounced, or declared, or treated as righteous or upright.'"[7]

Theologian J.I. Packer says, "There is no lexical grounds for the view of the medieval and Roman theologians that 'justify' means or connotes as part of its meaning 'making righteous' by subjective spiritual renewal. The tridentine [Council of Trent] definition of justification as not only the remission of sins but also the sanctification and renewal of the inward man is erroneous."[8]

Thus, if the Roman Catholic Church wishes to maintain its view of justification, it will have to explain why standard Greek dictionaries all show that the Catholic definition of "justification" is wrong (see endnote 7 for additional examples).

A Basic Misunderstanding

Unfortunately, some Catholics have misunderstood the Protestant position on justification, thinking that Protestants have little concern with a changed life, good works, or sanctification. To the contrary, Scripture is clear that good works and sanctification are crucial—indeed it is the very knowledge of grace itself (in a Protestant sense) that produces good works and growth in holy living.

For Protestants, both justification and sanctification occur by God's grace, not by works of righteousness—"Having begun by the Spirit, are you now being perfected by the flesh?" (Galatians 3:3 NASB).

Titus 2:11-14 states, "For the grace of God that brings salvation has appeared to all men. It teaches us to say 'No' to ungodliness and worldly passions, and to live self-controlled, upright and godly lives in this present age, while we wait for the blessed hope—the glorious appearing of our great God and Savior, Jesus Christ, who gave himself for us to redeem us from all wickedness and to purify for himself a people that are his very own, eager to do what is good."

Romans 1:5 refers to "the obedience that comes from faith" (see also Ephesians 2:8-10; 1 Peter 5:12; 2 Peter 3:18; Colossians 1:6; cf. 2:23). But again, good works and sanctification have nothing to do with our justification.

Thus, what justification means to Protestants is that believers are to plead the merits of Christ before the throne of God, instead of their own merits. This is why biblical Christians accept the "gift of righteousness" (Romans 5:17) and "glory in Christ Jesus, and . . . put no confidence in the flesh" (Philippians 3:3). As a result of being justified by God the moment one believes, sanctification through the power of the Holy Spirit also begins. But through sanctification one does not attain that which God has already given—and eternally declared to be settled (Hebrews 10:14).

Now let us briefly examine the Catholic views of sanctification.

In a "John Ankerberg Show" debate between Fr. Mitchell Pacwa, S.J., and Protestant theologian Dr. Walter Martin, Dr. Martin stated, "The error of Roman Catholic theology at this point is that it confuses justification with sanctification." In setting forth the Catholic position, Fr. Pacwa replied as follows:

> The error we see in Protestant theology is they separate justification from sanctification, rather than seeing that as one process. . . . It's one process rather than this radical distinction [of Protestants]. . . . To say that it is two separate processes is to separate Christ Himself, who is sanctification and justification. . . . [We believe] that [justification and sanctification are] one long process—and [something] we don't want to separate. And that's what we see as a mistake in Protestant theology.[9]

Clearly, Catholics do see justification and sanctification as one long process of individual growth in personal righteousness. Catholics believe sanctifying grace combined with our works allows one to eventually reach the point where God declares a person ultimately just *because* that person has actually cooperated with God in becoming just.

On the other hand, Protestants see a once-for-all completed act of justification as a declaration of God whereby the sinner is pronounced just. The sinner is not personally righteous because justification occurs at the very point of saving faith. A believer has not even had the time to become righteous. Therefore he or she could not possibly have attained actual, objective righteousness before God. And yet the Bible declares this brand-new believer is declared righteous—no matter how sinful his or her life may have been or is.

This is the whole message of the biblical gospel—that God declares sinful people and enemies of righteousness (Romans 5:8-10; Ephesians 2:1-10) to be perfectly righteous because of their trust in Christ. And He does this before they have any opportunity to become righteous on their own.

The biblical evidence reveals that justification cannot be the same as sanctification. If so, then what does the Bible teach sanctification is?

Biblical Sanctification

According to the Bible, "to sanctify" means "to be set apart to God." The noun *hagiasmos* refers to separation unto God as well as the proper course of life for those so separated.[10] "Sanctification is a process by which one's moral condition is brought into conformity with one's legal status before God. . . ."[11]

Basically there are three aspects of sanctification: one past (when God pronounced us justified and also sanctified us—that is, He set us apart to begin serving Him), one present ("referring to the continuing work of the Holy Spirit in the moment by moment life of the believer making him or her actually holy"[12]), and one future (after death, in heaven when God will complete our total sanctification).

The sanctification that is already past concerns the point at which we became believers and at which we were set apart to God for His purposes. Thus, Hebrews 10:10 NASB, in referring to God's will, says, "By this will we have been sanctified [set apart to God] through the offering of the body of Jesus Christ once for all."

Again, there is a second or present aspect of sanctification and this includes the results of our initially being set apart to God to do His will and what logically flows from it. This concerns our growth in holiness and the Christian life (Romans 6:13-16; Titus 2:14; 1 Thessalonians 2:12).

In Hebrews 10:14 NASB we see the clear difference between justification and sanctification. This Scripture reads, "For by one offering He has perfected for all time [justification] those who are [being] sanctified [further set apart]." The NIV reads, "Because by one sacrifice he has made perfect forever those who are being made holy."

Because no one ever becomes sinlessly perfect in this life, there is a progressive sanctification or growth in holiness throughout the Christian life (2 Corinthians 3:18; Ephesians 4:11-16; 2:10; 1 Thessalonians 4:3-7).

The third aspect of sanctification is the believer's glorification. Here, in every sense of the term, the believer is now sinlessly perfect and completely set apart to God. This occurs after death, when the sin nature is removed forever and when at the resurrection the believer inherits his eternally glorified body which is like that of Christ's (Philippians 3:21). Here we see the believer's final sanctification: "Those he justified, he also glorified" (Romans 8:30).

Again, sanctification involves a past reality ("You were sanctified," that is, there was a definite time when God set you apart to serve Him—1 Corinthians 6:11); a present reality ("But sanctify the Lord God in your hearts"—1 Peter 3:15 KJV); and a future application, which really refers to the doctrine of glorification or final and ultimate sanctification unto God (1 John 3:2; 1 Thessalonians 5:23,24).

Another way to look at this is to realize that justification is salvation from the penalty of sin (past action) while sanctification is salvation from the power of sin (a continuing process) and glorification is salvation from the presence of sin (future action).[13] Sanctification is our spiritual growth *in* grace, not our attempt to *earn* grace.

What this means is that after justification the essence of the Christian life is a growth in sanctification, or the actual setting apart of ourselves to God for His purposes. This includes growth in personal holiness. This is why Jesus prayed in John 17:17, "Sanctify them through thy truth, thy word is truth" (KJV). In other words, it is ultimately the believer's regular study and obedience to the Word of God which produces sanctification. Thus, sanctification—not justification—is a work of God in which believers cooperate (Ephesians 2:10; 4:15,16; Colossians 2:19; Philippians 2:13).

Catholic Confusion

It should be evident from our previous discussion that Roman Catholicism has made justification *the process of sanctification*—and therefore entirely confused the two. Catholicism has wrongly made justification a process, just like the biblical concept of sanctification. Catholicism teaches that justification can be increased, lost through mortal sin, or regained.

But the only reason that justification can be lost in the Catholic religion is because it depends on man's cooperation, and men do not live perfectly. Even though the Catholic Church teaches that justification is of God, the believer must still cooperate with God in specific actions such as the sacraments. The *Catechism of the Catholic Church* (1994) says, "The purpose of the sacraments is to sanctify men."[14]

Unfortunately, by rejecting the immediate nature of justification and making justification a lifelong process of sanctification, the Roman Catholic Church has brought great confusion in the minds of Catholics regarding the biblical *distinctions* between these two doctrines.

The confusion can be seen in statements like the following from Canon 24 of the Council of Trent:

> If anyone says that the justice [justification] received is also not increased before God through good works, but that the works were only the fruit and the signs of the justification received, not also a cause of its increase, let him be anathema.[15]

Also from the new 1994 *Catechism of the Catholic Church*,

> Since the initiative belongs to God in the order of grace, no one can merit the initial grace of forgiveness and justification, at the beginning of conversion. Moved by the Holy Spirit and by charity, we can merit for ourselves and for others the graces needed for our sanctification, for the increase of grace and charity, and for the attainment of eternal life.[16]

In addition, the *Catechism* states: "By giving birth to the 'inner man,' justification entails the sanctification of his whole being."[17] Thus, "justification is not only the remission of sins, but also the sanctification and renewal of the interior man."[18] "Justification detaches man from sin ... and purifies his heart of sin. Justification ... frees from the enslavement to sin, and it heals."[19] Finally, "Justification is conferred in Baptism, the sacrament of faith. It conforms us to the righteousness of God, who makes us inwardly just by the power of his mercy."[20]

To the contrary, according to the Bible justification means that true Christians may be assured that in God's eyes they *now* possess the perfect holiness necessary for them to gain an assured entrance to heaven. Why? If the death of Christ forgave all our sins and fully satisfied the divine penalty due them, and if God declares believers absolutely righteous on the basis of their faith in Christ, then nothing else is needed to permit their entrance into heaven. Thus, because of justification (i.e., because Christ's righteousness and merits are reckoned to believers as far as God is concerned), Christians now possess perfect holiness in this life, and possess it from the moment of saving faith. Neither sacraments such as baptism or penance, nor indulgences, nor saying the Rosary, nor suffering in purgatory can now possibly be necessary for believers to enter heaven. This is what the biblical doctrine of justification means. It means that the final judgment of God has been brought into the present, and once passed, it is irrevocable.

Once acquitted of all charges, no one—absolutely no one—goes back to the judge and asks for acquittal again. If there is complete justification for the believer, then obviously "there is no need for confession to a priest, forgiveness by a priest, or penance from a priest."[21] "Those accepted now are secure forever. Inquisition before Christ's judgment seat (Romans 14:10-12; 2 Corinthians 5:10) may deprive them of certain rewards (1 Corinthians 3:15), but never of their justified status. Christ will not call into question God's justifying verdict, only declare, endorse and implement it."[22]

Torment and Release

Several hundred years ago there was a Catholic monk undergoing tremendous pain and inner torment over his personal relationship with God. This pious man ardently sought peace with God in every possible manner he could think of. He did everything the Church told him to do—and everything else he could possibly do in order to find peace with God. He openly wept before God, performed torturous penances, spent hours in the confessional, and severely beat his body. But such peace with God was never found. The more he looked into his heart and recognized the sin that was there, the more that he despaired of ever living a good enough life to earn God's ultimate favor.

After having done everything possible a man could do in order to earn merit before God and find reconciliation with God, this Catholic monk ended up in a state of utter depression.

But then one day he came across a passage in the Bible that revolutionized his life forever. In Romans 1:16,17 he saw and clearly understood that there is a righteousness which comes from God, a righteousness apart from works that he could never provide, and one that God offers as a free gift. It was not something that had to be earned by his own works of merit and self-torture. This righteousness from God was not anything that could be earned by man. He realized that justification was a declaration, a legal pronouncement by God of his new and perfect status before God forever.

Sanctification was something that followed justification and was therefore not the basis of his acceptance before God. "Night and day I pondered until I saw the connection between the justice of God and the statement that 'the just shall live by faith.' Then I grasped that the justice of God is that righteousness by which through grace and sheer mercy God justifies us through faith. Thereupon I felt myself to be reborn."[23]

This Catholic monk's simple realization of what the Bible taught began the Protestant Reformation. The monk was none other than Martin Luther.

The life of Martin Luther illustrates the real frustration of trying to earn our own peace with God by lifelong works and merit. Keeping the law to obtain grace only leads to spiritual bondage, an increase of sin, and even hatred for God (Romans 5:20; 7:8; 8:2-4,6-9; Galatians 3:21-25). Only God knows how many Catholics (and Protestants) have given up on God because they concluded they could never please Him or obey His laws.

In our next chapter, we will begin to understand part of the weight carried by Martin Luther and many other pious and committed Roman Catholics today. And we will begin our look at what is meant when Pope John Paul II teaches that "a good life is the condition of salvation."[24]

.6.

The Catholic Sacraments

The fact that Christianity is a religion of salvation is expressed in the sacramental life of the Church. . . . Baptism and the Eucharist [are] sacraments which create in man the seed of eternal life.[1]

—Pope John Paul II

No one needs to be troubled over his relationship to God the way Martin Luther was. Anyone immediately can rest assured that God has declared full pardon for him from the penalty due his sins. Faith in Christ also results in full peace with God through simple faith in Jesus Christ (Romans 5:1,9-11; 1 John 5:13).

Unfortunately, Catholicism teaches that a believer can only achieve and maintain his peace with God through the performance of the sacraments. In this chapter we will discuss the sacraments and show how they can logically work against a believer's assurance before God. For if forgiveness of sins and salvation depends on what we do and achieve as a lifelong process through the sacraments, how can we possibly know our performance will be properly maintained up until the end?

The sacraments of Catholicism involve particular spiritual activities or responsibilities partaken of by believers, such as penance and the Holy Eucharist. The sacraments are presided over by a Catholic priest who acts as a mediator between God and man. These special activities are said to dispense God's grace (the word "grace" here is used to mean a spiritual substance or power) and God's favor.

How do the sacraments function in the life of a Catholic believer? In essence, they allow the person the specific means through specific works of merit to maintain his or her justification, increase it, and finally attain heaven.

Even though the Church declares that it is Christ who performs the sacraments and dispenses grace in the life of the believer, and therefore the effects of the sacrament are not produced by the righteousness of the believer, it is nevertheless the believer's responsibility to accept and/or perform the sacraments. The believer must be baptized, confirmed, partake of the Eucharist, do penance, and so on. If the believer does not do this, he simply cannot be saved. This is why the most recent *Catechism of the Catholic Church* (1994) unequivocally states, "The Church affirms that for believers the sacraments of the New Covenant are necessary for salvation."[2]

In this chapter we will examine the sacraments and show why Catholicism views them as necessary to salvation—and that, therefore, Rome teaches a salvation based on both faith in Christ and our own works.

The Seven Sacraments of Rome

In contrast to Protestantism which accepts two sacraments (baptism and communion), Roman Catholicism teaches there are seven sacraments, all of which are believed to have been instituted by Jesus Christ. The seven sacraments are baptism, the Holy Eucharist, penance, matrimony, anointing of the sick, confirmation, and Holy Orders.

Rome's sevenfold sacramental system was apparently not initiated until the twelfth century and was not made a permanent part of the Catholic faith until as late as the fifteenth century. (This means that for over 1000 years Christians were not required to accept the current sacramental system which Rome today maintains is necessary for salvation.) Nevertheless, for today's Roman Catholic, "His whole life from the cradle to the grave, and indeed beyond the grave in purgatory, is conditioned by the sacramental approach."[3]

The 1994 *Catechism* emphasizes the crucial importance of the sacraments for the Catholic believer when it declares, "The whole liturgical life of the Church revolves around the Eucharistic sacrifice and the sacraments."[4] Therefore, understanding the sacraments in Catholicism is essential to understanding Catholicism itself.

In Catholicism, the sacraments are said to "work by their own working" to "confer grace to the soul." The 1994 *Catechism of the*

Catholic Church puts it this way: "The sacraments act *ex opere operato* (literally: 'by the very fact of the action's being performed')."[5] (This explains why in some pagan countries overzealous Catholic priests have, apparently, actually thrown buckets of water on natives—hoping to infuse the graces of baptism merely by the act itself.)

In brief, the sacraments are believed to be effective in dispensing grace as a substance or power to the individual Catholic when he partakes of each specific sacrament.

The effects of sacraments are not dependent upon the attitude or merits of either the priest or the recipient—contrary to the rule that holds for all other activities. This is so because the sacramental act is in essence an act of Christ Himself, operating through His servant, the priest (called "another Christ"). And in the words of Pope Paul VI [*Mysterium fiedi*, no. 38]: "Let no one deny that the sacraments are acts of Christ, are holy of themselves, and owing to the virtue of Christ, they confer grace to the soul as they touch the body."[6] (But the sacrament must be received by the Catholic in the necessary moral condition.)

The results of each of the sacraments may be summarized as follows:

1. *Baptism* (not repeated) cleanses from original sin, removes other sin and its punishment, provides justification in an initial form, spiritual rebirth (John 3:3) or regeneration, and is "necessary for salvation."[7]

2. *Confirmation* (not repeated) bestows the Holy Spirit in a special sense leading to "an increase of sanctifying grace and the gifts of the Holy Spirit" as well as other spiritual power and a sealing to the Catholic Church.[8] Confirmation gives strength from the Holy Spirit to defend the Catholic faith and to avoid temptation. (In a sense, the larger process of justification begins at confirmation because justification cannot begin prior to faith, which is defined as "man's assent to revealed [i.e., Catholic] truth," nor can it occur before baptism.)[9]

3. *Penance* (or reconciliation) removes the penalty of sins committed after baptism and confirmation. Mortal or "deadly" sins are remitted and the "justification" lost by such sins is restored as a continuing process.[10]

4. *Holy Eucharist.* Christ is resacrificed or "re-presented" and the benefits of Calvary are continually applied anew to the believer.[11] This occurs at the Mass.

5. *Marriage* grace is given to remain in the bonds of matrimony in accordance with the requirements of the Catholic Church.[12]

6. *Anointing of the sick* (formerly extreme unction) bestows grace on those who are sick, old, or near death and helps in forgiveness of sins and sometimes the physical healing of the body.[13]

7. *Holy Orders* (not repeated) confers special grace and spiritual power upon bishops, priests, and deacons for leadership in the Church as representatives of Christ "for all eternity": "Holy Orders is the Sacrament of the New Law instituted by Christ, through which spiritual power is given together with the grace to exercise properly the respective office. The sacrament gives a permanent character, meaning that it cannot be repeated, and that it ordains one for all eternity."[14]

What Catholicism offers its one billion members is, in effect, a *priestly* or a "sacerdotal" religion. In such a system, salvation is mediated through the functions of the priesthood (in this case through the Catholic sacraments). Only Catholic priests and those above them can perform the sacraments.

Sacraments and the One True Church

The priestly system helps us understand why Rome teaches the Catholic Church is the one and only true Church. It also helps us comprehend the historic position of Rome that salvation is possible only through the Catholic Church. Rome holds this view because it believes that salvation comes *only* through the means of grace dispensed by the priest through the Catholic sacraments. Logically then, a person who does not partake of the sacraments cannot be saved. The Church *itself* is thus the true instrument of salvation.

Recent changes in Rome indicate that this is no longer completely true—technically, people can be saved apart from the Roman Catholic Church, but neither easily nor necessarily without consequence. Although Rome used to teach that outside the Church there was absolutely no possibility of salvation, a priest who taught this traditional belief was recently censored by the Church which claimed his teaching was heretical.

In essence, other churches and religions are now seen to have varying degrees of truth or vestigial remnants of truth; people may be saved in other churches and even in other religions, but anyone who desires the one true Church must join Rome because only Rome has the *full* truth.

This also underscores the historic basis for Rome denying salvation to Protestants and Vatican I referring to Protestants as heretics and schismatics. Vatican II has softened the tone, apparently seeing more grace operating outside the Church, and now merely refers to Protestants as "separated brethren"—an apparent attempt to help them return to their "Mother Church."

A standard Catholic text, *Fundamentals of Catholic Dogma*, while conceding that God can in some extreme circumstances communicate grace without the sacraments, nevertheless asserts, "The sacraments of the New Covenant are necessary for the salvation of mankind."[15] And, "The sacraments are the means appointed by God for the attainment of eternal salvation. Three of them [baptism, penance, Holy Orders] are in the ordinary way of salvation so necessary that without their use salvation cannot be attained."[16]

The Nature and Function of the Sacraments

The Catholic Encyclopedia discusses the nature and function of the sacraments as follows:

> It is necessary to set forth the essential elements of a sacrament. These are: (a) a sensible sign instituted by God, which gives sanctifying grace; (b) both matter and form present with each sacrament; the matter is the material used, the form the accompanying words and action; and (c) a minister, someone authorized to give the sacrament with the intention of doing what the Church intends.... The sacraments produce grace.... Sanctifying grace is given by reason of the rite itself (*ex opere operato*), and grace is not given if the sacrament is not received with the necessary moral disposition. In addition, each sacrament confers a special grace, called sacramental grace. As defined by the Council of Trent, it is the teaching of the Catholic Church, that every one of the sacraments of the New Law was instituted by Christ. ... Vatican II declares: "The purpose of the sacraments is to sanctify men, to build up the body of Christ, and finally to give worship to God. Because they are signs they also instruct."[17]

The sacraments are mediated through men who are properly trained by the Church and who believe they are representing God. They are held to dispense God's grace and favor. As noted above, each of the seven sacraments is believed to confer a special grace termed "sacramental grace."

Through the sacraments, "internal grace is that received in the interior of the soul, enabling us to act supernaturally."[18] Further, "The supernatural gift of God infused into the very essence of the soul as a habit is habitual grace. This grace is also called sanctifying or justifying grace, because it is included in both."[19]

In essence, "The soul becomes good and holy through the infusion of grace" in the sacraments.[20] This increases one's justification.

The real difference, then, between the Protestant and Catholic view of sacraments is not in the number of sacraments (two versus seven). Rather, it is in what the sacraments are believed to do—in their meaning and purpose.

Protestantism sees both baptism and communion primarily as symbols and/or memorials of vital theological truths. Baptism, for example, symbolizes the believer's death to his old life and resurrection to new life in Jesus Christ (Romans 6:1-13). Communion commemorates the death of Christ for our sins and also reminds the believer that not only did Christ die for all the believer's sins (Colossians 2:13), but He also rose from the dead as proof of the believer's justification before God (Romans 4:25).

But Catholicism sees the sacraments as actually changing a person inwardly, through a continual form of regeneration and spiritual empowerment. In Protestantism a sacrament underscores a promise of God; in Catholicism it is an outward sign of an actual infused grace or spiritual power.

In other words, the sacraments infuse a special grace into the soul of a Catholic in order to meet a special need. They are, therefore, an outward sign of an infused grace.

This explains why the basis for a doctrine like justification in Catholic theology is not the fact of Christ's righteousness being imputed (transferred or credited) once for all to a believer solely by faith. Rather, it is the fact that—through the sacraments—Christ's righteousness is infused into our very being (initial justification) so that we progressively become more and more righteous. And on that basis (the fact we progress in actual righteousness), we are eventually declared righteous, and then after death "ultimately righteous." Thus, in Catholicism final justification occurs primarily by means of the sacraments and progressive spiritual growth—not by faith alone.

The Catholic Sacraments • 71

If we look at the sacraments collectively, we can see that each one is intended to perform a special function at a special time. Just as baptism, confirmation, and marriage are pivotal points in a person's life, so also penance, the Mass, and anointing of the sick are steps on the road to heaven.

Rome's Unchanging Stance

Why is it that Rome has not changed its official position on justification? In one sense it cannot because of its stance on the sacraments.

In 1547 the Council of Trent decreed the following concerning the sacraments:

> Wherefore, in order to destroy the errors and extirpate the heresies that in our stormy times are directed against the most holy sacraments . . . which are exceedingly detrimental to the purity of the Catholic Church and the salvation of souls, the holy ecumenical and general Council of Trent . . . has thought it proper to establish and enact these present canons.[21]

The canons include the following declarations that these sacraments are necessary for salvation.

The Sacraments in General (Canon 4)

> If anyone says that the sacraments . . . are not necessary for salvation . . . and that without the desire of them men obtain from God through faith alone the grace of justification . . . let him be anathema.[22]

Baptism (Canons 3, 5)

> If anyone says that in the Roman Church, which is the mother and mistress of all churches, there is not the true doctrine concerning the sacrament of baptism, let him be anathema. . . . If anyone says that baptism is optional, that is, not necessary for salvation, let him be anathema.[23]

Penance (14th Session, November 25, 1551)

> Penance was indeed necessary at all times for all men who had stained themselves by mortal sin.... This sacrament of penance is for those who have fallen after baptism [and is] necessary for salvation, as baptism is for those who have not yet been regenerated.[24]

Confession (Canons 6, 7, 9)

> If anyone denies that sacramental confession was instituted by divine law or is necessary to salvation ... let him be anathema.... If anyone says that in the sacrament of penance it is not required by divine law for the remission of sins ... let him be anathema.... If anyone says that the sacramental absolution of the priest is not a judicial act but a mere service of pronouncing and declaring to him who confesses that the sins are forgiven ... or says that the confession of the penitent is not necessary in order that the priest may be able to absolve him, let him be anathema.[25]

Mass (Canons 3, 6, 9)

> If anyone says that the sacrifice of the Mass is one only of praise and thanksgiving; or that it is a mere commemoration of sacrifice consummated on the cross but not a propitiatory one; or that it profits him only who receives, and ought not to be offered for the living and the dead, for sins, punishments, satisfactions, and other necessities, let him be anathema.[26]

Trent continues in Canons 6 and 9, "If anyone says that the canon of the Mass contains errors and is therefore to be abrogated, let him be anathema. If anyone says that the Mass ought to be celebrated in the vernacular tongue only let him be anathema."[27]

It is clear from the above citations that the Roman Catholic Church opposed the biblical and Reformation view of justification by faith alone when it decreed that the sacraments were necessary for salvation and part of the process for a person to attain final justification. As Catholic theologian Ludwig Ott says, for the Catholic, "eternal blessedness in heaven is the reward for good works performed on this earth."[28] Indeed, unless these are maintained throughout life, a Catholic, irrespective of his faith in Christ, can still go to hell.

Justification is therefore not a completed, final, forensic act of God who declares the believer righteous as a result of his simple faith in Christ. We are dealing with a completely different system of religion. This should be clearly recognized by both Evangelicals and Catholics.

In order to show that the Catholic Church still holds to what the Council of Trent codified in 1547, we will now examine the sacraments as they are taught today. Space does not permit discussing each sacrament in detail; however, to illustrate the sacraments we will discuss baptism and Holy Eucharist in the pages that follow. In the next chapter, we will also examine penance.

Baptism Is Necessary for Salvation

The Catholic Church teaches that baptism remits original sin, actual guilt, and all punishment due to sin.[29] It also teaches that baptism confers 1) the start of justification, 2) spiritual rebirth or regeneration, and 3) the start of sanctification. The 1994 *Catechism* teaches that baptism and the Catholic Church are necessary for salvation: "Baptism is *necessary for salvation* for those to whom the Gospel has been proclaimed and who have had the possibility of asking for this sacrament. The Church does not know of any means other than baptism that assures entry into eternal beatitude. . . . *God has bound salvation to the Sacrament of Baptism*."[30] Further, "Baptism is birth into the new life in Christ. In accordance with the Lord's will, it is *necessary for salvation* as is the Church herself, which we enter by baptism."[31]

Further, "By Baptism all [past] sins are forgiven, original sin and all personal sins, as well as all punishment for sin," and "Baptism makes us members of the Body of Christ. . . . Baptism incorporates us into the Church."[32]

The *Catechism* also teaches that:

> Baptism not only purifies from all sins, but also makes the neophite "a new creature," an adopted son of God, who has become a "partaker of the divine nature." . . . The Most Holy Trinity gives the baptized sanctifying grace, the grace of justification: . . . giving them the power

> to live and act under the prompting of the Holy Spirit
> through the gifts of the Holy Spirit . . . allowing them to
> grow in goodness through the moral virtues. Thus the
> whole organism of the Christian's supernatural life has
> its roots in Baptism.[33]

Here we see once again that justification is confused with sanctification. We also see that baptism is a major step in progressive justification. In fact, "The different effects of Baptism [include] regeneration and renewal. Thus the two principal effects are purification from sins and new birth in the Holy Spirit."[34]

Given all that the sacrament of baptism is said to do, it is hardly surprising that baptism is said to be essential for salvation and that salvation cannot be had without it.

Catholic apologist Karl Keating teaches, "The Catholic Church has always taught that justification comes through the sacrament of baptism" and "baptism is the justifying act."[35] Thus, "the justification that occurs at baptism effects a real change in the soul."[36]

The Catholic Encyclopedia also stresses the importance of baptism in the scheme of salvation:

> The effects of this sacrament are: 1) it cleanses us from
> original sin; 2) it makes us Christians through grace by
> sharing in Christ's death and resurrection and setting up
> an initial program of living . . . ; 3) it makes us children of
> God as the life of Christ is brought forth within us. . . .
> Vatican II declared: ". . . baptism constitutes a sacramen-
> tal bond of unity linking all who have been reborn by
> means of it. But baptism, of itself, is only a beginning.
>
> . . . baptism is necessary for salvation."[37]

Notice, baptism is only the beginning of justification. Baptism is said to make it possible for a person to cooperate with divine grace, allowing for further growth in righteousness. Subsequent good works increase grace (spiritual power) and help perfect justification. So, baptism does not automatically save one forever, in that Catholicism holds that salvation can be lost through mortal ("deadly") sin or other means. But again (except in very rare cases), salvation cannot be had without baptism.

In *Outlines of the Catholic Faith*, an authoritative Catholic source, we read the following about baptism:

> The Sacrament of Baptism cleanses us from original sin.
> In those who have the use of reason Baptism also re-
> moves actual sin and the temporal punishment due to
> sin. In Baptism we are reborn as children of God, made
> members of his Church, and heirs to the kingdom of
> heaven. Baptism permanently relates us to God and is
> necessary for salvation. . . . The theological virtues of
> Faith, Hope and Charity are infused with grace into the
> soul by Baptism. Baptism imprints an indelible character
> on the soul and can be received only once.[38]

Because Catholicism teaches baptism places "an indelible mark
on your soul"[39] the Church of Rome holds that once a Catholic,
always a Catholic. As we have seen, however, to always be a Catholic does not necessarily mean one cannot end up in eternal judgment in hell.

As the 1994 *Catechism* emphasizes, "To die in mortal sin without
repenting and accepting God's merciful love means remaining separated from him forever by our own free choice. The teaching of
the Church affirms the existence of hell and its eternity. Immediately after death the souls of those who die in a state of mortal sin
descend into hell, where they suffer the punishments of hell, 'eternal fire.'"[40]

Of course, this is not possible if justification is an act whereby
God declares a person eternally righteous, based on Christ's death
for them, as Hebrews 10:14 says: "Because by one sacrifice [Christ's
atoning and substitutionary death on the cross for sinners] he
[Jesus] has made perfect [in standing through justification] forever
those who are being made holy [in the process of sanctification]."

Nevertheless, the fact that Catholicism teaches baptism is an
essential requirement for salvation underscores their system of
works salvation. The *Fundamentals of Catholic Dogma* declares, "Baptism by water is, since the promulgation of the gospel, necessary for
all men without exception, for salvation."[41]

Nowhere in all the Bible can this teaching be demonstrated. If
baptism conferred all the above upon the believer, it would be
strange indeed that the apostle Paul himself would even think of
saying that "Christ did *not* send me to baptize, but to preach the
gospel" (1 Corinthians 1:17, emphasis added).

Please let this sink in. Paul clearly teaches that God did not send
him to baptize, but to preach the gospel. Here we see the marked
difference between biblical Protestantism and Catholicism.

Catholicism claims that baptism forgives sins, regenerates, justifies, and sanctifies. It is therefore absolutely essential to salvation.

But if the Catholic Church is correct, then how could Paul possibly say what he has just said and emphasized? If Catholic dogma were biblical, we would expect Paul to say, "God absolutely did send me to baptize because apart from baptism no one will ever be saved." But that is not where Paul's emphasis lies. It lies with the preaching of the gospel and not with baptism! Why? Because it is the preaching of the gospel which teaches us that salvation comes by grace through faith alone to anyone. Faith allows Christ to truly regenerate, justify, forgive sins, and sanctify us.

In essence, to say that baptism is necessary for salvation is to undercut the basic biblical teaching of salvation by faith alone (Ephesians 2:8,9).

The Mass Is Necessary for Salvation

Roman Catholicism teaches that in the Mass the sacrifice of Jesus Christ Himself is actually re-presented to the faithful and its benefits are applied to them.

Although the Catholic Church maintains that the Mass in no way detracts from the atonement of Christ, it still believes that it is principally through the Mass that the blessings of Christ's death are applied to believers. Therefore, the blessings of Christ's death are not procured solely by faith alone in what He accomplished at the cross.

Let us begin our discussion of the Mass by evaluating what the 1994 *Catechism* says about it. This *Catechism* describes the Mass as "the source and summit of the Christian life"; "the sum and summary of our faith"; and "the Sacrament of sacraments."[42]

In the Catholic Mass, of course, we find Rome's doctrine of transubstantiation. This view details that the bread and wine each literally *become* the body and blood of our Lord Jesus Christ.

Thus, "It is by the conversion of the bread and wine into Christ's body and blood that Christ becomes present in this sacrament," and "In the most blessed sacrament of the Eucharist . . . the whole Christ is truly, really and substantially contained."[43] The Catholic Church also believes that all of Christ, blood and body, are present in both the bread and wine. Therefore, even though usually only the Catholic priest is allowed to partake of the wine, the layman nevertheless partakes of His blood through partaking of the bread.[44]

Furthermore, because Christ is actually present in His entirety in the Eucharist, the Catholic Church believes that the Eucharist should be worshiped. This is why priests and Catholics genuflect when the host is present—because it is really *Christ* present. "The Catholic Church has always offered and still offers to the sacrament of the Eucharist the cult of adoration [worship], not only during Mass, but also outside of it, reserving the consecrated hosts with the utmost care, exposing them to the solemn veneration of the faithful, and carrying them in procession."[45]

The following statements from the 1994 *Catechism* show in what manner the blessings of Christ's death are thought to be applied to believers during the Mass. These show that participation in the Eucharist is also part of the process of justification:

> When the Church celebrates the Eucharist...the sacrifice Christ offered once for all on the cross remains ever present. "As often as the sacrifice of the Cross is celebrated on the altar, the work of our redemption is carried out."[46]

> The Eucharist is thus a sacrifice because it re-presents (makes present) the sacrifice at the cross, because it is its *memorial* and because it *applies* its fruit. ... [e.g.,] its salutary power [is] applied to the forgiveness of the sins we daily commit.[47]

> The sacrifice of Christ and the sacrifice of the Eucharist are one single sacrifice...."In this divine sacrifice which is celebrated in the Mass, the same Christ who offered himself once in a bloody manner on the altar of the cross is contained and is offered in an unbloody manner."[48]

> The Eucharistic sacrifice is also offered for *the faithful departed* [in purgatory] who "have died in Christ but are not yet wholly purified," so that they may be able to enter into the light and peace of Christ. ...[49]

> Holy Communion... *preserves, increases, and renews the life of grace received at Baptism.* ... The Eucharist cannot unite us to Christ without at the same time cleansing us from past sins and preserving us from future sins. ... [It] *wipes away venial sins.* ... [And] the Eucharist *preserves us from future mortal sins.*[50]

> By this sacrifice he pours out the graces of salvation on his Body which is the Church.[51]

In light of all that is accomplished through a Catholic's participation in the Holy Eucharist, is it any wonder that the Church feels this is the "Sacrament of all sacraments"?

Clearly, it 1) carries out the work of redemption; 2) forgives sins; 3) helps purify those in purgatory; 4) "increases the life of grace received at baptism"; 5) cleanses past sins and sanctifies or preserves from future sins—even mortal ones; and 6) pours out the grace of salvation upon all the Church. Who then can deny that participation in the Mass is necessary for salvation and also is a form of salvation by faith/works?

Where does the Catholic Church derive all of these teachings—from the Scripture itself or from Catholic tradition? It can only be from Catholic tradition because Scripture itself contradicts this view.

The Mass and Christ's Atonement?

At issue in the debate between Evangelicals and Catholics on the matter of salvation is Rome's insistence that the Mass in no way detracts from the atonement of Christ.

But how can this be true? The Mass itself, because of Rome's belief in Christ's actual presence in the wine and host, is defined throughout Catholicism as being "truly propitiatory." In other words, it truly forgives sins. Because the Mass pardons sins, it is held to be necessary for salvation. From a Protestant perspective, the natural question is this: If Christ died for all sin on the cross, and faith alone reaches out to Christ who gives this benefit freely, is the Catholic sacrifice of the Mass even necessary?

Catholics and Protestants agree that sin is an affront to God's holiness, calling forth God's condemnation. They agree a propitiation is an offering that is made to God in light of His offended justice so that He becomes favorable to the sinner. But Protestants disagree with the following: "Hence the Mass as a propitiation is offered to effect the remission of sins."[52]

Instead of Christ's once-for-all offering at Calvary being sufficient, the Council of Trent upholds the standard Catholic view: "This sacrifice [of the Mass] is truly propitiatory. . . . For by this oblation the Lord is appeased . . . and he pardons wrongdoing and sins, even grave ones."[53] Further, the *Fundamentals of Catholic Dogma* states, "In the Sacrifice of the Mass, Christ's Sacrifice on the cross is made present, its memory is celebrated, and its saving power is applied," and "As a propitiatory sacrifice the Sacrifice of the Mass effects the remission of sins and the punishment of sins."[54]

The Catholic Church has always emphasized the fact that Christ is resacrificed in the Mass (Catholics use the term "re-presented") as a propitiation to God. And the authoritative Council of Trent affirmed that the sacrifice of the Mass is propitiatory both for the living and the dead because it offers in an unbloody manner *the same Christ* who once offered Himself in a bloody manner on the altar of the cross"—therefore:

> It [the Mass] is rightly offered not only for the sins, punishments, satisfactions and other necessities of the faithful who are living, but also for those departed in Christ, but not yet fully purified [i.e., those in purgatory].[55]

The doctrine of transubstantiation, that the bread and wine actually become the body and blood of Christ, was codified in its present form by Thomas Aquinas (1225-74). Nevertheless, this doctrine cannot be established biblically:

> Catholic theologians make much of such passages as John 6:48-58, Matthew 26:26, and 1 Corinthians 11:23-30 in an attempt to teach that Christ and the apostles taught this doctrine. But the evidence is not as one-sided as might first appear. . . . That our Lord was using highly figurative language is evident from the fact that both the Jews and His disciples were interpreting His words literally [John 6:] vs. 52, 60, 61 and He deliberately went out of His way to contradict such a literal interpretation: "The words that I am speaking to you are spirit and they are life: the flesh does not profit anything" (verses 63).

> Our Lord clearly taught that *belief* in Him was the metaphorical equivalent of "eating" His flesh and blood (John 6:35, 36). And as we have seen, He expressly stated that the words "bread," "flesh," "blood," and "eat," in a fleshly or literal interpretation, profited nothing.[56]

In other words, Jesus was telling His disciples to "eat" (ingest and digest) His *words*, not literally His physical flesh and blood.

Pope Pius XII in his encyclical (a general letter) *Mediator Dei* reaffirmed the Council of Trent when he stressed that the sacrifice of the Mass was not a "mere commemoration" of the passion and death of Christ, as Protestants teach, but "is truly and properly the offering of a sacrifice wherein by an unbloody immolation [something offered as a sacrifice], the High Priest does what He [Jesus] had already done on the Cross, offering Himself to the Eternal Father as a most acceptable victim."[57]

Vatican II continued this view of the Mass, also reaffirming the position of Trent: "One and the same is the victim, one and the same is He Who now offers by the ministry of His priests, and Who then offered Himself on the Cross; the difference is only in the manner of offering."[58]

As a result, Vatican II teaches that at the Mass, "the faithful gather, and find help and comfort through venerating the presence of the Son of God our Savior, offered for us [now] on the sacrificial altar."[59]

According to Karl Keating in *Catholicism and Fundamentalism*, "The Church insists that the Mass is the continuation and re-presentation of the sacrifice of Calvary."[60] Emphasizing it is not a recrucifixion of Christ where Christ suffers and dies again, he cites John A. O'Brien who says, "The Mass is the renewal and perpetuation of the sacrifice of the Cross in the sense that it offers anew to God the Victim of Calvary . . . and applies the fruits of Christ's death upon the Cross to individual human souls."[61]

In essence, the real problem of the Mass for Protestants is this: Catholicism teaches that Christ is still offering Himself today in thousands of Masses conducted regularly throughout the world.[62] We stress that here the Mass is not merely the symbolic offering of the Eucharist or the thanksgiving of the faithful. Instead, "It is the supreme moment in the Church's worship when the priest claims to offer Christ as a sacrifice for the living and the dead."[63]

The Catholic Encyclopedia states,

> We may establish that the Eucharist is a true sacrifice. The true nature of a sacrifice is realized in the Mass. By declaration of the Council of Trent, Christ is recognized as the offering Priest, the Victim offered, and the immolation in the sacramental order. These essentials of the sacrifice are present in the three main actions of the Mass: the Offertory, the Consecration, and the Communion.[64]

The Biblical View of Christ's Atonement

But a continual resacrificing of Christ is not what we find taught in the Bible. Rather, Christ is pictured as having accomplished His work once and for all and having sat down at the right hand of the

Father (Hebrews 1:3; 8:1). The finality of Christ's sacrifice stands in stark contrast with the Catholic conception of the constant "renewal" of that sacrifice in the Mass.

Consider the book of Hebrews. Hebrews repeatedly uses terms such as "once," "once for all," and "forever" to emphasize both the perfection and the finality of Christ's death on the cross (Hebrews 9:12,26,28; 10:12,14).

If Christ offered one sacrifice for sins forever and thus obtained eternal redemption for us (Hebrews 9:12; 10:10-14), what is the need for a perpetual "bloodless sacrifice" of Christ over and over again, literally millions of times? How can the Mass apply a forgiveness of sins that was already fully earned by Christ on the cross and applied to the believer at the very point of saving faith (John 5:24; 6:47)?

The writer of Hebrews reminds every believer of what God Himself has personally told them: "Their sins and lawless acts I will remember no more." The writer then goes on to state, "And where these have been forgiven, there is no longer any sacrifice for sin" (Hebrews 10:17,18). If there is *no longer a sacrifice for sin*, what can possibly be the purpose of the Mass as a sacrifice for sins? Catholicism wrongly teaches that by participating in the Mass—through a specific sacramental act or work—the believer can actually help to forgive his own sins and maintain and increase his "justification" (i.e., to Catholics the progressive sanctification that finally merits eternal life).

Clearly, this is another form of salvation by works. It is why Catholicism teaches that participation in the Eucharist is part of a whole system of progressive salvation which, in the end, actually *merits* heaven for the believer.

It should also be obvious why the sacraments are said to be essential for salvation, and the Eucharist is held to be the "sacrament of sacraments." One cannot logically deny that participation in the Eucharist is essential for salvation.

In contrast, the Scripture is clear: "one sacrifice for sins forever"; "once for all"; "It is finished," etc. (Romans 6:10; Hebrews 7:27; 9:26-28; 10:10-14; 1 Peter 3:18; John 19:30). Thus, in the book of Hebrews the "once for all" sacrifice of Christ is clearly contrasted with the perpetual offerings of the Levitical priest. We are told that Christ was not to offer Himself repeatedly, for then He would have had to suffer repeatedly since the foundation of the world:

Nor did he enter heaven *to offer himself again and again*, the way the high priest enters the Most Holy Place every year with blood that is not his own. Then Christ would have had to suffer many times since the creation of the world. But now he has appeared *once for all* at the end of the ages *to do away with sin* by the sacrifice of himself. Just as man is destined to die once, and after that to face judgment, so Christ *was sacrificed once* to take away the sins of many people; and he will appear a second time, not to bear sin, but to bring salvation to those who are waiting for him (Hebrews 9:25-28, emphasis added).

Thus, the Bible teaches that Jesus appeared "once for all" to put away sin by the sacrifice of Himself. This final sacrifice is further contrasted with the Levitical priestly sacrifices which "can never take away sins" (Hebrews 10:11). Indeed, it is the very idea of a repetition of sacrifices which proves their insufficiency. Otherwise, they would "have ceased to be offered" (Hebrews 10:2 NASB).

When the Bible teaches that "but when [Christ] had offered *for all time one sacrifice for sins*, he sat down at the right hand of God. . . . Because by one sacrifice he has made perfect forever those who are being made holy" (Hebrews 10:12,14, emphasis added), it undermines the very basis of the Catholic Mass: continual sacrifice. As H.M. Carson, a Baptist minister in North Ireland and author of *Dawn or Twilight: A Study of Contemporary Roman Catholicism* points out,

Any service, therefore, which purports to renew the sacrifice of Calvary is a plain denial of the overwhelming testimony of Scripture to the perfection of the Lord's one offering. The doctrine of the Mass implies the imperfection and insufficiency of the sacrifice of Calvary, for the latter needs now to be supplemented by the daily offering at the altars of the Church of Rome.[65]

In other words, Jesus' perfect sacrifice, reflected by His own cry from the cross, "It is finished" (John 19:30), leaves no room at all for the Catholic resacrifice of Christ at the Mass based on the idea that Christ is actually present in the bread and wine.

Because of the dogma of transubstantiation, Roman Catholicism teaches that Christ continues to offer Himself as a holy sacrifice for sin at every Mass. Many Protestants have argued that if this does not undermine the finality and sufficiency of the atonement, they can think of little else that does.

The Problem of the Sacraments

In the end, for Catholicism it is still *my* work and *my* merit that makes it possible for God to restore me to the process of justification and/or salvation. In the end it is something *I* do that keeps me out of hell. But this teaching is not biblical.

All through the New Testament it is the merit of Jesus Christ alone that reconciles us, justifies us, and assures our entrance into heaven. The problem with the Catholic sacraments is that they are a constant reminder and demand for works that must be performed in order to finally merit heaven after death. The biblical doctrine of justification does away with all this by teaching that the believer can know he has a perfect standing with God and the assurance of heaven the moment he places his total faith in Christ to save him.

The above discussion clearly demonstrates that Catholicism does teach that salvation occurs through the sacraments—works of merit performed by individual Catholics in order to help secure their own redemption. These teachings are why "the sacraments as works of human merit, which must be mediated through the church, represent a denial of justification by faith alone and an infringement upon the sovereign freedom of God."[66]

The Council of Trent—whose decrees, as we have shown, still remain authoritative today—declared as anathema (divinely cursed) anyone who would deny the seven sacraments of Rome: "If anyone says that the sacraments . . . were not all instituted by our Lord Jesus Christ, or that there are more or less than seven . . . or that any one of these seven is not truly and intrinsically a sacrament, let him be anathema."[67] Further, "If anyone says that the sacraments are not necessary for salvation and that without them . . . men obtain from God through faith alone the grace of justification let him be anathema."[68]

But anyone who, in the light of Scripture, carefully examines the Roman Catholic sacraments would have to conclude that these sacraments do involve works of merit. They are supposed to increase justification. They actually do *merit* heaven for Catholics because without them no one will ever *get* to heaven. In other words, no Catholic gets to heaven unless he accomplishes and performs the proper sacramental actions.[69]

This is why the 1994 *Catechism* states, "From the time of the apostles, becoming a Christian has been accomplished by a journey and initiation in several stages."[70]

But according to the Bible, "becoming a Christian" is not a journey, nor does it happen in several stages. It happens instantaneously at the point of true faith in Jesus Christ for the forgiveness of sins.

For Protestants, *being* a Christian may be considered a journey, after being justified. Not so in Catholicism. *Becoming* a Christian involves a lengthy, indeed lifelong journey of various stages of initiation, sanctification, justification, and final salvation after death—with no certainty of ultimate success in this life.

What Kind of Works?

The response of Catholic scholars to such a critique is to say that the works of initial grace are done entirely in the power of Christ and therefore are not human works of righteousness meritorious for salvation. In essence, the argument is that the Catholic Church claims it is *not* teaching a system of salvation by personal merit and works of righteousness. But consider the following discussion from the 1994 *Catechism*, which clearly states, "We can then merit for ourselves . . . the attainment of eternal life":

> The merit of man before God in the Christian life arises from the fact that God has freely chosen to associate men with the work of his grace. The fatherly action of God is first on his own initiative, and then follows man's free act and through his collaboration, so that the merit of good works is to be attributed in the first to the grace of God then to the faithful. . . .

> Since the initiative belongs to God in the order of grace, no one can merit the initial grace of forgiveness and justification, at the beginning of conversion. Moved by the Holy Spirit and by charity, we can then merit for ourselves and for others the graces needed for our sanctification, for the increase of grace and charity, and for the attainment of eternal life.[71]

Let us consider this argument here. The Catholic Church is claiming that because our initial movement toward salvation is solely by God's grace, ultimately Catholicism does not teach a system of salvation by faith and works. The Catholic Church is attempting to argue that grace-*inspired* works are not works for salvation! As philosopher and theologian Dr. Norman Geisler argues, "It makes no difference whether these works are *prompted* by grace, they are still meritorious works as *a condition* for eternal life. They are not based on grace and grace alone."[72]

No more authoritative analysis of the Council of Trent has been penned than by Lutheran theologian Martin Chemnitz. At this point we ask the reader to consider carefully his evaluation of this issue of meritorious works in the religion of Roman Catholicism. It is clear from both the sixteenth chapter of the Council of Trent as well as Chemnitz's masterful analysis that Rome did teach—and that the Catholic does believe—a sinner merits eternal life from his good works:

> First, that they [Rome] teach that the regenerate through their works truly merit not only other spiritual and bodily rewards but also eternal life itself, which is to be paid as a reward for the good works and merits of the regenerate. Second, that they think that rewards are given to good works not from the grace, mercy, and fatherly liberality of the heavenly Father but as a matter of debt, because nothing is lacking in the good works of the regenerate that they should not be judged to have satisfied the divine law fully according to the state of this life and to have truly merited eternal life. These things are found in the 16th chapter of the Council of Trent.
>
> The Council of Trent says that the good works of the regenerate truly merit eternal life. Thus they simply repeat and strengthen the fictions of the Scholastics concerning the *meritum condigni*, that the works of the regenerate in this life, because they have been performed in love, worthily merit eternal life, that is, that eternal life must be given as something owed by divine justice to good works. For thus they define the *meritum condigni*.
>
> And let the reader observe that to the Tridentine fathers it seemed just too shameless to ascribe eternal life solely to our merits, therefore, as they sought to give some indication of modesty, they divided eternal life, for honor's sake, between the merit of Christ and the merit of our works.[73]

When Roman Catholic scholars insist they do not teach salvation by works, they are fudging. As in Mormonism and other so-called "Christian" religions, they must make an artificial distinction between two categories of works in order to do so.

In Mormonism, this distinction is between Mosaic works (no longer required) and "gospel works" (required for salvation). In Catholicism, the distinction is between "works of the law" (not required) and "works of the church" (meritorious works required for salvation) or between "self-righteous works" and "self-denying works."

No Biblical Distinction

The problem is that such distinctions cannot be upheld biblically. For example, what good work is there that is not in harmony with the divine law—and therefore still a "work of the law"? And again, even works prompted by grace are still works.

When Paul condemns salvation by works, we do not find an artificial distinction upheld. All works are condemned as a way of salvation. Thus, even Gentiles who don't have the Mosaic law (Romans 2:14) cannot be justified by works (Romans 3:21-24).

Paul himself does not distinguish "works of the law" from simply "works" or "works of righteousness" (Ephesians 2:8,9; Titus 3:5-7). As far as salvation is concerned, they all suffer the same condemnation.

Finally, Catholics may claim that we can attain a right standing before God apart from merit (as in our initial justification), but this does not address the real issue. As Dr. Geisler points out:

> Catholic insistence that a right standing can be obtained without works misses the point. Namely, that this standing for Catholics does not entail the gift of eternal life. Further, the Catholic argument that this is a gift that is merited by work (though not deservedly earned) is insufficient. For even if one is given, say, a million dollars from someone for getting a loaf of bread for him (which he obviously did not earn), nonetheless, he did do some work and, hence, it was not by grace alone. Likewise, if someone spends a lifetime of works (however long) as a condition for receiving eternal life, then it was clearly not by grace alone.
>
> [Further,] the argument by some Catholic apologists that one need not work for eternal life but simply avoid mortal sin misses the mark for two very important reasons. First, the question is not how one loses salvation but how he obtains it to begin with. Second, and most importantly, regardless of

whether one only loses salvation by a mortal sin (not by lack of works) or not, if he lives for receiving justification he still has to work as a condition for receiving eternal life. And if this is so then it is not totally by grace.[74]

The sacraments of Rome are proof that a system of salvation by merit is taught and therefore that the Catholic Church teaches another gospel (Galatians 1:8,9). In the end, salvation is procured by 1) God's grace, 2) individual faith, and 3) individual performance (that is, the sacraments).

In conclusion, when one thoroughly examines what Rome teaches concerning the sacraments, especially baptism and the Holy Eucharist, it becomes impossible to deny that a system of salvation by works is taught in Roman Catholicism—no matter what Catholics may claim otherwise.

.7.

Penance, Confession, and the Rosary

*W*hat does the Catholic Church teach concerning the lifelong process of justification and salvation in relationship to penance, confession, and the Rosary?

The Catholic Church teaches that after baptism, if a man or woman commits mortal sin, he or she will lose his or her justification. In order to regain justification a person must perform the sacrament of penance.

Penance is a particular act or series of acts considered as satisfaction offered to God as a reparation for sin committed. Penance may involve what is known as "mortification" or self-punishment such as wearing an irritating shirt woven of coarse animal hair,[1] prayer (e.g., the Rosary), or a religious pilgrimage to a shrine of Christ or Mary,[2] or any number of other deeds.

The Catholic View of Penance

According to *The Catholic Encyclopedia*, Jesus Christ Himself instituted the sacrament of penance for "the pardon of sins committed after baptism."[3] Thus, "In the Sacrament of Penance, the faithful obtain from the mercy of God pardon for their sins against Him."[4]

As noted, the sacrament of penance is designed specifically to deal with sins committed after baptism. Why? Because the grace that is received or infused in baptism can be entirely lost by mortal ("deadly") sin. Mortal sin is held to be deadly because it actually destroys the grace of God within a person, making salvation necessary again. Thus, a new sacrament (penance) is necessary in order to restore an individual to the state of grace first received at baptism.

In fact, without penance a person *cannot* be restored to salvation.

This is one reason why the Council of Trent actually referred to the sacrament of penance as a "second plank" of justification:[5]

> Those who through sin have forfeited the received grace of justification, can again be justified when, moved by God, they exert themselves to obtain through the Sacrament of Penance the recovery, by the merits of Christ, of the grace lost. For this manner of justification is restoration for those fallen, which the holy Fathers have aptly called a second plank after the shipwreck of grace lost.[6]

As the *Catechism of the Catholic Church* (1994) emphasizes,

> Christ instituted the Sacrament of Penance for all sinful members of his church: above all for those who, since baptism, have fallen into grave sin, and have thus lost their baptismal grace. It is to them that the sacrament of Penance offers a new possibility to convert and to recover the grace of justification. The Fathers of the Church present this sacrament as "the second plank [of salvation] after the shipwreck which is the loss of grace."[7]

Even though the *Catechism of the Catholic Church* maintains that "only God forgives sins,"[8] it nevertheless teaches that God forgives sins through *penance*. After discussing different forms of penance in the Christian life, such as fasting, prayer, almsgiving, the Eucharist, Scripture reading, praying the Liturgy of the Hours, praying the Our Father, etc., it says this: "Every sincere act of worship or devotion revives the spirit of conversion and repentance within us and contributes to the forgiveness of our sins."[9]

Further, the *Catechism* teaches that "the disclosure or confession of sins to a priest is an essential element of the sacrament."[10]

In fact, Catholicism teaches the sacrament of penance has three parts: first, "contrition"—a person must be sorry for his sins; second, "confession"—a person must fully confess each one of his mortal sins to a priest; and third, "satisfaction"—a person must do works of satisfaction such as fasting, saying prayers, almsgiving, or doing other works of piety the priest gives him to do.

Complete spiritual health cannot be had, according to the Roman Catholic Church, apart from acts of penance: "Raised up from sin, the sinner must still recover his full spiritual health by doing something more to make amends for the sin: he must 'make satisfaction for' or 'expiate' his sins."[11]

Penance As a Form of Salvation

On the basis of what we have discussed, salvation through good works is evident in the doctrine of penance. As *The Catholic Encyclopedia* states: "The result of mortal sin is the loss of sanctifying grace, the loss of the gifts of the Holy Spirit, remorse, and the punitive effect of *eternal separation from God*. To avoid these consequences, the reception of the Sacrament of Penance is required to return to the love of God."[12]

In other words, apart from performing the sacrament of penance, a Catholic who commits mortal sin is destined for eternal punishment in hell. Escaping such a fate results from the penitent acts of the believer (that is, a form of salvation by works).

But none of this is biblical. Biblically, prior to salvation *all* sin, especially unbelief in Jesus, is mortal. Even the smallest sin against God is sufficient to condemn a person eternally. But after salvation *no* sin is mortal, no matter how grave, because Christ paid the full divine penalty for every sin, big or small, on the cross. This complete forgiveness, God's pardon, has been freely given to the believer (Ephesians 1:7; Colossians 2:13).

Further, according to Scripture, salvation is based on God's grace and election, "not by works but by him who calls" (Romans 9:12). Salvation "does not, therefore, depend on man's desire or effort, but on God's mercy" (Romans 9:16).

If salvation is by grace and election, then it depends entirely on God. Therefore no saved person can ever be lost and no mortal sin can ever cancel a person's justification.

What this means is that Catholics who believe their mortal sins are forgiven by the work of penance are being deceived concerning what the Bible really teaches. If Christ alone truly saves them, then their mortal sins—all of them—are already fully forgiven by the death of Christ solely through their faith in Jesus (see chapter 11).

But if Catholics are *not* saved, then all the penance in the world cannot forgive their sins, whether such sins are "mortal" or the less serious "venial" ones. Biblically, it is faith in Christ alone who forgives all our sins—not penance or any other sacrament.

The sacrament of anointing of the sick is related to penance and also "removes sin":

Its reception completes the effects of the Sacrament of Penance, removes the remnants of sin, brings grace to the soul, disposes the recipient to undergo his sufferings with the conscious joining of these with the sufferings of Christ, and sometimes brings health to the body.[13]

Catholicism maintains that the works of satisfaction accomplished by the penitent sinner are done through the power of Jesus and the grace of God. But the key point is that they *are* works done by an individual—they are his or her works and they *do* earn for the individual God's merit or favor.

Is Catholicism's doctrine of penance truly biblical? Is Catholicism correct in saying that it is absolutely necessary for a person to do penance before God will forgive him and allow him to continue in the process of justification?

The Protestant View of Penance

Protestants believe that Catholicism's sacrament of penance infers that the sacrifice of Christ was not sufficient to atone fully for man's sin and that Christ's sacrifice must be supplemented by man's good works. They believe that it is solely the merits of Christ's sacrificial death on the cross which are imputed or transferred to the believer that cancel out the sinner's debt. Again, this is why Protestants maintain that justification and forgiveness take place in a single moment—the moment the sinner, through faith, asks Christ for forgiveness of his sins.

Roman Catholics believe that much more than faith is needed in order for a person to obtain forgiveness. They insist there must be both faith and works and that by these the grace of justification increases. As the Council of Trent declared, "If anyone says that the good works of the one justified . . . does not truly merit an increase of grace, [and the obtaining of] eternal life, let him be anathema."[14]

But Protestants respond, "Only Jesus Christ can atone for man's mortal sins, and He did this once for all, when He died on the cross and completely satisfied the divine law" (see chapter 11).

Protestants maintain that what God desires in the sinner before He grants forgiveness is not works of satisfaction or self-punishment for sins through lifelong penance, but repentance, which is a change of heart, a turning away from sin, and a complete trust in the work of Christ for the forgiveness of sin.

The Necessity of Confession

At the Council of Trent the Catholic Church codified priestly confession as absolutely necessary for the restoration of justification:

> The Universal Church has always understood that the complete confession of sins was also instituted by our Lord, and by divine law necessary for all who have fallen after baptism; because our Lord Jesus Christ left behind Him priests, His own vicars, as rulers and judges, to whom all the mortal sins into which the faithful of Christ . . . may have fallen should be brought in order that they may, in virtue of the power of the keys, pronounce the sentence of remission or retention of sins.[15]

Although it is frequently lost upon the faithful, the Catholic Church has made it clear that the priest does not have intrinsic authority to forgive a person's sins—his only authority is a derived one in that he is a representative for Christ, and that Christ is working through him.

Thus, when the priest says, "I absolve you," he does not mean that he alone in his own power is absolving a person from their sins. It is Christ through him. But that priestly confession is still necessary for justification.

Further, because Christ actually is thought to be in Person working through the priest, his absolution is as valid as if done by Christ Himself.[16] In *Fundamentals of Catholic Dogma* we are told, "Confession is the self-accusation by the penitent of his sins before a fully empowered priest, in order to obtain forgiveness from him by virtue of the power of the keys. . . . The Sacramental confession of sins is ordained by God and is necessary for justification."[17]

The Council of Trent places an anathema on anyone who denies the necessity of confession when it declares:

> If anyone denies that sacramental confession was instituted by divine law or is necessary to justification . . . let him be anathema [cursed by God]. . . . If anyone says that the sacrament of penance is not required by divine law for the remission of sins . . . let him be anathema. . . . If anyone says that the sacramental absolution of the priest is not a judicial act but a mere service of pronouncing and

declaring to him who confesses that the sins are forgiven . . . or says that the confession of the penitent is not
necessary in order that the priest may be able to absolve
him, let him be anathema.[18]

While the Catholic Church officially maintains that the priest per
se does not forgive the believer's sins, it is difficult to deny that in
the minds of many Catholics the priest is actually forgiving the
same sins for which Jesus died on the cross.

Catholicism also teaches that confession before a priest must be
sincerely done to be valid. The individual Catholic must genuinely
be sorry that he has committed the sin, and he must also resolve not
to repeat it. He must agree to make restitution to any individual that
his sin might have harmed, and finally he must be willing to accept
any penances imposed by the priest.[19] Only after he does all of this
is forgiveness effective.

All this raises some questions. How easy or difficult is it for a
person to be forgiven by God through the priest in order to continue
his justification? How secure is one's knowledge that his sins are
really forgiven when the forgiveness depends on what he does?
What if the person wasn't completely sorry he did the sin? What if
he isn't sure he won't do it again? What if the penances are not done
properly or completely or the restitution is unsatisfactory?

What if mortal sins like being drunk, skipping Mass, using birth
control, envying, thieving, etc., are committed regularly—every
day or every week? In essence, penance and confession pose problems for the Catholic who wishes to have certainty his lost justification is now reinstated so he may continue its increase. Penance and
confession are supposed to restore, maintain, and build one's justification, but do they—and how does the Catholic really *know*?

On the other hand, the Bible teaches a person's mortal sins are
forgiven—all of them, past, present, and future—when a person
believes in Christ. The real reason we confess our sins to God (1 John
1:9) is not to acquire a forgiveness already obtained, but to be
reminded of the forgiveness we have and to retain our sensitivity to
sin so that we may continue to grow in sanctification.

Catholicism claims that its evidence for the practice of confession
stems from two sources: first, from Jesus' own words in John 20:23,
and second, from the allegedly unanimous agreement of the Church
Fathers.

Jesus said in John 20:23, "If you forgive the sins of any, their sins
have been forgiven them; if you retain the sins of any, they have

been retained" (NASB). (Catholics believe this power originates from the "keys of the kingdom" Jesus gave to Peter and his alleged successors in Matthew 16:19.) But does this verse teach that Christians must confess their sins to a priest, or is Jesus describing what God will do as a result of the apostolic preaching of the gospel?

The Protestant View of Confession

John is not saying that the apostles or anyone else has the power to "forgive" sins in a priestly confessional, as Rome teaches. Instead, the apostle is teaching that when we go out and preach the gospel, as Jesus commanded us to, we are doing exactly what His Father sent Him to do. If men accept the gospel, then we have the right to inform them on the basis of the promises of Jesus, "Your sins are forgiven because you have placed your trust in Jesus Christ." If men reject the gospel, we also have the right to inform them on the same basis, "Your sins are not forgiven; they cannot be forgiven until you believe in Jesus Christ."

The apostle John is actually teaching that *all* Christians have this declaratory power, not just Catholic priests. In other words, every Christian—great and small—has the right to tell a new believer on the basis of Christ's promises that his sins have already been forgiven him by Jesus Christ.

The Bible does not state that any priest has the exclusive right to forgive sins on Christ's behalf. This is a prerogative of all believers which comes under the biblical teaching of the universal priesthood of believers—the fact that every believer in Christ is "a priest unto God" (1 Peter 2:5,9).

Protestants, therefore, do not believe that it is necessary for a person to confess his sins to a priest before God will forgive him. Protestants assert that all believers have been given the right of access to God through Christ and are able to go directly to God in prayer. First Timothy 2:5 declares, "For there is one God and one mediator between God and men, the man Christ Jesus." If Christ is the true mediator between God and man, as the Bible plainly says, then men should confess their sins to Him, not to a priest.

Biblically, there is no necessity for the often-humiliating experience of the confessional if Jesus Christ alone has already forgiven us the full divine penalty for our sins. There is also no fear that someone will not perform the acts of penance properly before God will grant forgiveness. There is no reason to be concerned about obligations to the Church, no need for confusion over whether or not one's sins are truly forgiven, and no reason to be terrified of purgatory for errors committed in this life.

Protestants also assert that 1 John 1:9 denies the Catholic view of priestly confession because, in context, it speaks of confession only to God, never even mentioning a priest: "If we confess our sins, he is faithful and just to forgive us our sins, and to cleanse us from all unrighteousness" (KJV).

While the Bible does teach that we are to "confess [our] sins to one another" (James 5:16 NASB); it never mentions confession to a priest. Priestly confession is a teaching that has evolved from Catholic tradition.

The reason why Protestants confess their sins to one another and not to a priest has nothing to do with the issues of the ultimate forgiveness of sins before God. Rather, it has to do with individual reconciliation among true believers in Christ. Again, there is no reason to confess our mortal sins to a priest if Christ's death on the cross has already paid for their full divine penalty.

In conclusion, both penance and priestly confession negatively impact the biblical doctrine of the atonement and the joyous promises surrounding the doctrine of justification by faith. It has been our experience that in individual Catholic practice the teachings of penance and (as we will see in chapter 9) purgatory work to undermine full confidence in Christ's free gift of justification by grace alone through faith in Christ alone.

The Rosary

The importance of the Rosary is difficult to overestimate.[20] According to Catholic tradition, it allegedly supplies a Catholic with spiritual power and, many believe, forgiveness of sins—as well as many blessings and graces from God. Pope Paul VI stated in his apostolic exhortation *Marialis Cultus* (February 2, 1974) that the Rosary was the pious practice which, correctly, has been called "the compendium of the entire Gospel."[21] Thus, he emphasized, "The Rosary should be considered as one of the best and most efficacious prayers that the Christian family is invited to recite."[22]

The Rosary is comprised of both mental prayer and vocal prayer. In mental prayer the participant meditates on the major "mysteries" (particular events) of the life, death, and glories of both Jesus and Mary.

The vocal aspect involves the recitation of 15 "decades" (portions) of the "Hail Mary" which involves contemplating 15 principal virtues that were practiced by Jesus and Mary. One Catholic author writes, "So the Rosary is a blessed blending of mental and vocal prayer by which we honor and learn to imitate the mysteries and the virtues of the life, death, passion and glory of Jesus and Mary."[23]

The 15-volume *Catholic Encyclopedia* observes of the Rosary that through a "long series of papal utterances it has been commended to the faithful" and that according to tradition, St. Dominic himself claimed Mary had revealed to him that the Rosary was "an antidote to heresy and sin."[24] Various popes have emphasized that the Rosary appeases God's anger, makes salvation more easily attainable, and brings the favors of Mary to the Catholic believer for "Jesus and Mary reward in a marvelous way those who glorify Him."[25]

Consider the following blessings authoritatively pronounced upon recitation of the Rosary (the first is given by an alleged vision of Mary):

> When you say your Rosary the angels rejoice, the Blessed Trinity delights in it, my Son finds joy in it too and I myself am happier than you can possibly guess. After the Holy Sacrifice of the Mass, there is nothing in the Church that I love as much as the Rosary. . . . I shall see to their salvation if only they will sing the Rosary, for I love this type of chanting.[26]

> The Rosary recited with meditation on the mysteries brings about the following marvelous results: it gradually gives us a perfect knowledge of Jesus Christ; it purifies our souls, washing away sin; it gives us victory over all our enemies; it supplies us with what is needed to pay all our debts to God and to our fellow men, and finally, it obtains all kinds of graces for us from almighty God.[27]

In another alleged supernatural encounter between the famous Catholic saint Dominic, the Virgin Mary, and a group of demons, Mary commands the demons to answer her servant Dominic immediately. We are told that Mary, by her divine power, has forced them to proclaim "the whole truth and nothing but the truth" about the importance of the Rosary and how to say it properly. Listen carefully to the following encounter. The demons reply to Mary:

> Oh you who are our enemy, our downfall and our destruction, why have you come from heaven just to torture us so grievously? O Advocate of sinners, you who

snatch them from the very jaws of hell, you who are the very sure path to heaven, must we, in spite of ourselves, tell the whole truth and confess before everyone who it is who is the cause of our shame and our ruin? . . .

Then listen well, you Christians: the Mother of Jesus Christ is all-powerful and she can save her servants from falling into hell. She is the Sun which destroys the darkness of our wiles and subtlety. We have to say, however reluctantly, that not a single soul who has really persevered in her service has ever been damned with us; one single sigh that she offers to the Blessed Trinity is worth far more than all the prayers, desires and aspirations of all the saints. We fear her more than all the other saints in heaven together and we have no success with her faithful servants. . . .

Now that we are forced to speak we must also tell you this: nobody who perseveres in saying the Rosary will be damned, because she obtains for her servants the grace of true contrition for their sins and by means of this they obtain God's forgiveness and mercy.[28]

Even some Catholics might wonder at such an alleged account. Regardless, in a great deal of Catholic literature we are told that the Rosary is so powerful that it will certainly help to forgive sins and even to save a soul from hell. In other words, it too is part of the process of maintaining and increasing justification—something certainly believed in by millions of Catholics.

Catholics are told that even if a person is on the brink of damnation and has one foot in hell, "even if you have sold your soul to the devil as sorcerers do who practice black magic," and are a heretic, nevertheless, "if you say the Rosary faithfully until death, I do assure you that, in spite of the gravity of your sins 'ye shall receive a never fading crown of glory.'"[29]

But the Bible says not a word about recitation of the Rosary. This is another illustration of how Catholic tradition has undercut the authority of the Bible. For those who trust the Rosary to forgive sin, Christ's atoning work itself is denigrated.

Strong Reaction for a Good Reason

Perhaps it is now a bit easier to understand the strong Protestant reaction to Catholic doctrines such as the sacraments, confession, and the recitation of the Rosary. The Bible teaches that full forgiveness of sin, including all its penalty, occurs solely by grace through faith in Jesus Christ alone, based upon the complete adequacy of His propitiatory atonement.

Catholic teaching, on the other hand, implies that the benefits of the death of Christ in some sense can be applied in other ways than by faith in Christ alone.

Protestants believe it is a serious matter for the Roman Catholic Church to teach that there are many additional ways besides personal faith in the death of Christ through which forgiveness of sins can occur. Catholicism's beliefs are far removed from the simple biblical declarations of "believe in the Lord Jesus, and you will be saved" (Acts 16:31), or "by one sacrifice he has made perfect forever those who are being made holy" (Hebrews 10:14), or "in Him we have redemption through His blood, the forgiveness of our trespasses, according to the riches of His grace" (Ephesians 1:7 NASB), or "having forgiven us all our transgressions" (Colossians 2:13 NASB).

That Catholicism teaches justification by works in these and other practices is demonstrated by Karl Keating in his book *Catholicism and Fundamentalism*. He emphasizes that, in Catholicism, men and women learn that they will merit heaven by their good works and personal righteousness, but that to merely "accept Jesus" as Savior supposedly accomplishes nothing. He also says that Catholics must maintain their justification until death or they will lose it and go to hell. In other words, one can have lived a perfect life in Catholicism for 70 years and, by one small omission, still go to hell. What kind of assurance can this bring?

> For Catholics, salvation depends on the state of the soul at death. Christ ... did his part, and now we have to cooperate by doing ours. If we are to pass through those [heavenly] gates, we have to be in the right spiritual state. . . . The Church teaches that only souls that are objectively good and objectively pleasing to God merit heaven, and such souls are ones filled with sanctifying grace. . . . As Catholics see it, anyone can achieve heaven, and anyone can lose it. . . . The apparent saint can throw away justification at the last moment and end up no better off than the man who never did a good deed in his life. It all depends on how one enters death, which is why dying is by far one's most important act. . . .

[What this means is that] "accepting Jesus" has nothing
to do with turning a spiritually dead soul into a soul alive
with sanctifying grace. The soul [that "accepts Jesus"]
remains the same [i.e., dead]. . . . The Reformers saw
justification as a mere legal act by which God declares the
sinner to be meriting heaven. . . . The Catholic Church,
not surprisingly, understands justification differently. It
sees it as a true eradication of sin and a true sanctification
and renewal. The soul becomes objectively pleasing to
God and so merits heaven. It merits heaven because now
it is actually good. . . .

The Bible is quite clear that we are saved by faith. The
Reformers were quite right in saying this, and to this
extent they merely repeated the constant teaching of the
Church. Where they erred was in saying that we are
saved by faith alone.[30]

But again, if the Bible really does teach that justification is entirely by grace, then justification is by faith alone. To add meritorious works would mean that justification is by faith and works.

The Bible leaves no doubt that the very concepts of "grace justification" and "works justification" involve entirely opposing
principles. A study of the biblical books of Galatians and Romans
will prove this.

One cannot have a justification based 75 percent on grace and 25
percent on works. Justification occurs entirely by one means or
entirely by the other. Even a salvation 99 percent by grace and
1 percent by works is still not salvation by grace. As Scripture itself
emphasizes, "And if by grace, then it is no longer by works; if it
were, grace would no longer be grace" (Romans 11:6).

Consider a final example. In "My Ticket to Heaven," a popular
Catholic tract that has sold over five million copies, readers are told
that their "ticket to heaven" is good works and permanently ab-
staining from mortal sin. Thus, "If I do my part, God will do His
part."[31] This booklet is labeled as "a Tract of Justification," and a
"straightforward presentation of Christian faith," but its principal
effect is to produce the fear of never achieving heaven since justification is so clearly laid out as involving a practical perfectionism.
No one can possibly do what this booklet says they must do in order
to maintain and increase their justification so that they will go to
heaven.

Although written by a priest of 40 years, it never once mentions personal faith in Jesus Christ as the basis for salvation or justification.

In conclusion, the Bible teaches that practices such as penance, confession, and the Rosary play no part whatever in the forgiveness of sins or the maintenance of justification. Rather, the Bible over and over again repeats the wonderful news that when Jesus died on the cross He paid the full divine penalty for all sin so that forgiveness and justification could be offered to every man and woman as a free gift of God's grace and mercy.

.8.

Indulgences

*S*urprises can be good or bad depending upon their nature. Sometimes even Catholics are surprised to learn what their Church really teaches. Indulgences and purgatory are among such surprises for many modern Catholics, as this chapter and the next will reveal.

The requirement that Catholics gain indulgences and attend purgatory is yet another consequence of Rome's unbiblical view of justification. Why? Again, according to Rome, justification is a life-long process that may be increased, lost, regained, etc. Because Catholic justification does not involve the full forgiveness of sins, including all of their punishment, Rome has instituted various ways to solve the problems raised by the inadequacies of its own view of justification.

Through penance, Catholicism offers forgiveness of sin and rein-states justification after baptism, while indulgences and purgatory respectively remit and institute the punishments for sin that Rome still thinks are necessary. In other words, according to Rome, one can be forgiven a sin by God and yet still be required to suffer for it. Surprise!

The paradox is that in its practice of indulgences Rome attempts to remit or refrain from inflicting the temporal punishment due certain sins so that the Catholic will not have to suffer punishment. But then it turns right around and tells almost all Catholics that when they die, they will have to suffer temporal punishment for their sins in purgatory. Surprise again! (At least indulgences can be instituted for Catholics wherever they are—on earth or in purgatory.)

Thus, contemporary Catholic apologist Karl Keating informs Catholics that they are in error if they think the Church has "dropped its old belief in indulgences," which have the power to remove them from purgatory more quickly. Further, "Many Catholics simply don't know what indulgences are."[1]

What Indulgences Are

Indulgences are gained by various acts of piety offered by the Church, and are the remission of part or all of the temporal punishment due to forgiven sins in virtue of the merit of Christ and His Church. *Fundamentals of Catholic Dogma* defines an indulgence as "the extra-sacramental remission of the temporal punishments of sin remaining after the forgiveness of the guilt of sin."[2] In other words, the *guilt* for sins may have been removed by the atonement of Christ and the sacraments, but all the *punishment* for them is not. "We can be forgiven [our sins], yet still have to suffer."[3]

The Catholic Encyclopedia explains the rationale for indulgences and the basis on which the Church claims to offer them when it declares,

> The remission of the temporal punishment due for sins and hence, the satisfaction owed to God for one's sins is called an indulgence. Indulgences granted by the Church may be gained for oneself or for the souls in purgatory. The granting of indulgences is founded upon three doctrines of Catholic faith: the treasury of the merits of the communion of saints, Christ himself, and the Blessed Virgin and the saints.[4]

Rome claims that in granting indulgences it "dispenses and applies with authority the treasury of the satisfactions of Christ and the saints" to believers for specific acts they perform.[5]

In other words, punishment for sin is canceled out by the good deeds of Catholic saints, the Virgin Mary, and Jesus Christ applied to the believer who performs the requirements of the indulgence.

> This treasury includes as well the prayers and good works of the Blessed Virgin Mary. They are truly immense, unfathomable and even pristine in their value before God. In the treasury, too, are the prayers and good works of all the saints, all those who have followed in the footsteps of Christ the Lord and by his grace have made their lives holy and carried out the mission the Father entrusted to them. In this way they attained their own salvation and

at the same time cooperated in saving their brothers in the unity of the Mystical Body.[6]

Catholicism maintains that indulgences are necessary because it holds that when people sin, God's justice requires a punishment beyond that given to Christ on the cross. The 1994 *Catechism* teaches the following: "The doctrine and practice of indulgences in the Church are closely linked to the effects of the Sacrament of Penance."[7] In other words, amends must be made to God by some means, whether by indulgences or through the miseries and trials of life, or through death, or through purifying sufferings in purgatory.

Indulgences are offered to the faithful as a means to escape God's punishment. But on what basis does the Catholic Church offer such indulgences? It is supposedly on the basis of the merit of others having special spiritual quality. Because Christ, Mary, and the relatively small number of Catholic saints have all provided "superabundant satisfactions" to God through their merits, the Church believes it can offer these same merits to the Catholic believer in exchange for remission of punishment.

In essence, because of the infinite merits of Christ plus those of the Virgin Mary and the Catholic saints, the Church argues it has the prerogative to administer the benefits of these indulgences "in consideration of the prayers or the pious works undertaken by the faithful."[8]

Types of Indulgences

There are two kinds of indulgences. First, those which are "easy" to gain (called partial indulgences) and second, those which are more difficult to obtain (called plenary indulgences). The difference concerns how much punishment for sin they supposedly remove.

Plenary indulgences remove all temporal punishment due to sin, while partial indulgences only remove part of the punishment due to sin.[9] Again, "This punishment [for sin] may come either in this life, in the form of various sufferings, or in the next life, in purgatory. We don't get rid of here [through indulgences] what we suffer there [in purgatory]."[10] In other words, any punishment for sin that is not remitted through indulgences in this life must then be endured in purgatory.

Supposedly, the requirements for a plenary indulgence are tougher than for a partial.[11] Thus, plenary indulgences (remitting all temporal punishment for sin) were offered to those who partook in the

Crusades against the Muslims (ironically, the Muslims were told something similar from their religious leaders).

But on the other hand, today merely performing the sign of the cross is an indulgence having great merit:

> The Sign of the Cross is the most frequently used sacra-
> mental of the Church. The sign is a repetition in motion
> of the symbol of our salvation, the cross on which Christ
> died. . . . The faithful, as often as they devoutly sign them-
> selves with the sign of the cross, are granted an indul-
> gence *of three years*; whenever they make the same holy
> sign with blessed water, they may gain an indulgence of
> *seven years*.[12]

Devotion to Mary and the Rosary are also "highly indulgenced" by Roman Catholicism:

> While the devotion to the Blessed Mary through recita-
> tion of the Rosary is recommended for all, it is strongly
> advised for all who study for the priesthood. . . . One of
> the many indulgences attached to the devotion [of Mary]
> is that the faithful who recite the Rosary together in a
> family group, besides the partial indulgence of ten years,
> are granted a plenary indulgence twice a month, if they
> perform this recitation daily for a month, go to confes-
> sion, receive Holy Communion, and visit some Church
> or public oratory.[13]

Indulgences are also granted for visits of the faithful to various Catholic shrines, some of which were built in honor of Marian appa-ritions (appearances of Mary).[14]

But indulgences are received only by performing the specific work and/or requirements to which the indulgence is attached.

For example, three conditions are necessary to gain a plenary indulgence in addition to performing the specific requirements of that indulgence: sacramental confession, Eucharistic communion, and prayer for the pope—as well as the absence of all willful attach-ment to sin (even "minor" venial sin).

As noted earlier, under proper conditions indulgences are actu-ally applied to the dead in purgatory for the reduction of the degree of suffering and/or the length of time this place must be endured.

To its credit, the modern Catholic Church claims that if a person ever bought an indulgence merely to get some soul out of purgatory or for buying forgiveness of sins, that this was wrong. The Church also claims it never officially condoned the massive abuses of the practice in earlier years, although it did clearly share in the responsibility for them.

Nevertheless, indulgences are said to play an important role in the salvation both of individuals on earth as well as in purgatory after death. It must also be pointed out that the remission of punishment due sin only occurs after the guilt and eternal punishment of sin have been remitted by adherence to Catholic practice. Supposedly, Rome can say, "The Church grants such indulgences after the guilt of sin and its eternal punishment have been remitted by sacramental absolution or by perfect contrition."[15]

Full Efficacy at Stake

Once again, when we see teachings like this—that the "guilt of sin and its eternal punishment" are supposedly remitted by the sacraments or by "perfect contrition"—we can only question Catholicism's commitment to the full efficacy of Christ's atonement.

In conclusion, the Catholic Church claims that it has the power to grant indulgences. These are necessary for the remission of the alleged temporal punishment due sin and are accomplished by a specific act or work (e.g., the recitation of the Rosary) which then allegedly applies the merits of Christ and the earned merits of Mary and the Catholic saints to Catholic believers today—even to those in purgatory. This allows believers on earth and in purgatory to escape at least some of the punishments due their sins.

The problem with this belief in indulgences is evident from the biblical teaching on the atonement. The necessity for indulgences assumes that the death of Christ did not forgive all divine punishment for sin. We are either forgiven or we are not forgiven. The Bible teaches God "forgave us all our sins" (Colossians 2:13). Therefore, no punishment whatever is owed to God for them in this life.

This takes us to our next topic in the Catholic process of salvation. Unfortunately, indulgences may remove some of the punishment due sin in this life, but Rome teaches that they cannot remove it all—in other words, further punishment for sin and its guilt is also required in purgatory after death.

.9.

Purgatory

*I*n Dostoyevski's *The Brothers Karamazov*, Aloysha comments of hell, "Even if there were material fire, they would be genuinely glad of it, for I fancy that in material agony the much more terrible spiritual agony would be forgotten, even though for a moment." This comment illustrates the terrible nature of hell and brings us to a discussion of the Catholic doctrine of purgatory.

The Catholic Doctrine of Purgatory

The Roman Catholic teaching on purgatory was officially proclaimed as dogma in 1438. This means that until that year, belief in the doctrine was not required. Not so today. Today it completes the final justification of the Catholic. Despite the hope of some, the Church has not reversed its teachings on this frightening subject: "Purgatory is a defined doctrine of the Catholic faith. As a Catholic you must believe in it."[1]

Purgatory is a temporary hell that almost all Catholics must attend in order to work off the temporal punishment for their sins: "Very possibly, this will [include] the large majority of the saved."[2] Specifically, it is to cleanse the guilt of sins already forgiven and to deal with sins already confessed but not atoned for. (It makes one wonder what happened during the atoning death of Christ.)

Catholicism believes that penance may not only be performed by good works in this life but also through hellish suffering endured in purgatory after death. As a result, those in purgatory are labeled as "the Church Suffering who have died in grace and whose souls are being purged in purgatory."[3] In essence, "The temporal punishments for sins are atoned for in the purifying fire [of purgatory] . . . by the willing bearing of the expiatory punishments imposed by God."[4]

The Council of Trent taught that the sacrifice of the Mass "is rightly offered not only for the sins, punishments, satisfactions and other necessities for the faithful who are living, but for those departed in Christ but not yet fully purified [in purgatory]."[5] Trent thus declared to the Church the following mission: "that the sound doctrine of purgatory . . . be believed and maintained by the faithful of Christ, and be everywhere taught and preached."[6]

The Justification of Purgatory

Purgatorial suffering is justified on the basis that only perfect people enter heaven. Because no one can enter heaven with any stain of sin whatsoever, "therefore anyone less than perfect must first be purified before he can be admitted to [heaven]."[7]

Here, we may once again see how the fragmentary and deficient nature of the Catholic doctrine of justification absolutely requires a doctrine like purgatory. Catholics are indeed correct: Only those people who are perfect get into heaven. The issue, then, is how one gets to be perfect. Is it on the merits of Christ and His righteousness alone which are freely given to the believer by faith, or is it by our own good works, our maintaining and increasing of justification, and our suffering here and in purgatory?

If the personal righteousness and suffering of Christ for our sin were insufficient, then what these lacked must be made up by the believer's own increasing righteousness and suffering for sin in purgatory.

"Only perfect people" get to heaven, and so in Catholicism all sin and its punishment must be removed prior to entering heaven because, say what Catholics may, Christ's righteousness and atonement obviously did not supply all that was necessary for the believer's salvation. Thus, purgatory institutes the final cleansing of sin and punishment for sin which alone provide the believer's entrance into paradise.

Although technically the souls in purgatory cannot make "true" satisfaction for their sins,[8] the fact of being in purgatory and enduring punishment for them is believed to both cleanse individuals of the remnants of sin and permit such persons entrance into heaven as newly perfected people.[9]

Further, in purgatory the person pays for the penalty of venial or mortal sin, even if the guilt of those sins has already been forgiven by the sacrament of penance.[10] In other words, purgatory completes final justification for the good Catholic. After a life of faithful contrition and confession, penance, indulgences, attending Mass, maintaining faith, and working diligently to maintain justification in order to remain in God's grace, the Catholic then dies and suffers the hellish punishments of God to complete the justification that could only be partially accomplished in this life.

As *The Catholic Encyclopedia* teaches,

> The souls of those who have died in the state of grace suffer for a time a purging that prepares them to enter heaven. . . . The purpose of purgatory is to cleanse one of imperfections, venial sins, and faults, and to remit or do away with the temporal punishment due to mortal sins that have been forgiven in the Sacrament of Penance. It is an intermediate state in which the departed souls can atone for unforgiven sins before receiving their final reward. . . . [Further,] such "purgatorial punishments" may be relieved by the offerings of the living faithful, such as Masses, prayers, alms, and other acts of piety and devotion.[11]

Biblically, all this is nonsense. If God has already declared a person righteous through justification, then he or she is already perfect in His sight. The Bible does not teach that in order to enter heaven, purgatorial suffering is necessary. For "by one sacrifice he [Jesus] *has made perfect* forever *those who are being made holy*" (Hebrews 10:14, emphasis added).

Three Views of Purgatory

Without biblical support, Catholicism has advanced three basic views of purgatory. The first assumes that purgatory is as terrible as hell itself. In fact, it *is* hell—only its punishments are temporary:

> Purgatory [is] *a hell which is not eternal*. Violence, confusion, wailing, horror, preside over its descriptions. It dwells, and truly, on the terribleness of the pain of sense which the soul is mysteriously permitted to endure. The fire is the same fire as that of hell, created for the single and express purpose of giving torture. Our earthly fire is as painted fire compared to it. Besides this, there is a special and indefinable horror to the unbodied soul in becoming the prey of this material agony. The sense of imprisonment, close and intolerable, and the intense

palpable darkness are additional features in the horror of the scene. . . . To these horrors we might add many more. . . . Bellarmine [taught], "Many theologians have said, not only that the *least pain of purgatory was greater than the greatest pain of earth, but greater than all the pains of earth put together.* This then is a true view of purgatory, but not a complete one."[12]

The second view is that in spite of such unutterable torments in hell, the millions of sufferers simultaneously experience the bliss of the presence of Mary and Christ. Apparently, this does not cancel out the torments but it somehow makes them more bearable. In this view one experiences suffering and bliss simultaneously.[13]

Third, more recent views imply that the suffering in purgatory is not the same as that in hell. But it must still be terrible—and all the more reason for Catholics to stay in good standing with the Church. As Hardon's *Catholic Catechism* notes, "Their suffering is intense on two counts. . . . Most Catholic theologians hold, with Bellarmine [canonized in 1930], that in some way the pains of purgatory are greater than those on earth."[14] Further, as Hardon points out (p. 297), "They clearly see their deprivation was personally blameworthy and might have been avoided if only they had prayed and done enough penance during life."

Indeed, only God knows the untold billions of dollars and endless number of fear-inspired indulgences this unbiblical doctrine of purgatory has produced over the centuries. Unfortunately, the burden of purgatory is also carried by the entire family as they realize they have the power to reduce the horrible suffering of their loved ones by their own good works, by suffering through penance and indulgences, by participation in the Mass, or by financial payment through the purchase of Mass cards.

Another Denial

Biblically, again, all this is not only unscriptural, it constitutes another denial of the completed work of Christ on the cross. That work of Jesus Christ assures us that salvation is a free gift—not something we may secure only through enduring great suffering.

The Scriptures commonly cited in defense of purgatory (Matthew 5:25,26; Luke 16:19-31; 1 Corinthians 3:12-23; Hebrews 12:29; 1 Peter 3:19; Revelation 21:27) can only be so appropriated under Catholic premises. By themselves they do not teach purgatory, as standard commentaries on these verses will show.

In fact, the only place purgatory can possibly be inferred from is the Catholic Apocrypha (2 Maccabees 12:46). Here, the troops of Judas found the corpses of slain warriors and discovered amulets of the idols of Jamnia under their shirts. The story relates that these men had perished in divine judgment for their idolatry. As a result, all the troops of Jamnia "betook themselves to supplication, beseeching that the sin committed might be wholly blotted out." Judas then collected from each man the sum of 2000 drachmas of silver, "which he forwarded to Jerusalem for a sin offering. In this he acted quite rightly and properly. . . . Hence he made propitiation for the dead, that they might be released from their sin."[15] Here it is plain to see that purgatory is not even mentioned. It must be read in from somewhere else.

Catholic scripture alone is not the only rationale that is given for acceptance of the doctrine of purgatory. Catholics believe that the "Apostles' Creed," which refers to the "communion of saints," offers warrant for belief that the actions of believers here on earth can impact the condition of believers in purgatory. Allegedly, this is part of what the idea of the "communion of saints" means: that alms, Masses, and prayers for the Catholic dead can be done by the living to reduce their suffering in purgatory. But an appeal to the Apostles' Creed is misplaced, as pointed out by our late friend, Dr. Walter R. Martin:

> Further than this, it should be carefully observed that for Catholics, "the communion of saints" is sufficient warrant for believing in Purgatory. The statement, however, comes from the Apostles' Creed and refers to the "fellowship (communion) of Saints" or all true believers on earth—not in the mythical Purgatory of Roman Catholic Tradition. The Apostles' Creed is not Scripture anyway and was not written by the Apostles at all, but is a second century document.[16]

The Consequences of Purgatory

All Catholic ideas concerning purgatory can be seen to be lacking in any exegetical support from Scripture by consulting any good commentary. At issue is the consequence and implication of purgatory historically, which tend to reveal its true weight on men's souls. The telling of the emotional and financial weight will have to be reserved for a later book; here we can only briefly address the occult implications.

In our earlier book we documented how the Catholic doctrines of purgatory, indulgences, and the communion of saints have resulted in an openness to visits of the alleged dead and a greater subjection to Catholic dogma.[17]

Thus, throughout the history of the Catholic Church there have been "widespread and constant"[18] apparitions from the alleged dead (including Mary) which are invariably seen to support unique Catholic teachings. As an example we could cite *The Dogma of Purgatory*, containing both Catholic seals of approval (the *nihil obstat* and *imprimatur*), signifying a book is "free of doctrinal or moral error."[19] This book is full of stories of the alleged spirits of deceased Catholics appearing to the faithful and warning them of the torments of purgatory. The result? Inevitably it is a greater bonding to Roman Catholic beliefs and practice.[20]

Doctrines that the alleged Mary and other dead Catholic souls have strongly reinforced in the lives of individual Catholics include: the Mass and host,[21] the Rosary,[22] indulgences,[23] purgatory,[24] Mary worship,[25] and trust in and worship *(dulia)* of Catholic saints and angels.[26]

Further, thousands of supernatural visions and appearances of Mary to both living Catholics and those in purgatory (who in turn recount the event to the living) have resulted in the institution of Catholic shrines, days of religious observance, and/or Holy Orders.[27] Currently, there are literally hundreds of sites of Marian apparitions around the world.[28]

But all this raises a question. Would the truly saved dead, or the biblical Mary, or holy angels support teachings and practices that were against the Word of God? If not, perhaps we have little recourse but to assign such supernatural phenomena to another source.

If Mary, the dead in purgatory, and dead Catholic saints from heaven actually appear to the living and give false teachings, how is one to distinguish such phenomena from that found in spiritism in general? On what authoritative and logical basis are we to distinguish them?

Historically, Catholic tradition has maintained a strong tie to accepting communications from the allegedly sanctified dead: "The Church has never frowned on the invocation of the poor souls [in purgatory]—a practice that is widespread among the faithful, and which has been advocated by many theologians," and "Apparitions of the souls that are in purgatory are a frequent occurrence."[29]

Catholicism teaches that not only may the living help the dead (for example, by indulgences for the souls in purgatory) but that the dead (i.e., souls in purgatory, the saints, and Mary) may also help the living. As one Catholic priest stated, "Oh! If it were but known how great is the power of the good souls in Purgatory with a Heart of God, and if we knew all the graces we can obtain through their intercession, they would not be so much forgotten. We must, therefore, pray much for them, that they may pray much for us" and "with the intention of obtaining in return through the assistance of their prayers, the favors which we desire."[30] Thus, "the Church has always recognized the intercessory power of [dead] saints."[31] Indeed, "patron saints" exist for no less than 300 different occupations— and even nations—around the world.[32]

Our concern at this point is how easily belief in such doctrines may, at the individual level, progress into actual spiritistic contact under the guise of seeking the assistance of the departed Catholic saints, souls in purgatory, Mary, guardian angels, etc. In our earlier book we documented that this does occur and is thus a violation of the prohibitions against contacting the dead given in Deuteronomy 18:10-12: "Let no one be found among you who . . . consults the dead. Anyone who does these things is detestable to the Lord."

The conclusion of our last three chapters is this: Although the Bible teaches that full forgiveness of sin and its punishment comes solely and entirely by grace alone, through faith in Christ alone, based on His atonement alone, Catholicism denies this and teaches that forgiveness of sin and its punishment comes through any or all of the following: 1) penance and priestly confession; 2) the recitation of the Rosary; 3) indulgences; and 4) purgatorial suffering after death. Because the true merit of man—achieved through these and other means—is in some sense responsible for a Catholic's final justification and salvation, Catholicism cannot logically deny that it teaches a form of salvation by works.

.10.

Redefining Biblical Words

*I*n chapter 6 of *Alice in Wonderland*, Lewis Carroll revealed the philosophical acumen of Humpty Dumpty when he wrote,

> "When I use a word," Humpty Dumpty said, in a rather scornful tone, "it means just what I choose it to mean— neither more nor less."

> "The question is," said Alice, "whether you *can* make words mean so many different things."

> "The question is," said Humpty Dumpty, "which is to be the master—that's all. . . . When I make a word do a lot of work . . . I always pay it extra."

As lawyer and philosopher Dr. John Warwick Montgomery pointed out in *The Shape of the Past*, words require specific definition by the user. When words are not defined properly, various problems can be created.[1]

The Catholic doctrines on salvation are in part upheld by the unique definition Rome gives to key biblical words. But the question is, "Are these words properly defined in their biblical sense?"

The Semantic Problem

The problem faced in a discussion of this subject is similar to that in many other religions and even cults that claim allegiance to the Bible and yet through various means reject its authority. Among such groups are Mormons, Christian Scientists, Jehovah's Witnesses, and The Way International. Typically, biblical authority is undermined because the Bible is read through the eyes of a new source of authority that is itself antibiblical. Whether it is in the occult writings of Joseph Smith (Mormonism), or of Mary Baker Eddy (Christian Science), the Watchtower Society (Jehovah's Witnesses) or Victor Paul Wierwille (The Way International), the teachings of the Bible become distorted because now their true interpreter has become an alien source of information rather than the biblical words themselves.[2] Unfortunately, this is also the case with Catholic tradition, and it occurs as well through both Protestant and Catholic use of higher criticism.

It is because of the larger Catholic theology (tradition) into which biblical words and concepts are placed that their final meaning is frequently unbiblical. Sometimes Catholic scholars use biblical terminology and sound as if they are evangelical. But they tend to confuse even many Protestants about what Catholicism is really teaching on salvation.

For example, Catholic writers often speak of "salvation by grace" and cite biblical Scriptures to that effect. In response to the Protestant charge that "the Catholic Church teaches we earn salvation by good works," Karl Keating offers the following reply: "The Catholic Church has never taught such a doctrine. In fact, it has constantly condemned the notion that we can earn salvation. Only by God's grace, completely unmerited by works, is one saved. The Church teaches that it's God's grace from beginning to end which justifies, sanctifies, and saves us."[3]

While this sounds orthodox, we must realize that these words mean something quite different to a Catholic than to a Protestant. Keating and other Catholics are simply reiterating the position of the Council of Trent that no one can do good works or please God apart from grace (that is, the prior infusing of sanctifying grace). But—and this is key—Catholic theology goes on to teach that the works which come after God infuses grace, though inspired by grace, are also what help to save a person. As Pope John Paul II emphasizes, "Man is justified by works and not by faith alone."[4]

So it is crucial to understand that once terms such as "faith," "grace," "salvation," "redemption," and "justification" are filtered through larger Catholic theology, they become so altered that they lose their biblical meaning.

This distinction in meaning is frequently unnoticed by both Catholic and Protestant laymen. Keating is entirely correct when he points out, "As in so many matters, fundamentalists [e.g., conservative Christians] and Catholics are at loggerheads because they define terms differently."[5] For example, the manner in which certain words are used in the Council of Trent on justification sound biblical,[6] but once interpreted in light of larger Catholic theology, they mean something entirely different than what the Bible means.

Catholics themselves frequently admit their interpretation of biblical words differs from that of Reformation Protestantism. For example, *The Papal Encyclicals* admit: "Faith has different meanings for a Catholic and a Protestant."[7] Thus, "in this [definition of] faith sacraments and good works are included."[8]

Keating provides us with two additional examples: 1) he defines "redemption" as something distinct from actual salvation, and 2) he sees faith as intellectual assent to Church doctrine:

> The truth is that we are all redeemed—Christians, Jews, Muslims, animists in the darkest forests—but our salvation is conditional.[9]

> For Catholics, faith is the acceptance of revealed truths, doctrines, on God's word alone. This is called theological or confessional faith. For fundamentalists, faith is trust in Christ's promises, not belief in a set of dogmas. This is called fiducial faith.[10]

Biblically, however, redemption is something that only a believer has, and it is clearly stated to include the forgiveness of sins: "In him *we have redemption* through his blood, the forgiveness of sins" (Ephesians 1:7, emphasis added). Muslims, Hindus, and animists do not have redemption, biblically speaking, because they do not believe in Christ, and thus are *not* saved.

When Keating distinguishes redemption and salvation in the manner he does, he makes a Catholic distinction that is unbiblical. Biblically, faith is trust in Christ, despite what Rome teaches. Faith certainly involves belief in doctrine, but it also includes more than mere intellectual assent that such doctrines are true. As R.C. Sproul once commented in a lecture on justification by faith, "It is one thing for me to affirm that Jesus Christ is the Son of God and it is another thing for me to trust my life to Him for all eternity."[11]

Which Definitions?

Unfortunately, devout Catholics do not question their Church's teaching about the definition of biblical terms because they have been told by their leaders that, "Over the Book [Bible] stands the Church."[12] The Church has final authority over the Bible and therefore it is the Church's *interpretation* of biblical words that is authoritative. In the end, it is the Church's definition of biblical terms—not the biblical definition—that is accepted.

The Papal Encyclicals correctly point out that Protestants turn to the Bible alone to determine whether or not a doctrine is true. Nevertheless, *The Papal Encyclicals* also confess,

> This is just the reverse of the Catholic's approach to belief. As the Catholic sees it . . . it is not for him to "judge" the divine message, but only to receive it. Since he receives it from a living, teaching organ, he does not have to puzzle over the meaning of the revelation because the ever-present living magisterium [teaching office] can tell him exactly what the doctrine intends.[13]

Catholics turn to the Church because they have been promised that the Church exercises an inerrant authority to properly interpret the Bible for them. In other words, the Catholic man or woman can, in full trust, accept whatever the Church teaches about salvation and never have to worry that the Church might be wrong.

Catholics are assured that "the Bible . . . is interpreted infallibly only by the teaching authority invested by Jesus in the Catholic Church."[14] In the words of Vatican II, "The task of authentically interpreting the word of God, whether written or handed on [tradition], has been entrusted *exclusively* to the teaching office of the Church."[15]

But what is wrong with Rome's claim? In his definitive critique of the Council of Trent, Lutheran theologian Martin Chemnitz (1522-86) correctly noted that the Catholic popes and teaching office had reserved for themselves the prerogative of a biased interpretation of Scripture predicated largely upon Catholic tradition. In the words of Chemnitz, the end result was an entirely new interpretation "so that we must believe not what the Scripture says simply, strictly, and clearly but what they through their power and authority interpret for us. By this strategy they seek to escape the clearest passages [of Scripture] concerning justifying faith . . . the intercession of Christ, etc."[16] This situation remains true today in Catholicism. Consider only two key terms—"grace" and "faith." First, Catholicism teaches that salvation (i.e., forgiveness of sins) occurs through God's grace—but a form of grace that makes possible necessary works of human merit which also help a person attain salvation. Thus, salvation is by grace *and* works. As *The Catholic Encyclopedia* asserts, God's grace is a supernatural power that "makes it possible for them [Catholics] to place [perform] acts directed toward eternal salvation."[17] And further, the "means of salvation given by Christ" are defined specifically as "the sacraments and sacrifice [Mass]" of Catholicism.[18]

Biblically, however, "salvation" is not so defined. Grace is not a divine empowerment of men to help them attain their own salvation; rather it is a divine disposition toward men that offers them salvation entirely as a free gift of God's mercy. The following Scriptures prove this:

> I will . . . love them freely (Hosea 14:4).

> [Believers] are justified freely by his grace (Romans 3:24).

> The gift of God is eternal life in Christ Jesus our Lord (Romans 6:23; cf. 5:15,16).

> How much more will those who receive God's . . . gift of righteousness reign in life (Romans 5:17).

> It is by grace you have been saved, through faith—and this not from yourselves, it is the gift of God—not by works (Ephesians 2:8,9).

The same kind of distortion can be seen when we consider the term "faith."

Is Faith Really a "Work"?

For Protestants, a person's faith is not a meritorious work that contributes to or helps provide justification. Rather, faith is only an instrument which allows a sinful person to reach out to Christ, who is the sole reason, grounds, and basis upon which God justifies.

In Catholicism, faith (at least in part) is said to be a supernatural gift from God which holds out the truths of revelation, begins the process of salvation, and is carried through life by the supernatural power of God—unless certain sin intervenes.

But there are also statements by Catholic theologians which declare that faith per se is a work and therefore is something meritorious. For example, after speaking of faith as "a free gift twice over," John A. Hardon, S.J., of the Jesuit School of Theology in

Chicago, writing in *The Catholic Catechism* nevertheless declares, "The act of faith is a work that pertains to salvation."[19]

The Papal Encyclicals declare, "In the Catholic doctrine of faith, sacraments and good works are included."[20]

In commenting on Romans 1:16, *A Catholic Commentary on Holy Scripture* also argues that faith includes works: "Faith [should] be understood in the sense of dogmatic faith, which accepts all the doctrines of the Gospel as true and obeys all its precepts as divine commandments. For in this faith, sacraments and good works are included."[21]

The official 1992 Lutheran response to the 1983 declaration of the Lutheran-Roman Catholic Dialogue Report VII (see chapter 19) emphasized the Catholic position as stating that faith is "incomplete without trust in Christ and loving obedience to him." It also pointed out that for Catholics faith must be "intrinsically qualified" by love (i.e., by the sanctified life of the sinner). The Lutheran response disagreed: "But to imply in any way that the sanctified life of the sinner must somehow 'intrinsically qualify' justifying faith to accomplish justification before God is not only to misunderstand the nature of faith, but also to call into question the all-sufficient work of Christ itself."[22]

In that Trent and Rome teach that salvation is clearly (in part) by works, it would seem difficult to separate faith here from merit. If other non-faith works are meritorious, then one would logically assume that faith is also—since faith, even though instituted by God, clearly requires a natural human response. Thus, in part, faith as merit does provide our justification in that the work of baptism produces faith which then begins the process of justification, which itself is the first part of salvation, the start of sanctification, etc.

If faith is meritorious from the Catholic perspective, it is not so from the Protestant view. So from the Protestant perspective, let us return to our earlier illustration of how faith is only the instrument by which we are saved and is not deserving of merit on our part.

Picture that burning building and the frightened man trapped on the third floor. He is urged to jump—in other words, to have faith in the firemen below that they will catch him in their net. But if the man jumps, his faith will only be that belief which caused him to jump. It will not be that which actually saves his life. Rather, it will be the firemen holding the net who actually save him.

In a similar manner, concerning salvation, it is not ultimately the instrument of faith which actually saves us; rather, it is Christ in whom our faith is placed that saves us. People everywhere exercise faith in something, but it is only faith in *Christ* that saves. Our faith merely reaches out to Christ who rescues us because faith places us into Christ's hands. As a result, Christ tells all those who believe in Him, that "they shall never perish" because "no one can snatch them out of my hand" (John 10:28).

In conclusion, if the biblical words relating to salvation are interpreted normally in their own context, apart from Catholic tradition, they tell us that salvation is a free gift that we only need to receive by grace through faith alone.

.11.

Two Ways of Reading the Bible

M ost of us remember the heartwarming movie *Fiddler on the Roof* with Herbert Bernardi's stalwart musical exaltation of "Tradition!" Tradition, of course, is good; family, social, and cultural traditions all play an important role in our lives.

But is all tradition good? Thoreau said, "No way of thinking or doing, however ancient, can be trusted without proof." Auguste Comte may have observed, "The dead govern the living," but Pierre Bayle declared, "It is pure illusion to think that an opinion which passes down from century to century, from generation to generation, may not be entirely false." In other words, duration alone is not a test of what is true or false.

It should be clear to our readers by now that we have been reading the Bible alone to arrive at our conclusions. Our approach here underscores another major difference between Evangelicals and Catholics. Some people believe we are to read the Bible alone to determine Christian doctrine and practice. Others believe we are to read and give equal weight to both the Bible and Church tradition. The question this raises is, "Will these two approaches—reading the Bible versus reading the Bible and observing tradition—bring a person to completely different conclusions on the subjects we have been discussing?" Roman Catholics claim that if Protestants would allow the Bible and Catholic tradition to speak to them that they would come away with a different conclusion than what they have arrived at.

We agree. Anyone will indeed reach a different conclusion by reading the Bible alone versus reading the Bible and including Catholic tradition. We have explained some of the reasons for this in Appendix B.

Tradition As Used in the Bible

This takes us to a discussion of how the word "tradition" is used in the Bible. On the one hand, Catholics argue that the Bible itself teaches the validity of Roman Catholic Church tradition. They cite the apostle Paul who said, "Hold firmly to the traditions, just as I delivered them to you" (1 Corinthians 11:2 NASB), and "stand firm and hold to the traditions which you were taught, whether by word of mouth or by letter from us" (2 Thessalonians 2:15 NASB).

On the other hand, both Jesus and Paul also *condemned* tradition. For example, Jesus said that the religious authorities of His day had "[broken] the command of God for the sake of your tradition" (Matthew 15:3), and the apostle Paul said that Christians were to avoid "the tradition of men" (Colossians 2:8 NASB).

Obviously, the word "tradition" is being used in different contexts. Resolving the proper use of the word "tradition" will tell us whether or not the Bible teaches that we are to accept Roman Catholic tradition as being of equal authority with Scripture. The Catholic Church maintains, "Therefore, both sacred tradition and sacred Scripture are to be accepted and venerated with the same sense of devotion and reverence. Sacred tradition and sacred Scripture form one sacred deposit of the Word of God, which is committed to the Church."[1] But if this is true, sacred tradition should never contradict Scripture. Unfortunately, it does.

It is evident from every biblical usage of the term "tradition" that neither Jesus, Paul, nor any other biblical writer ever encouraged Christians to accept teaching or tradition that denied what God had already revealed was true.

When the apostle Paul wrote that Christians should accept the traditions, he was clearly referring to apostolic, divinely inspired teachings that either he had received from the other apostles or from God Himself (Galatians 1:11,12). It was this information that he then passed on: "And for this reason we also constantly thank God that when you received from us the word of God's message [apostolic tradition based on divine revelation—see Galatians 1:11,12], you accepted it not as the word of men, but for what it really is, the word of God, which also performs its work in you who believe" (1 Thessalonians 2:13 NASB).

Paul told the Corinthians, "I delivered to you as of first importance what I also received [divinely authoritative apostolic tradition], that Christ died for our sins according to the Scriptures" (1 Corinthians 15:3 NASB).

In fact, the apostle Paul opposed every false teaching that rejected the gospel, whether it came from within the church (e.g., the Judaizers, Acts 15:1) or outside the church (e.g., the Gnostics, Colossians 2:18,23). He opposed all teaching not in conformity to the revealed Word of God because he could do nothing else (cf. 1 Corinthians 9:16; Galatians 1:6-8). Therefore, Paul could never advocate that Christians accept any tradition that opposed the Word of God, no matter how authoritative it claimed to be. If a leader's teaching or any particular tradition violated what God said was true, it was simply not to be accepted.

Therefore, if Catholic tradition is in harmony with what God has revealed, there is nothing wrong with accepting it. But if Catholic tradition denies and opposes what God has revealed in His Word, then it must not be accepted by any Christian.

All this explains why Evangelicals reject Catholic tradition. Again, following Vatican II, Catholicism maintained that both sacred Scripture and sacred tradition form "one sacred deposit" of the Word of God. The problem is that Catholic tradition is replete with errors and contradictions and clear denials of biblical teaching. It is Catholic tradition that is the source of all the unbiblical teachings we have been discussing (see Appendixes B and D for illustrations).

For example, priestly loyalty to Rome and its tradition explains why, according to one of the most thorough polls of American clergy ever made, "over three-quarters of Roman Catholic priests reject the view that our only hope for heaven is through personal faith in Jesus Christ as Lord and Savior. They hold instead that 'heaven is a divine reward for those who earn it by their good life.'" Priestly loyalty to Rome also reveals why "four-fifths of all priests reject the Bible as the first place to turn in deciding religious questions; rather, they test their religious beliefs by what the Church says."[2]

The reason why the majority of Catholic priests reject the biblical doctrine of salvation is because as priests, loyal to the pope, they are required to reject the idea that divine authority resides only in the Bible. For them, divine authority resides in the Catholic Church and its tradition. Priests, therefore, look primarily to the Church for answers to religious questions because they believe that only the Catholic Church can infallibly determine proper doctrine through its supposedly infallible interpretation of the Bible and Catholic tradition. Thus, a study of Catholic history will show that it is the Church and not the Bible which has developed Catholic doctrine over the years (again, see Appendix B).

Salvation in the Bible

But now compare Catholic tradition to what the Bible alone teaches about salvation and how a person acquires eternal life.

The Bible declares that salvation is something that comes freely to any individual who simply places genuine trust in Jesus Christ for forgiveness of sins. In other words, full and complete forgiveness of sins occurs immediately and strictly on the basis of individual trust in Christ's atoning death on the cross. Please read carefully the following Scriptures which prove this:

> Yet to all who received him, to those who believed in his name, he gave the right to become children of God (John 1:12).

> For God so loved the world that he gave his one and only Son, that whoever believes in him shall not perish but have eternal life (John 3:16).

> All the prophets testify about him [Jesus] that everyone who believes in him receives forgiveness of sins through his name (Acts 10:43).

> He forgave us all our sins (Colossians 2:13).

> In him we have redemption through his blood, the forgiveness of sins, in accordance with the riches of God's grace (Ephesians 1:7).

> He himself bore our sins in his body on the tree . . . by his wounds you have been healed (1 Peter 2:24).

> For it is by grace you have been saved, through faith—and this not from yourselves, it is the gift of God—not by works, so that no one can boast (Ephesians 2:8,9).

> Not having a righteousness of my own that comes from the law, but that which is through faith in Christ—the righteousness that comes from God and is by faith (Philippians 3:9).

> He [Jesus] sacrificed for [our] sins once for all when he offered himself (Hebrews 7:27b).

> Therefore he is able to save completely those who come to God through him, because he always lives to intercede for them (Hebrews 7:25).

> But he [Jesus] entered the Most Holy Place once for all by his

own blood, having obtained eternal redemption. . . . [He] offered for all time one sacrifice for sins. . . . Because by one
sacrifice he has made perfect forever those who are being
made holy. The Holy Spirit also testifies to us about this. . . .
He says: . . . "Their sins and lawless acts I will remember no
more" (Hebrews 9:12; 10:12,14,15,17).

Do any of the above verses teach that salvation or forgiveness of
sins comes by baptism, good works, through religious sacraments,
or by any other means of human effort or merit? Do these verses
ever hint that salvation comes by being good or by personal character or effort? No, these Scriptures are clear. God Himself teaches
that complete forgiveness of sins occurs solely by faith in what was
already accomplished by Christ on the cross 2000 years ago.

This is why Romans 1:17 teaches, "For in the gospel a righteousness from God is revealed, a righteousness that is by faith *from first
to last*, just as it is written: 'The righteous will live by faith'" (emphasis added).

Because salvation is by grace through faith alone, once a person
has trusted in Christ, then he or she may *know* that all their sins are
forgiven—all sins past, present, and future.

Assurance of Salvation in the Bible

Catholics (by virtue of Church teaching), and many Protestants
also (by virtue of poor teaching), have no assurance or certainty of
their own salvation. Further, both Catholics and even many Evangelical Protestants reject the doctrine of eternal security (that the
true believer in Christ can never lose his salvation).

But we think that not only does God want us to know that we can
have assurance of salvation in this life, but He also wants us to know
that we will *never* be lost.

When Christ paid the full divine penalty for our sins 2000 years
ago, all our sins were future. If the Bible teaches our sins are forgiven at the point of true faith in Christ, this must logically include
all of them, even all future sins. Thus, "He forgave us *all* our sins"
(Colossians 2:13, emphasis added). Therefore, come what may in life
(please read Romans 8:28-38), the person who trusts in Christ alone
for salvation will go to heaven when he dies because God Himself
informs the believer that he now possesses "an inheritance that can
never perish, spoil or fade" because it is "kept in heaven for you"
(1 Peter 1:4). The salvation God offers is perfectly secure precisely

because it involves a gracious act of God and is in no way dependent upon human merit or good works for its accomplishment. It is simply a free gift (Romans 3:24).

Because salvation occurs by God's grace and is in no way dependent upon anything we do to earn it, and because the divine penalty for all sin was fully paid by Jesus on the cross, the Bible teaches that those who have genuinely received Christ as their personal Savior may from that point forward be fully assured that they now possess eternal life. Consider the following Scriptures carefully:

> I tell you the truth, whoever hears my word and believes him who sent me *has* eternal life and will not be condemned; he has crossed over from death to life (John 5:24, emphasis added).

> I tell you the truth, he who believes *has* everlasting life (John 6:47, emphasis added).

> I write these things to you who believe in the name of the Son of God so that you may *know* that you *have* eternal life (1 John 5:13, emphasis added).

Again, these verses teach that God wants believers to know they now possess eternal life merely by their personal trust in Jesus. If any person now possesses *eternal* life, it cannot be lost, can it?

Unfortunately, the above Scriptures do not reflect the teachings of the Catholic Church, which maintain that salvation is a provisional, lifelong process partially earned by a person's own works and individual merit.

Biblically, of course, salvation *can* be viewed as a process, but only in this manner: that sinless perfection and glorification are not received until after death. And so we struggle in this life to increase our sanctification and "work out" (Philippians 2:12), not work *for* the logical consequences of our having already been saved and of having already received the gift of eternal life. But this is not Roman Catholic teaching.

Biblically, true salvation—in the sense of our right standing before God and forgiveness of all sins—occurs at a point in time (the point of receiving Christ as personal Savior), even though the practical implications of salvation (progressive sanctification or growth in holiness) are worked out over a lifetime.

Thus, 1) complete reconciliation with God (full forgiveness of sins and cancellation of the penalty of sin); 2) regeneration (being made spiritually alive to God and the imparting of eternal life), and

3) justification (the crediting of Christ's full and complete righteousness to the believer) all occur in an instant, at a moment in time: the point of faith.

They are irrevocable since they are all gifts from God, and God says that He never takes back what He gives: "For God's gifts and his call are irrevocable" (Romans 11:29). This includes God's calling to salvation and His election (Ephesians 1:4,5,11; Acts 13:48).

Catholicism, on the other hand, teaches that a right standing before God is something that does not happen fully in this life, nor can it occur in a moment of time. It is something that comprises a lengthy process that is only earned after a lifetime of good works and obtained merit and (in all likelihood) hellish purgatorial suffering after death.

Lack of Assurance in Catholicism

All Catholics agree that they do not and cannot have absolute assurance of salvation in this life. In other words, if a Catholic man or woman were to die today, he or she could have no assurance of going to heaven.

Many Protestant commentators have also taken note of this unfortunate fact. For example, G.C. Berkouwer observes, "At the Council of Trent, Rome rejected the Reformed confession of the assurance of salvation with unmistakable clarity."[3]

The late evangelical authority Dr. Walter Martin, during his life had many conversations with individual Catholics and Catholic priests. In one of his books he discusses the scriptural proof that the believer in Christ *now* has peace with God (e.g., Romans 5:1 NASB, "Therefore having been justified by faith, we have peace with God through our Lord Jesus Christ"). He then says:

> We make bold to say, however, that no Roman Catholic who really believes the teachings of his Church has that peace with God—and I believe it can be proved. If you ask any Roman Catholic, "Do you know that God has completely forgiven you of your sins? Do you know that because Christ died in your place, as the Bible says, you have eternal salvation now? Do you know, right at this moment that you have passed from death to life?" The answer is negative.

> Every Roman Catholic whom I have ever spoken to on this subject, be he priest, theologian or layman, has said

to me, "I hope I will be saved; I truly hope so." Friends, there is no peace in just hoping![4]

Catholic theologians respond by stating that while full assurance of salvation is impossible, there is still an intermediate position between on the one hand the fear one won't be saved, and on the other the complete assurance of salvation, which they deny.

Supposedly there is a relative (not absolute) assurance that one will be saved. However, because this "assurance" is still based upon performances, merit, and faithfulness, we do not think this is assurance at all—especially given human nature (not to mention unregenerate human nature). As we saw, even the Council of Trent itself used the terms "fear" and "apprehension" concerning a person's knowledge of having obtained God's grace.

Again, if "to justify" means to make a person righteous by good works, a person is left to his or her own subjective condition as to the basis of his or her acceptance before God. A fluctuating justification that is lost every time a mortal sin is committed can hardly provide any security of salvation because, as we saw earlier, even the Catholic Church teaches that mortal sins are common occurrences: envy, drunkenness, failure to attend Mass, using birth control, etc.[5]

And as we saw in chapter 7, someone may have lived a perfect life in Catholicism for 70 years, and at the very moment of death—by one small omission—still go to an eternal hell: "The apparent saint can throw away salvation at the last moment and end up no better off than the man who never did a good deed in his life. . . . Dying is by far one's most important act."[6]

Again, the specific condition of the soul at the moment of death determines one's eternal destiny. If this is "assurance," it would seem to be an assurance only of despair. Given the weakness of faith (especially a faith that is a human work and not based upon God's perseverance), when confronted by the immense power of "the world, the flesh and the devil," who can possibly know the condition of their dying—that it will be favorable for salvation?

Death is no reliable friend. It can come in a flash at an unguarded moment or leave no hint of its presence for decades. And a lot can happen in decades. Who, then, can ever know their dying moments will arrive with goodwill and not enmity?

Remember, the requirements for even relative assurance of salvation in Catholicism are not easily maintained over an entire lifetime. These requirements include saving faith, loyal membership in the Church, obedience to the commandments, love of God and neighbor, participation in the sacraments of the Eucharist, penance, etc., plus prayer, good works, indulgences and, certainly last but not least, persevering in God's grace until death and at the point of death, dying in the right condition.[7]

Is this the assurance that God has provided for His people?

Of course, a Protestant cannot have any assurance of salvation either, unless he also believes what God has declared is true.

Personal Responsibility

This brings us to a key issue in the Christian life: the importance of personal commitment to biblical study. God Himself encourages believers in Jesus Christ to do just this, and not to rely solely upon the interpretation of another, whether that interpreter be a person, church, or teaching office.

For example, consider the following two Scriptures, Acts 17:11,12 and 2 Timothy 2:15. In the first, the apostle Paul and Silas have been sent from Thessalonica to preach in Berea. God says, "Now these [Bereans] were more noble-minded than those in Thessalonica, for they received the word of God with great eagerness, *examining the Scriptures daily*, to see whether these things were so. Many of them therefore believed, along with a number of prominent Greek women and men" (Acts 17:11,12 NASB, emphasis added).

Here we see that the Bereans did not even take the apostle Paul's word that he had interpreted the Bible correctly. They examined the Scriptures daily for themselves to see if what Paul had told them was really true. Nor was this some minor issue.

The apostle Paul had been preaching to the Bereans that Jesus Christ was the prophesied Jewish Messiah. Indeed, few subjects were more controversial. The Jewish leaders and authorities had already warned the people not to believe in the name of Jesus, whom they had classified as a false teacher. But the people chose to examine the Scriptures first before uncritically accepting what their religious leaders told them. As a result, they came to believe that Jesus was, in fact, the true Messiah and that the religious leaders were in error. Thus, "Many of them therefore believed."

This Scripture instructs us that, whether we are Catholic or Protestant, and regardless of what we may have been taught in our churches, it is our personal responsibility to "examine the Scriptures daily" to see whether or not what we have been taught is true.

In *On Liberty* John Stuart Mill well said, "Truth gains more even by the errors of one who, with due study and preparation, thinks for himself, than by the opinions of those who only hold them because they do not suffer themselves to think."

Again, the topic of salvation is so crucial that no one should trust solely in what another person claims; they should only trust in what God has said in His Word. This is why we are to study the Scriptures: "Be diligent to present yourself approved to God as a workman who does not need to be ashamed, handling *accurately* the word of truth" (2 Timothy 2:15 NASB, emphasis added).

As Dr. Walter Martin observes,

> It is worthwhile to note that the Holy Spirit did not instruct us to have Scripture interpreted for us by anyone as is the Catholic position. We are to interpret it under His guidance, the Person of the Holy Spirit (John 16:13), who will keep us sound in the great truths of the Divine revelation.[8]

If we remember that the Bible teaches the following basic points about salvation, we can perhaps understand why many Christians are so concerned over Catholic teaching—and why hundreds of thousands of Catholics are converting to Protestantism. So let us recall the important points of salvation according to the Bible. The one who believes what the Bible teaches can *now* have the assurance of salvation and of attaining heaven at death:

1. Salvation, or an eternally valid right standing before God, occurs solely due to the death of Christ (what Christ accomplished on the cross) entirely apart from the agency of the Church and its practices (1 John 2:2; 1 Peter 2:24; Romans 10:13; John 14:6; Acts 4:12).

2. On the cross Jesus Christ paid in its entirety the full divine penalty for all sin (Hebrews 10:12,14). Church sacraments, the Mass, or purgatorial suffering after death are unnecessary to remove the divine penalty for sin in this life or the next.

3. In terms of our standing before God, full salvation occurs at a point in time (1 Corinthians 5:17-21; 1 Peter 2:24). It is not a lifelong process that occurs or increases over time, which is sanctification.

4. Complete salvation is secured solely by personal faith—by trusting in Jesus Christ for the forgiveness of sins (John 1:12;

Romans 10:9,10; Ephesians 2:8,9). Good works enter the picture only as a result—not a cause—of our salvation (Ephesians 2:10; Romans 12:1,2). Thus, good works are not even a partial cause of our salvation (Romans 11:6). According to the Bible, activities such as baptism, penance, and other sacraments contribute nothing to the salvation of a believer (e.g., Galatians 3:13,21; 4:9,10; 5:1,4).

5. At the moment of saving faith a person is fully—not partially—justified (Romans 3:28; 5:1). In other words, a person is declared righteous by God Himself—fully and finally. All his sins are forgiven and God declares him legally righteous (perfectly righteous in God's own eyes), even though he continues to remain a sinner because of the presence of a sinful nature (Roman 3:28–4:6; James 2:10; 3:2; 1 John 1:8-10). What this means is that in an instant of time a person has passed over from spiritual death to spiritual life, and that nothing else is required for him to go to heaven (see John 5:24). Once justified, a person can never lose her or his justification (see Romans 8:30-38; 11:29). Thus, justification is not a slow process of spiritual growth whereby infused grace and supernatural power permits a man to actually become righteous before God; it is infinitely more.

6. At the moment of saving faith a person has also been regenerated—God has made him alive spiritually and imparted eternal life to him. Regeneration does not occur at the point of baptism; rather, it occurs at the point of saving faith. The fact that regeneration involves the imparting of eternal life underscores the finality of biblical salvation (John 6:47; 1 John 5:13).

7. Because a person now possesses eternal life, his salvation, as a result, can never be lost (Ephesians 1:11,12; 1 Peter 1:3-5). Such a person is eternally secure from the point of saving faith, regardless of his sins or his works (Romans 8:28-38).

No Need to Fear

In conclusion, a person does not need to fear that he or she may lose salvation from the commission of mortal sin or by any other cause. Consider the following chart comparing words in their scriptural and Catholic meaning:

Grace

Bible: A disposition of God toward men expressing His mercy and love so that the believer is now treated as if he were innocent and perfectly righteous.

Catholicism: Often a substance or power separate from God which is placed into a believer to enable him or her to perform meritorious works and earn the "right" to heaven.

Salvation

Bible: The instantaneous reception of an eternally irrevocable right standing before God—secured at the point of faith entirely by grace. Salvation is given to those whom the Bible describes as "ungodly," "sinners," "enemies," and "children of wrath" (e.g., Romans 5:6-10; Ephesians 2:1), and thus to those who are not objectively righteous.

Catholicism: The lifelong process whereby God and men cooperate in the securing of forgiveness of sin. This is achieved only after death (and/or purgatorial cleansing from sin) and is dependent on man's personal securing of objective righteousness before God; otherwise, there is no salvation.

Reconciliation
(through atonement)

Bible: All sins (past, present, and future) are forgiven at the point of salvation because Christ's death satisfied all God's wrath against sin.

Catholicism: In practice, sins are only potentially forgiven and so must be worked off through a process mediated by the Church and its sacraments over the lifetime of the believer.

Regeneration

Bible: The instantaneous imparting of eternal life and the quickening of the human spirit, making it alive to God.

Catholicism: (In part) The lifelong process of infusing grace (spiritual power) to perform works of merit.

Justification

Bible: The legal declaration of Christ's righteousness reckoned or imputed to the believer at the point of faith solely as an act of God's mercy and grace.

Catholicism: Spiritual rebirth and the lifelong process of sanctification which begins at the point of the sacrament of baptism and yet which can be lost by mortal sin.

Clearly the Bible and Rome have a difference of opinion. Although Roman Catholicism claims it believes in the biblical view of grace, the saving power of Christ's death, reconciliation, and justification (and even that it does not teach salvation by works), unfortunately, none of this is true.

In his landmark book *Crossing the Threshold of Hope*, a text self-described as "having no precedent in Catholic history," Pope John Paul II stressed not only his love for ecumenicism and the Second Vatican Council—which he participated in from first to last and described as the "seminary of the Holy Spirit"—but he also emphasized to Catholics and Protestants, "What unites us is much greater than what separates us. . . ." He added that even *doctrinal* obstacles must be overcome for the church to have true unity: "The road to unity . . . is itself a process, which must gradually overcome many obstacles—whether of a doctrinal or a cultural or a social nature. . . . Above all, it is necessary to *recognize the unity that already exists*."[9]

Is this perhaps an attempt to employ the *idea* of unity as a means to help Protestants overcome *their* doctrinal "deficiencies" which are supposedly obstacles to full Christian unity?

.12.

Evangelicals and Catholics Together?

Now it is required that those who have been given a trust must prove faithful.

—1 Corinthians 4:2

A growing movement exists in America today hoping that Roman Catholics and Evangelical Christians will join forces and recognize that the things that unite them outweigh the things that divide them. But having examined some of the biblical doctrines that have divided Protestants and Catholics for 450 years, those who claim to really have reached agreement on these matters must explain:

1. Precisely what they agreed to.

2. Historically who was right and who was wrong so that agreement could now be reached (or did both sides come to a new historical understanding?).

3. How the affirmations agreed to were supported, not opposed by God's Word (documenting that, in fact, the affirmations did not deny scriptural teaching).

4. How the doctrine of justification, which has been the main point of contention, was finally resolved.

In our world today, it must be kept in mind that an agreement

133

could possibly be forged by fringe leaders from both sides who totally ignore Scripture. But such an agreement would not be biblically based and would be rejected by both Protestants and Catholics who love Christ and hold to the authority of Scripture.

But the reason that the recent "Evangelicals and Catholics Together" statement caused a lot of interest was because 40 respected Evangelical and Catholic leaders who hold to the authority of the Bible said they had come to an agreement. Who were they?

The Participants

Among the Evangelical participants were Dr. Bill Bright, founder of Campus Crusade for Christ; Dr. Os Guiness with Trinity Forum; Dr. Mark Noll of Wheaton College; Dr. James I. Packer with Regent College; the Reverend Pat Robertson, founder of the Christian Broadcasting Network; Charles Colson, founder of Prison Fellowship; Dr. Richard Land with the Christian Life Commission of the Southern Baptist Convention; Dr. Larry Lewis with the Home Mission Board of the Southern Baptist Convention; and Dr. John White with Geneva College and the National Association of Evangelicals.

Among the Roman Catholic participants were John Cardinal O'Connor, Archdiocese of New York; Father Avery Dulles, Fordham University; Monsignor William Murphy, Chancellor of the Archdiocese of Boston; Father Richard John Neuhaus, Institute of Religion and Public Life; Archbishop Francis Stafford, Archdiocese of Denver; Father Augustine DiNoia, Dominican House of Studies; Father Matthew Lamb, Boston College; and Ralph Martin, Renewal Ministries.[1] (For more detailed information, see endnote 1.)

Also included was Catholic lawyer Keith Fournier, author of *Evangelical Catholics* (we discuss his book in chapter 15), who is with Regent University's American Center for Law and Justice.

Now it is easy to understand how some Evangelicals and Catholics would wish to put aside as many differences as possible in order to help address the moral crises destroying so many lives everywhere.

But this agreement goes beyond mere concern with social issues as the old Moral Majority did. In other words, this agreement is more than different groups working for social causes. It is based upon different groups uniting together as one spiritual family under the banner of Christianity.

While we can clearly sympathize with the motives of these tenderhearted people, united social action must not be at the expense of truth, and unity should never be allowed to eclipse the most important spiritual truth of all: the gospel.

Our contention is this: In spite of the announced unity, is it a true unity? Is there a true biblical basis for Catholics and Evangelicals to unite spiritually? And can those who announced this unity demonstrate the basis on which this unity was arrived at?

We have already shown why the doctrine of justification by faith alone and the true nature of the gospel are watershed issues that can be of no less importance today than the same issues debated during the Reformation days. We have documented biblically why salvation is by grace through faith alone. Works (even those cooperating with faith and done in the power of Christ) are not in any way contributing factors to obtaining salvation. Having realized this, we are now prepared to examine the "Catholics and Evangelicals Together" statement.

Catholics and Evangelicals Together?

It should be noted that the thrust of this document is cultural cooperation in the face of a culture rapidly disintegrating morally. We do not deny that Catholics and Evangelicals can work together for the betterment of society, or as the report itself correctly points out, to counter the secularism and threats of Islam against the Christian Church. We agree with this. But the task of moral and cultural revitalization is not the key issue *here* where the gospel is at stake.

Many leaders on both sides have hailed this important document as a historic event—even as the most historic event since the Reformation. What was agreed to by both sides?

Throughout this document a major new assumption was made concerning the relationship between Evangelicals and Catholics. The Evangelicals agreed that all Roman Catholics are genuine Christians, and the Roman Catholics agreed that all Evangelicals are genuine Christians.

This new relationship can be seen in the following statements:

> Evangelicals and Catholics are brothers and sisters in Christ.[2]
>
> We are called [together] and we are therefore resolved to explore patterns of working and witnessing together in order to advance the one mission of Christ.[3]
>
> We recognize that there is one church of Christ.[4]

> We confidently acknowledge the guidance of the Holy Spirit.[5]

> We are bound together by Christ and his cause.[6]

> We thank God for the discovery of one another as brothers and sisters in Christ.[7]

> Together we search for a fuller and clearer understanding of God's revelation.[8]

In these statements there is no doubt whatever that the signers of this document are declaring that Evangelicals and Catholics are Christians together. Confidently, the Evangelical and Catholic leaders affirmed in many places that:

> As Christ is one, so the Christian mission is one. . . . The mission that we embrace together is the necessary consequence of the faith that we affirm together.[9]

> This is a time of opportunity—and . . . responsibility—for Evangelicals and Catholics to be Christians together.[10]

> As Evangelicals and Catholics, we pray that our unity in the love of Christ will become ever more evident as a sign to the world of God's reconciling power.[11]

> We do know that God who has brought us into communion with himself through Christ intends also that we be in communion with one another.[12]

But if this is really true, why is it that scholars from both sides ever since the Reformation have refused to recognize the other as genuine Christians? On what scriptural or theological basis can it be said that these leaders have resolved the main issues which have divided the two communities for 450 years?

Unfortunately, we are not told. Rather, those who drafted this statement simply proclaim this surprising new unity:

> In this statement we address what we have discovered . . . about our unity.[13]

> We together, Evangelicals and Catholics, confess our sins against the unity that Christ intends for all his disciples.[14]

The mission that we embrace together is the necessary consequence of the faith that we affirm together.[15]

What Is the Basis of the New Unity?

The basis of the new unity proclaimed by the leaders who signed this report can be found in numerous statements scattered throughout their document. In essence, the new unity is said to be based on the familiar biblical phrase "in Christ." The agreement states:

> Evangelicals and Catholics are brothers and sisters in Christ.[16]

> However difficult the way, we recognize that we are called by God to a fuller realization of our unity in the body of Christ.[17]

> We do know that God who has brought us into communion with Himself through Christ intended that we also be in communion with one another.[18]

We agree that all who accept Christ as Lord and Savior are brothers and sisters in Christ. But this begs the question, "How does a person get in Christ?" Because the document does not tell us this, we disagree with the assumption that both Evangelicals and Catholics are brothers and sisters in Christ.

Historically, Evangelicals have held that the only way a person gets in Christ is by admitting that he is a sinner and placing his total trust in Christ's atoning work for him. If he does not do this, he is not in Christ and, therefore, not a genuine Christian. So this little phrase is crucial to understanding this issue.

In the Bible, the apostle Paul always used the phrase "in Christ" to designate genuine Christians. He never once used the phrase to designate non-Christians.

> Therefore if any man is *in Christ*, he is a new creature; the old things passed away; behold, new things have come (2 Corinthians 5:17 NASB, emphasis added).

> Greet Prisca and Aquila, my fellow workers *in Christ Jesus* (Romans 16:3 NASB, emphasis added).

> To the saints in Ephesus, the faithful *in Christ Jesus* (Ephesians 1:1, emphasis added).

> And I was still unknown by sight to the churches of Judea which were *in Christ* (Galatians 1:22 NASB, emphasis added).

When these people are designated to be "in Christ," this is an important designation to the apostle Paul. It is so important that he leaves no ambiguity whatever about how a person gets to be "in Christ." He goes to great lengths to show that it is not by sacraments or by works of any kind. It is not by accepting simultaneously two different paths of salvation. It is only by faith in Jesus Christ.

> For the wages of sin is death, but the free gift of God is eternal life in Christ Jesus our Lord (Romans 6:23 NASB).

> He saved us, not because of righteous things we had done, but because of his mercy (Titus 3:5).

> Therefore, my brothers, I want you to know that through Jesus the forgiveness of sins is proclaimed to you. Through him everyone who believes is justified from everything you could not be justified from by the law of Moses (Acts 13:38,39).

> For by grace you have been saved through faith; and that not of yourselves, it is the gift of God; not as a result of works, that no one should boast. For we are His workmanship, created in Christ Jesus for good works, which God prepared beforehand, that we should walk in them (Ephesians 2:8-10 NASB).

So how can Roman Catholics be considered "in Christ" if they continue to deny the only basis for coming to be in Christ—justification by grace through faith alone? Those who signed this document do not tell us. They just start from the false premise that all Catholics are "in Christ."

Common Convictions?

The agreement claims that the Evangelical Protestants and Catholics have been led "through prayer, study, and discussion to common convictions about Christian faith and mission."[19]

They commend their joint declaration to the prayerful consideration of Christians everywhere, including "the Eastern Orthodox and those Protestants not commonly identified as Evangelical," all of whom they claim "are encompassed in the prayer [of Jesus], 'May they all be one.'"[20]

But is this sentiment biblically accurate? The first thing that should be noted about Jesus' prayer for Christian unity in John 17 is that this unity is based on Jesus' assumption that those united to Him have already experienced regeneration or spiritual rebirth (John 3:3). He also clearly states this unity is based on the truth of Scripture:

> I manifested Thy name to the men whom Thou gavest Me out of the world; Thine they were, and Thou gavest them to Me, and they have kept Thy word.... Sanctify them in the truth; Thy word is truth.... And for their sakes I sanctify Myself, that they themselves also may be sanctified in truth. I do not ask in behalf of these alone, but for those also who believe in Me through their word; that they may all be one (John 17:6,17,19-21 NASB).

When Jesus referred to those "whom Thou gavest Me out of the world" He was referring to all believers that the Father had given to Him for salvation. In His prayer to the Father He spoke of those God had given Him: "To all whom Thou has given Him, He may give eternal life. And this is eternal life, that they may know Thee, the only true God, and Jesus Christ whom Thou hast sent" (John 17:2,3 NASB).

In Ephesians chapter 2 the apostle Paul also refers to the unity of believers and that, whether they are Jew or Gentile, they are made into one body in Christ Jesus. This occurs as a result of our belief in what He did at the cross:

> But now in Christ Jesus you who formerly were far off [the Gentiles] have been brought near by the blood of Christ. For He Himself is our peace, who made both groups into one and broke down the barrier of the dividing wall, by abolishing in His flesh the enmity, which is the Law of commandments contained in ordinances, that in Himself He might make the two into one new man, thus establishing peace, and might reconcile them both in one body to God through the cross, by it having put to death the enmity.... For through Him we both have our access in one Spirit to the Father (Ephesians 2:13-18 NASB).

In the above verses the apostle Paul makes clear that he is referring to those who are in Christ Jesus. He also says that it is Christ who is "our peace," who has reconciled all believers into a unity by abolishing "the Law of commandments."

Again, here it is clear that true unity between people is to be based on their belief in Christ's substitutionary death. If one group claims that salvation is to be maintained by keeping the commandments, then there is no possible way for a Christian group to have unity with them.

Finally, Paul says that it is through Christ that every believer has access "in one Spirit to the Father." In other words, only those who come to God through Christ and accept what He did for them on the cross can participate in Christ's unity and have access to the Father through the Holy Spirit.

Later, in Ephesians 4:13, Paul refers to all true believers attaining "to the unity of the faith, and of the knowledge of the Son of God, to a mature man, to the measure of the stature which belongs to the fulness of Christ" (NASB). Here the unity of the faith is based on proper knowledge of the Son of God and the fullness of what Christ has done for us.

Nowhere in the "Evangelicals and Catholics Together" statement do we hear from the Evangelicals' side how Roman Catholics (those that Evangelicals have historically defined as being "outside of Christ" and therefore as not participating in Christian unity) have now suddenly become biblically qualified to partake of that unity.

The apostle Paul never told the young Christians in his churches to unite in harmony with the Judaizers—even though the Judaizers also believed in the one true God, the deity of Christ, the inspiration of the Scriptures, and going to church. Why such a harsh stance? Because, in spite of believing all these good things, the Judaizers taught a different gospel and therefore were not "in Christ."

Needless Conflict?

The report goes on to state, "As Evangelicals and Catholics, we dare not by needless and loveless conflict between ourselves give aid and comfort to the enemies of the cause of Christ."[21] The question is, "Are those who wrote this document equating 'needless conflict' with disputes over the definition of what the gospel is?" Isn't it true historically that the very center of all "our communal and ecclesial separations [which] are deep and long standing"[22] has been the Protestant and Catholic disagreement over the gospel?

If so, one then wonders if the Evangelicals who signed this document would consider saying to Luther that the Reformation was a "needless conflict." Hopefully not. Why? Because the Reformation went to the heart of what the gospel message was.

In fact, in Scripture itself we are told that the gospel will precipitate conflict and that the gospel by its very nature is offensive to some and divisive to others (Matthew 10:22; John 15:18; 17:14; Romans 9:33; Galatians 5:11).

So biblically can it be maintained that Catholics and Evangelicals are part of the body of Christ while disagreeing on the gospel message itself? Is there any way to avoid conflict as long as this disagreement exists? The apostle Paul gives an emphatic "No" to this question in writing to the Galatians who were dealing with this same problem.

> I am astonished that you are so quickly deserting the one who called you by the grace of Christ and are turning to a different gospel—which is really no gospel at all. Evidently some people are throwing you into confusion and are trying to pervert the gospel of Christ. But even if we or an angel from heaven should preach a gospel other than the one we preached to you, let him be eternally condemned! (Galatians 1:6-8).

> This is the only thing I want to find out from you: did you receive the Spirit by the works of the Law, or by hearing with faith? (Galatians 3:2 NASB).

> Behold, I, Paul, say to you that if you receive circumcision, Christ will be of no benefit to you (Galatians 5:2 NASB).

> You have been severed from Christ, you who are seeking to be justified by law; you have fallen from grace (Galatians 5:4 NASB).

> I have confidence in you in the Lord, that you will adopt no other view; but the one who is disturbing you shall bear his judgment, whoever he is (Galatians 5:10 NASB).

Witnessing Together?

The declaration states:

The love of Christ compels us and we are therefore... resolved... to explore patterns of working and witnessing together in order to advance the one mission of Christ.[23]

Without ignoring conflicts between and within other Christian communities, we address ourselves to the relationship between Evangelicals and Catholics who constitute the growing edge of missionary expansion at present and, most likely, in the century ahead.[24]

The mission that we embrace together is the necessary consequence of the faith that we affirm together.[25]

But this raises the questions, "What exactly is the one mission that Catholics and Evangelicals are to embrace? Can it be truthfully said that we are witnessing together if both parties disagree on the basic gospel message which is to be proclaimed?"

Those who signed this agreement do not answer these questions, though they seem to be aware of the importance of the issues since they state, "We reject any appearance of harmony [or unity] that is purchased at the price of truth."[26]

But aren't statements about Christian unity, witnessing together, and advancing the one mission of Christ, when they are made without any biblical basis or explanation, projecting the appearance of harmony at the price of forfeiting truth?

Anyone who compares the gospel of Roman Catholicism with the gospel of Scripture must conclude that there can be no agreement between Evangelicals and Catholics. If Catholics now agree to doctrines they formerly rejected, then why didn't this agreement document *that*?

True Brotherhood?

The following information is a classic example of how those who crafted this document made statements which can be understood in two different ways:

Jesus Christ is Lord.... He is the One sent by God to be Lord and Savior of all, "and there is salvation in no one else, for there is no other name under heaven given among men by which we must be saved" (Acts 4).... We affirm together that we are justified by grace through faith because of Christ.[27]

Some of the Evangelical leaders who signed this agreement have written us and pointed to this paragraph as proof that they did not compromise the gospel and did affirm justification by faith. So why do we think this statement is ambiguous?

At first glance this statement certainly sounds good. But in light of:

1. 450 years of disagreement;

2. knowing that the men who wrote this agreement were aware of past history;

3. both Catholics and Protestants using the same words but defining them differently;

4. the fact that no explanation is given as to which set of definitions are used

—then we cannot possibly know the proper meaning of these words.

So is it the Catholic or Protestant position that is being presented here? What did the Roman Catholic men mean who signed this statement and used these words? Catholics historically have given different meanings to the terms "grace," "justification," and "faith."[28]

So our question is, "Why did the framers of this agreement—knowing that the doctrine of justification by faith has been and continues to be the watershed issue between Catholics and Protestants—not take the time to define terms precisely?" Why did they leave us guessing?

We also find it very interesting that there is the absence of the word "alone" in the above statement about justification. Catholics argue adamantly that it is not by grace through faith *alone* that a person is saved. Rather, they argue it is by faith and one's cooperation in the power of Christ with additional requirements given by the Church. If the Catholic signers of this document really did agree with Evangelicals that justification was by faith alone, then why didn't they just say that and place into this document the crucial, historic phrase that we are justified by grace through faith alone?

How Deep Are Our Disagreements?

Possibly the most eye-opening statement in this document is given when the authors set forth the following:

> However imperfect our commune with one another, how-
> ever deep our disagreements with one another, we rec-
> ognize that there is but one church of Christ.... How-
> ever difficult the way, we recognize that we are called by
> God to a fuller realization of our unity in the Body of
> Christ.[29]

Is it really true that no matter how "imperfect our commune,
however deep our disagreements, however difficult the way," we
are still united? Apparently they thought there is no issue that currently exists which is deep enough to keep us from calling each
other Christians.

In the document we are told, "All who accept Christ as Lord and
Savior are brothers and sisters in Christ. Evangelicals and Catholics
are brothers and sisters in Christ."[30] To see the weakness of this
statement, one only need change the wording slightly to read something like this: "All who accept Christ as Lord and Savior are brothers
and sisters in Christ. Mormons and Jehovah's Witnesses are our
brothers and sisters in Christ." But are they?

Mormons and Jehovah's Witnesses both claim to accept Jesus
Christ as "Lord and Savior," but this does not mean they agree with
us on the meaning of the words "Lord" and "Savior." Therefore,
this does not automatically make them Christian.

Most people realize that when Evangelicals and Catholics say
that they accept Jesus Christ as Savior, that yes, for both Jesus is the
Savior. But how a person receives Jesus' salvation is not agreed
upon by the Catholics and Evangelicals. Knowing this, why didn't
the authors of the agreement tell us what they meant?

In other words, if the Catholic Church teaches that salvation is by
faith-works, and therefore denies the free gift of salvation Jesus
offers by faith alone, biblically how can Jesus actually be the Savior
of those in the Catholic Church? And if He is *not* their Savior, how
can He be their Lord? If He can be, then don't Jehovah's Witnesses
and Mormons also have a legitimate claim to say that Christ is *their*
Lord and Savior? And if they can do that, isn't the meaning of
Scripture being twisted to suit anyone's private interpretation?

Is Christ really the Lord and Savior of all groups who claim Him,
in spite of the fact that they proclaim different ways a man can
receive salvation?

Jesus Himself says no:

> Not everyone who says to me, "Lord, Lord," will enter
> the kingdom of heaven (Matthew 7:21).

He who believes in Him [Christ] is not judged; he who does not believe has been judged already, because he has not believed in the name of the only begotten Son of God (John 3:18 NASB).

Agreement on Scripture?

Another puzzling statement made in this agreement has to do with the historic dispute over what constitutes the canon. The report merely declares: "We recognize together that the Holy Spirit has so guided His Church in . . . the formation of the canon of the Scriptures."[31]

Here are more ambiguous words. What do they mean? Scholars on both sides realize that Roman Catholicism accepts the Apocrypha as Scripture. Protestantism does not. Are Protestants now ready to concede that the Holy Spirit did guide the Catholic Church to bring the Apocrypha into the canon when it had already been rejected as false by Jesus Christ, the apostles, and the church for 15 centuries? Or is a denial of the Apocrypha as Spirit-inspired Scripture something Roman Catholics now agree to? Who knows? The agreement doesn't tell us. It just makes another vague statement.

United on the Christian Mission?

Further problems can be seen in the section that has to do with evangelization and missions. The authors of the document argue:

We do know that we must affirm and hope and search and contend and witness together.[32]

We are called and we are therefore resolved to explore patterns of working and witnessing together in order to advance the one mission of Christ.[33]

To any knowledgeable participant in either community, these comments raise such questions as:

- How can we witness together if we are proclaiming different gospels?

- What exactly have the signers of this agreement concluded is the one mission of Christ?

- How do Protestants answer those who ask about the anathemas against Protestant views of salvation found in the documents of the Council of Trent, Vatican I and II?

Sadly, the authors do not explain. They simply admit:

> Our communal and ecclesial separations are deep and long standing. We acknowledge that we do not know the schedule nor do we know the way to the greater visible unity for which we hope. We do know that existing patterns of distrustful polemic and conflict are not the way.[34]

It is not surprising that these Evangelicals and Catholics seeking to be united spiritually do not "know the way" to the visible unity for which they hope. After all, they admit they do not agree on the different authorities they accept. Among points of difference are:

- The sole authority of Scripture *(sola scriptura)* or Scripture as authoritatively interpreted only by the Catholic Church.

- The sole freedom of the individual to interpret the Bible or the sole authority of the magisterium (teaching office) of the Church.[35]

In brief, the two communities are following different "maps" on the way to unity. So is it surprising they do not know the way to the unity which they seek?

Protestants have held to the concept of *sola scriptura* (Scripture as the only final spiritual authority) because God Himself teaches that all Scripture is inspired and profitable for teaching, for reproof and correction (2 Timothy 3:16). This means that true unity comes only in Christ and only on the basis of what the Bible teaches about salvation. Until the participants can agree on these things, how can they proclaim they are united in "one mission"?

Can We Disagree and Still Be United?

In the report the authors recognize there are differences between them, but they maintain this does not seem to hinder their unity:

> In this search to understand the truth more fully and clearly, we need one another. We are both informed and

> limited by the histories of our communities and by our
> own experiences. Across the divides of communities and
> experiences, we need to challenge one another, always
> speaking the truth in love, and in order to build up the
> Body (Ephesians 4).
>
> We do not presume to suggest that we can resolve the
> deep and long standing differences between Evangeli-
> cals and Catholics. Indeed these differences may never
> be resolved short of the Kingdom Come. Nonetheless,
> we are not permitted simply to resign ourselves to differ-
> ences that divide us from one another.[36]

But stop and think for a moment. Can you imagine Luther and
Calvin saying to the medieval popes and Catholic hierarchy, "We
really need one another to understand the doctrine of justification
by faith"? Of course not.

How does this document refer to the past, to our spiritual heritage—both Protestant and Catholic? It says: "We are both informed
and limited by the histories of our communities."[37] What does this
mean? If we are both limited by the histories of our communities, for
Catholics does this refer to the Council of Trent and Vatican I and II?
Should these histories be discarded? For Evangelicals, does this
statement refer to the Reformation? If the Reformation were really a
limiting factor in the Evangelical community, should it not be discarded?

The paper continues, "We need to challenge one another, always
speaking the truth in love, and in order to build up the Body."[38] But
which Evangelical pastor would find it acceptable to allow Roman
Catholics to challenge the members of his own church with "the
truth" of the Catholic view of salvation?[39] Or on the other hand,
what Catholic priest would allow an Evangelical Protestant to teach
his congregation salvation is by Christ alone, through grace alone,
by faith alone?

The apostle Paul asked the Galatians who were being led astray
by those who offered a false gospel (see Galatians 5:4-12), "Have I
therefore become your enemy by telling you the truth?" (Galatians
4:16 NASB). What was the truth he spoke of?[40]

> You have been severed from Christ, you who are seeking
> to be justified by law; you have fallen from grace. For we
> through the Spirit, by faith, are waiting for the hope of

> righteousness. . . . You were running well; who hindered
> you from obeying the truth? This persuasion did not
> come from Him who calls you (Galatians 5:4,5,7,8 NASB).

The signers of the declaration are frank in listing some of the differences and disagreements that divide the two communities. They say these "must be addressed more fully and candidly in order to strengthen between us a relationship of trust and obedience to truth."[41]

Among the disagreements listed are the nature of the Church, the authority of Scripture versus tradition, biblical interpretation (by individual Christian or magisterium), the authority of the pope versus the priesthood of all believers, the nature of the sacraments, the role of Mary and the saints, and the nature of baptism as a sacrament of regeneration or as a testimony to regeneration.[42]

These disagreements just about say it all, even though the report acknowledges, "This account of differences is by no means complete."[43] This is true.

As noted, the study neglects to mention the nature of justification by *faith alone*—a small omission, to be sure. As if to regather its senses, the report concedes that, at least in some instances, the doctrinal beliefs of the authors of this document "reflect authentic disagreements . . . which comprise present barriers to full communion between Christians."[44]

But if these present barriers are granted by those who signed the report, does the Bible allow us to disagree on them and still be bound together as a spiritual family? Until these issues are resolved, is biblical unity possible? Can we really ignore the issue of justification by faith and admit anyone into the fellowship of the Christian family?

In this age of relativism, no one wants to offend anyone. But on these issues either Catholics are right and Evangelicals are wrong, or Evangelicals are right and Catholics are wrong, or both are wrong. But both cannot be right.

The authors of this agreement let slip the crux of the matter when they write, "Evangelicals hold that the Catholic Church has gone beyond Scripture, adding teachings and practices that detract from or compromise the Gospel of God's saving grace in Christ."[45] This is true. But then how can there be an agreement and spiritual unity between those who hold to the gospel and those who compromise it?

Undaunted by the above list of disagreements, the report encourages study, discussion, and prayer "for a better understanding of one another's convictions."[46] But that's the problem: one another's convictions. We do understand Roman Catholic convictions—convictions concerning Scripture and hermeneutics, the pope, sacraments, tradition, Mary, salvation, regeneration, justification, etc. The more we understand them, the more we remember why there was a Reformation. Biblically it will be impossible for Evangelicals or Catholics to reach agreement until one side radically changes its stance.

Among the many paradoxes found in this document is this one: "We are bound together in contending against all that opposes Christ and his cause."[47] But what if Roman Catholicism opposes the gospel? Does this mean Protestants should oppose them? And from the Catholic point of view, are Protestants still anathematized for holding to justification by faith alone?

After reading all of the ambiguous statements in this agreement, one of the most striking declarations is found under the section "The Mutual Affirmation of Witnessing About Christ." There we find this classic statement:

> The achievement of goodwill and cooperation between Evangelicals and Catholics must not be at the price of the urgency and clarity of the Christian witness to the Gospel[!][48]

Sheep Stealing?

The participants in this agreement take some very strong stands concerning "proselytization," or what it calls "sheep stealing":

> Today, in this country and elsewhere, Evangelicals and Catholics attempt to win "converts" from one another's folds. . . . In many instances, however, such efforts at recruitment undermine the Christian mission. . . .

> It is understandable that Christians who bear witness to the Gospel try to persuade others that their communities and traditions are more fully in accord with the Gospel. There is a necessary distinction between evangelizing and what is today commonly called proselytizing or "sheep stealing." We condemn the practice of recruiting people from another community for purposes of denominational or institutional aggrandizement. At the same

time, our commitment to full religious freedom compels us to defend the legal freedom to proselytize even as we call upon Christians to refrain from such activity.[49]

The *Oxford American Dictionary* (1986) defines "proselytization" as "to try to convert people to one's beliefs or opinions." So isn't the point of giving the gospel to those in a false religion to try and convert them, to try and rescue them from false teaching and opinions?

Then why would preaching the gospel to those who do not hold to the gospel undermine the Christian mission? Isn't this the very heart of the Christian mission and how Protestants have viewed Catholics who still need to hear about true grace (Ephesians 2:8,9)?

Further, when the report talks about persuading others that their traditions are "more fully in accord with the gospel," what does this mean? Are we to take this to mean that there are now *degrees* of being in accordance with the gospel?

If someone is 50 percent in agreement with the gospel, is that enough agreement to make him in accord with the gospel? What about 45 percent? 30 percent? 20 percent? 10 percent? Will someone who is only 10 percent in accord with the gospel undermine this unity?

Scripture tells us what the gospel is—not what 20 percent, 50 percent, or 90 percent is, but what 100 percent of the gospel is.

It's not how close a person gets to the gospel, as if somewhere along the line he gets close enough to be constituted a Christian. Rather, biblically a person is either in accord with the gospel or he is not (Romans 11:6).

Is Conversion a Continuing Process?

The report also discusses the importance of conversion. It cites the Baptist/Roman Catholic International Conversation (1988) as setting forth an agreeable definition of "conversion." That definition reads as follows:

> Conversion is a passing from one way of life to another new one, marked with the newness of Christ. It is a continuing process so that the whole life of a Christian should be a passage from death to life, from error to truth, from sin to grace. . . . We seek and pray for the conversion of others, even as we recognize our own need to be fully converted.[50]

This is another example of the equivocation found in the statements of this document. All knowledgeable people know that Catholics and Evangelicals mean something different when they say that "conversion is a continuous process."

For Evangelicals, conversion is only a continuing process when it refers to sanctification, our growth in holiness. As more commonly understood, conversion is the point at which salvation occurs. According to John 5:24, when a person believes, he has already passed "from death to life, from error to truth, and from sin to grace." In other words, conversion has already taken place. Again, for Evangelicals conversion happens the moment a person believes. At that moment he is forgiven and eternally saved. But from that moment of justification springs sanctification, which is a lifelong, progressive spiritual growth.

On the other hand, for Roman Catholics sanctification begins the process of holy living and continues throughout life in order to attain God's final justification. This is a teaching that no Evangelical familiar with biblical truth can accept.

When Catholicism refers to conversion as a continuing process, it also incorporates works done by the person in the power of Christ, and it states it is necessary for the Catholic to do these to attain ultimate salvation. That is why Protestants see Catholicism as teaching faith and works.

The surprising thing is that those who signed the report claimed to agree on the above statement concerning conversion. But is it right to make people think that agreement exists when it really doesn't? If there really was agreement, why didn't the signers tell us how they reconciled the historical disputes over the nature of conversion?

Different Ways of Being Christian?

The paper next argues, "There are different forms that authentic discipleship can take. . . . There are different ways of being Christian."[51] What does it mean to say there are "different forms" and "different ways of being Christian"? Is it now valid for Catholics and Evanglicals to both accept that there are either two or seven sacraments? Catholic tradition or Scripture alone? Does it matter whether one venerates Mary and the saints or believes it is wrong? Can we hold to both justification by faith alone and justification by faith and works? Is regeneration both something that occurs at a point in time and a continuing process begun in baptism?

If there are different ways of being Christian, are there different ways of gaining salvation? If so, what religions around the world should we exclude as being illegitimate ways of salvation and on what basis?

Some might argue that perhaps all that the authors of the agreement meant was that once a person becomes a Christian, there are different churches, there are different ways of serving Christ and showing one belongs to Him. Obviously, we agree—if that is what they mean. But then why did they place these words in the section on conversion? Further, why do most of the statements in this section divulge a Catholic sense of conversion? For example, "We seek and pray for the conversion of others, even as we recognize our own continuing need to be fully converted."[52] Also, "Conversion is . . . a continuing process so that the whole life of a Christian should be a passage from death to life."[53]

By defining "conversion" in an ambiguous way, it almost seems to convey the fact that the authors agreed that either the Evangelical or Catholic interpretation of conversion is acceptable. Is this what they mean by saying, "There are different ways of being Christian"?

Growth in Christian Discipleship?

All parties who signed this agreement go on to say, "We as Evangelicals and Catholics affirm that opportunity and means for growth in Christian discipleship are available in our several communities."[54] But is this really true?

Is it also true that when a person is converted, whether he has been converted in an Evangelical or Catholic context, that it doesn't matter which church he attends? The authors of the agreement said differences between Evangelicals and Catholics must be presented to that person. Then that person should be left alone to decide which community of believers he will join. They say that they "dare not interfere" with such decisions as:

> . . . differing beliefs about the relationship between baptism, new birth, and membership in the church [that] should be honestly presented to the Christian who has undergone conversion. . . .
>
> Those converted—whether understood as having received the new birth for the first time or as having experienced

the reawakening of the new birth originally bestowed in the sacrament of baptism—must be given full freedom and respect as they discern and decide the community in which they will live their new life in Christ. In such discernment and decision . . . we dare not interfere with the exercise of that responsibility.[55]

In essence, what seems to be implied here is that truth doesn't matter. Also whether or not a new convert joins an Evangelical Church or a Roman Catholic Church makes no difference. Apparently, the only thing that matters is that new converts are given the choice.

We must remind ourselves once again that Paul argued and reasoned and had great dispute and dissension with those who opposed the gospel. He never acted as if it didn't make any difference whether a person joined a true Christian community or a church of the Judaizers or Gnostics. Again, the Bible teaches, "Contend earnestly for the faith [with the article, the word "the" refers to the propositional truths—the doctrines which make up the faith] which was once for all delivered to the saints" (Jude 3 NASB).

Why on earth would Evangelicals go against biblical teaching to tell new converts that the Roman Catholic view of the new birth, baptism, salvation, etc., is equally valid with their own when, in fact, it really isn't?

Further, isn't the document mistaken when it assumes Evangelicals will agree that a Catholic has legitimately received the new birth via baptism only? Isn't it true that no Evangelical assumes this since he has been convinced by the Scriptures that this contradicts the gospel?

As Paul said, "For Christ did not send me to baptize, but to preach the gospel" (1 Corinthians 1:17 NASB).

In essence, the authors of the "Evangelicals and Catholics Together" statement seem to assert that no matter what an individual believes, as long as he is either a Protestant or a Catholic, he is Christian. All that is needed is to present to new converts that there are different ways of living the Christian life and different beliefs, but that everyone in those two camps is still saved. Where new converts choose to fellowship doesn't matter since neither side is wrong. What is important is that new converts be allowed to choose.

Is this how the Reformers acted toward the popes? Is this what Paul did with the Judaizers and Gnostics? Can we imagine the apostle Paul telling the Judaizers, "If you convert anyone, you tell them what I think is true, and if I convert anyone, I'll tell them what you think is true—then on Sunday they can come either to my house or your house and worship the Lord"?

The New Birth

Our final excerpt from the agreement has to do with the new birth:

> We encounter a major difference in our understanding of the relationship between baptism and the new birth in Christ. For Catholics, all who are validly baptized are born again and are truly, however imperfectly, in communion with Christ. . . . For Catholics, all the baptized are already members of the church, however dormant their faith and life.[56]

This says it all. If we can agree to disagree on something like this and still call Roman Catholics Christian, have we not abandoned the meaning of the words of Scripture?

The above statement also undergirds the Catholic teaching that all members of the Catholic Church, because of baptism, are life-long Catholics—however dormant their faith and life!

A critic of this document has responded:

> Do the Scriptures allow for such an idea? Can Christian life be present but dormant in a person who has never manifested evidence of life? Isn't this a Roman Catholic excuse for giving extreme unction and the blessings of the Church to those who have never evidenced any relationship to Christ?

> Would [Evangelicals] offer any hope of salvation to someone who had joined the Church at age three or four, and who had never again shown the slightest interest in the things of God? Of course, they would not. Then why would Evangelicals offer hope of heaven to anyone simply on the basis of their having been baptized as an infant? This does not question the security of the believer or the perseverance of the saints; what it does question is church membership alone as a reliable indicator of salvation![57]

The question is this, "Have Evangelical scholars been persuaded that all those who are in the Catholic Church, who don't live the

Christian life, really are saved ('in communion with Christ')?" If
Evangelicals can agree to this, then it is understandable why there is
no need for Protestants to attempt to convert Catholics.

But the Bible responds:

> They profess to know God, but by their deeds they deny
> Him (Titus 1:16 NASB).

> The one who says, "I have come to know Him," and does
> not keep His commandments, is a liar, and the truth is
> not in him (1 John 2:4 NASB).

> Even so faith, if it has no works, is dead, being by itself
> (James 2:17 NASB).

Four Crucial Reasons

In conclusion, should our Evangelical leaders have signed the
document titled "Evangelicals and Catholics Together: The Christian Mission in the Third Millennium"? There are four reasons why
we believe they should not have signed it:

1. *The Evangelical signers were aware of past church history.* None of
the signers were ignorant of the 450 years of church history and the
biblical doctrines that have divided Protestants and Catholics during that time. Evangelical leaders must have realized before they
signed their names to this agreement that the Evangelical community would want to know from them exactly *where* Roman Catholics
finally "saw the light" and realized they were wrong.

But nowhere in this document are we told that the Roman Catholics surrendered their beliefs concerning such doctrines as justification by faith plus works or that their basis of authority has changed
from Church tradition, the Councils, papal encyclicals, etc., to the
Bible alone.

If there was real agreement, why weren't the changes in belief
documented? Why weren't the reasons for the changes given? To
claim that Catholics and Evangelicals have agreed spiritually and
not give the evidence to support that claim implies there was no real
agreement.

2. *The affirmations in the agreement are ambiguous and not precise.*
Surely the Catholic and Protestant leaders who signed this document realized in advance that their constituents would want to
know exactly what was agreed to if a consensus was reached. What

happened? Leaders from both sides said they did reach a consensus, but precise explanations were not given. Instead, such terms as "justification by grace," "the one mission of Christ," "the Body of Christ," "conversion," and "the Gospel" were placed in ambiguous statements.

The final document placed these important words in contexts which allow them to be interpreted to fit the historical meaning of these words used by either Roman Catholics or Protestants. This can only lead one to conclude that this agreement has the appearance of unity and harmony, but it is really not based on biblical truth. To our way of thinking, if Catholics really had changed their minds on basic doctrines, then it seems they would have been only too happy to have made this clear in what they said. But none of this can be found in this document of agreement.

3. *Not all the statements made in this document are supported by Scripture.* The affirmations stated in this agreement, besides being unclear and vague, are only occasionally supported by Scripture and when they are, sometimes they distort Scripture. Also, this document made many statements that have no scriptural reference because Scripture would contradict them. In many other places in this document the Scripture passages which are quoted are robbed of their meaning because of prior assumptions.

For example, "All who receive Jesus Christ as Savior and Lord are brothers and sisters in Christ."[58] This is a truism. If a person is in Christ, we agree he is a fellow Christian. But this begs the question, "How does a person get in Christ?" If you apply the Bible to the prior assumption, namely, "How does a Roman Catholic person get in Christ?" the Bible doesn't support the statement that "all who receive Christ as Savior and Lord are brothers and sisters in Christ."

Another example would be, "Conversion is . . . a continuing process so that the whole life of the Christian should be a passage from death to life."[59] This statement can be true, but it can also be interpreted as a false statement if prior Catholic assumptions are read into it. Prior assumptions not supported by Scripture rob Scripture of its true meaning.

4. *The main doctrine separating Catholics and Evangelicals—justification by faith—is not dealt with clearly.* Here again, both Roman Catholic and Evangelical leaders must have been aware of the prior historical debate. Specifically they have known that their churches have been separated by the doctrine of justification by faith for more than 450 years. In part, they admit, "We do not presume to

suggest that we can resolve the deep and long-standing differences between Evangelicals and Catholics."[60] But if one of the deep and long-standing differences that remains is justification by faith, then there cannot be any agreement.

Was this issue resolved? Who was right? Who was wrong? Since this is the watershed issue upon which the church stands or falls, and since this doctrine is the heart of the gospel (Romans 1:17), then there can be no excuse for the leaders on both sides not being precise about this doctrine.

In essence, not enough was written, not enough was stated; and what was stated in the document causes us concern because the statements were ambiguous. To declare that there has been an agreement between Catholics and Protestants and then write vague pronouncements that can be interpreted by either side as they have always done in the past is to lead to the conclusion that this coalition came together for reasons other than those based on biblical truth.[61] (For detailed information, see endnote 61.)

Keep the Faith

We cannot judge the motives of another's heart. We assume that our Evangelical leaders signed this agreement out of good intentions. However, because they did sign it, and because of their stature and who they are, it is our view that they have muddied the waters concerning the nature of the true gospel to many people around the world. This imprecise definition of the gospel can only hurt the cause of Christian missions. This may have the effect of blinding millions of Roman Catholics and further lulling them into thinking they are on their way to heaven simply because they are devout Roman Catholics.

These are fearful things for us to write. But that's why God's Word instructs us, "Let not many of you become teachers, my brethren, knowing that as such we shall incur a stricter judgment" (James 3:1 NASB).

Let us say we have been surprised by the wide acceptance of this Catholic and Evangelical agreement. Many have already praised it, and we will shortly explain why so many others have accepted what is really a compromising document.

The words of the apostle Paul may give the reason:

The time will come when they will not endure sound doctrine; but wanting to have their ears tickled, they

will accumulate for themselves teachers in accordance to
their own desires; and will turn away their ears from the
truth, and will turn aside to myths. But you, be sober in
all things, endure hardship, do the work of an evangelist,
fulfill your ministry (2 Timothy 4:3-5 NASB).

In this same passage (verse 7), the apostle Paul contrasts this
spirit of compromise with his own determination: "I have fought
the good fight, I have finished the course, I have kept the faith."

Our prayer is for all true believers that they too may indeed
"contend earnestly for the faith which was once for all delivered to
the saints" (Jude 3 NASB).

.13.

Impact of Ecumenism

This [ecumenical] path is very dear to me.[1]
—Pope John Paul II

*W*hile the "Evangelical and Catholics Together" statement was said to be a declaration that does not speak officially for the Evangelical or Catholic communities, it has nevertheless had wide impact. Indeed, according to *World* magazine for April 9, 1994, "The paper has been circulated among top Vatican officials" and further, "Unnamed leading Evangelical figures on the world scene have also seen the declaration and have offered encouragement." *World* magazine itself called it "a landmark document."[2]

Both *Christianity Today* and "The Christian Coalition" referred to it as a "historic document."[3]

An editorial in *Christianity Today* noted, "For too long, ecumenism has been left to Left-leaning Catholics and mainline Protestants. For that reason alone, Evangelicals should applaud this effort and rejoice in the progress it represents."

The editorial also went on to assert that the document upheld both the authority of Scripture and justification by faith: "Both the formal and material principles of the Reformation—that is, the infallibility of holy Scripture and justification by faith—are duly affirmed in this statement."[4]

Whether or not *Christianity Today's* editorial is true or overly optimistic in light of past church history should be weighed in the balance of the information presented in our previous chapter.

However, praise for this statement came from other quarters as well. *Christian American* cited an editorial in the *Wall Street Journal*, April 4, 1994, which referred to the declaration in the following terms: "This is the wave of the future. It is as significant a coalition to the future of American Politics as the unification of blacks and Jews during the civil rights struggle."[5]

Christian American also quoted John White, president of Geneva College and former president of the National Association of Evangelicals, who said, "I really do think it's a historic moment."[6] Reverend Pat Robertson, a very influential Evangelical leader, was quoted as saying, "The time has come where we must lay aside minor points of doctrinal differences and focus upon the Lord Jesus Christ."[7] Dr. Larry Lewis, President of the Home Mission Board of the Southern Baptist Convention, a signer of the statement, said, "Many are calling it the most significant document since the Reformation."[8]

Evangelical Leaders Who Disapprove

Not all Evangelicals thought that the agreement signed between Evangelical and Catholic leaders was a good thing. For example, David Howard, immediate past international director of the World Evangelical Fellowship and a former missionary in Latin America, told *World* magazine that "in the discussion of evangelizing and proselytizing he saw the paper 'almost leaning' toward instructing Evangelical missionaries to send their converts to Catholic churches"; he was also left "with a sense of uneasiness and incompleteness. . . . I was not sure at the beginning or end what they're driving at."[9]

Noted theologian R.C. Sproul, in a telephone interview with *World*, "expressed alarm" over the theological content of the paper: "I'm afraid the document trivializes the Reformation," he declared, suggesting that the Evangelicals negotiated away justification—"what Luther called the article upon which the Church stands or falls." He also noted that the "'absence of the discussion of any forensic character of justification was dramatic.'"[10] In the foreword to this book he writes: "What has become blurred in the new irenicism is the critical issues raised during the Reformation regarding essential points of the gospel."

Dave Hunt responded to the new agreement as follows:

> I believe the document represents the most devastating blow against the gospel in at least 1,000 years. Already the declaration is being "translated into Spanish, Polish, Portuguese and Russian for circulation throughout Latin America and Eastern Europe." Soon it will have a revolutionary impact world wide. . . . [Yet] the very heart of the

gospel which evangelicals affirm is denied by Catholicism in all its creeds, catechisms, canons and decrees and dogmas, and those who dare to affirm it are anathematized. . . . To be saved, a Catholic would have to believe the true gospel and reject Catholicism's false gospel.

One can't believe two contradictory propositions at the same time. . . . One can't believe salvation is by faith and "not of works" and at the same time believe that good works earn salvation. . . . I have sent photocopies of pertinent sections from Vatican II, Trent and catechisms to some of these men, with no response to the issues. They cannot be excused on the grounds of ignorance. The most tragic result of this historic development will be to prevent the gospel from being presented to lost millions who have now been wrongly reclassified by evangelical leaders as Christians.[11]

Southern Baptist leader Dr. James Holly sent his critique of the agreement to other leaders across the Southern Baptist Convention:

Lip service is repeatedly given to biblical doctrine, while political pragmatism drives this document. . . . Even if Evangelicals and Catholics can agree upon common political and social goals, their irreconcilable theological differences mean that in order to "work and witness together" the truth of the Gospel must be subordinated to the practical goals agreed upon by this document. . . . The imprecision of this document is characteristic of ecumenical statements. What is the driving force behind this document? It isn't truth, because that is being compromised! And, if it is political cooperation, that is not a goal which requires theological homogeny! . . . Theological convergence between Roman Catholicism and Evangelicals can only take place with compromise by Evangelicals or with conversion by Roman Catholics. There is no middle ground for resolving the critical issues which divide us. . . . We do not have a "common evangelistic task" with Roman Catholics. We have an evangelistic task to the whole lost world, which includes the vast majority of Roman Catholics.[12]

Again, our own assessment of the "Evangelicals and Catholics Together" statement leads us to wonder why our friends were not more careful in making precise affirmations concerning the gospel. If there really was agreement with Catholics that the gospel is through grace alone, by faith alone, then wouldn't all sides have been glad to say that?

Surely our leaders must have known the Evangelical world would require from any agreement a clear definition of justification by faith alone in light of past church history. Then why isn't there a clear definition?

Among our Evangelical brethren who have signed this statement are those for whose ministries we have only the greatest respect. However, in light of the contents of this document, its ambiguity, its lack of clear statements on the gospel and justification by faith alone, we must disagree with our friends and hope they will reconsider their signatures to this document and either have their names removed and/or publicly disavow it. Below we explain our biblical motivation for saying this.

Guidelines: The God of Truth

Because God is a God of truth (Isaiah 65:16), He is concerned that His people honor the truth. Any concordance study on the word "truth" will immediately reveal how important this subject is. Consider the following Scriptures: "Serve Him in truth with all your heart" (1 Samuel 12:24 NASB). Jesus said, "God is spirit, and his worshipers must worship in spirit and in truth" (John 4:24); "If you hold to my teaching, you are really my disciples. Then you will know the truth, and the truth will set you free" (John 8:31,32); "For this reason I was born, and for this I came into the world, to testify to the truth" (John 18:37). The apostle Paul told the Corinthians, "We spoke all things to you in truth" (2 Corinthians 7:14 NASB). We are to "[speak] the truth in love" (Ephesians 4:15); and to understand "the grace of God in truth" (Colossians 1:6 NASB). Finally, we are to handle "accurately the word of truth" so that the way of truth will not be maligned (2 Timothy 2:15 NASB; cf. 2 Peter 2:2).

Because God places a premium on truth, He warns Christians about those who have gone astray from the truth (2 Timothy 2:18), oppose the truth (2 Timothy 3:8), lie against the truth (James 3:14), and He tells us that no lie can be of the truth (1 John 2:21).

In the end, truth cannot be escaped within any more than it can be escaped without. As Shakespeare wrote in *Measure for Measure*, "Truth is truth to th' end of reck'ning."

When confronted by that which opposes it, truth is by its very nature divisive. Truth is tough. Wasn't it Jesus who said, "Do not suppose that I have come to bring peace to the earth. I did not come to bring peace, but a sword. For I have come to turn 'a man against his father, a daughter against her mother . . . a man's enemies will be the members of his own household'" (Matthew 10:34-36)? Truth is divisive for the very reason that it stands against and opposes that which is not true.

Scripture not only emphasizes knowing the truth and avoiding error, it commands us to defend the truth. "Contend earnestly for the faith which was once for all delivered to the saints" (Jude 3 NASB).

The apostle John could say, "I have no greater joy than to hear that my children are walking in the truth" (3 John 4).

The apostle Paul constantly attempted to reason with and persuade both Jews and Greeks as to the truth of the Christian message: "Every sabbath he [Paul] reasoned in the synagogue, trying to persuade Jews and Greeks" (Acts 18:4; cf. 17:2-4,17). Paul told Titus to "[hold] fast the faithful word . . . both to exhort in sound doctrine and to refute those who contradict" (Titus 1:9 NASB).

Because of this strong emphasis of standing for the truth, there were regular controversies over it. When the Judaizers came down from Antioch, they were teaching Christians that they could not be saved unless they were circumcised according to the custom taught by Moses (i.e., unless they obeyed the Mosaic law). The apostle Paul debated such men: "This brought Paul and Barnabas into sharp dispute and debate with them" (Acts 15:2).

This particular debate was resolved when the apostle Peter himself emphasized that salvation was by grace alone and the Gentiles did not have to keep the Law: "Now then, why do you try to test God by putting on the necks of the disciples a yoke that neither we nor our fathers have been able to bear? No! We believe it is through the grace of our Lord Jesus that we are saved, just as they are" (Acts 15:10,11).

However, at a later time, even Peter felt the pressure to please both sides and as a result compromised the gospel. Paul saw what Peter was doing and "did not give in to them for a moment, so that the truth of the gospel might remain with you" (Galatians 2:5).

What did the apostle Paul do?

> When Peter came to Antioch, I opposed him to his face, because he was clearly in the wrong. . . . The other Jews joined him in his hypocrisy, so that by their hypocrisy even Barnabas was led astray. When I saw that they were

not acting in line with the truth of the gospel, I said to Peter in front of them all, "You are a Jew, yet you live like a Gentile and not like a Jew. How is it, then, that you force Gentiles to follow Jewish customs? We who are Jews by birth and not 'Gentile sinners' know that a man is not justified by observing the law, but by faith in Jesus Christ. So we, too, have put our faith in Christ Jesus that we may be justified by faith in Christ and not by observing the law, because by observing the law no one will be justified" (Galatians 2:11,13-16).

Exercise in Diplomacy?

In light of these Scriptures, it seems that the "Evangelicals and Catholics Together" statement is more an exercise in Catholic/Evangelical diplomacy than biblical truth. In our view, the persons who convened this project and spent two years preparing it probably knew the difficulties they would face; such a conclusion seems evident throughout the document.

Careful reading reveals that the report was written with diplomatic skill. As noted, in many instances the wording is carefully drafted so that both Catholics and Evangelicals can accept a given statement on its surface. But if Catholics and Evangelicals were to sit down and define what they mean by the terms used in this document, 450 years of church history tell us that they could not possibly agree. If they really did agree and achieved a new breakthrough, then why didn't they let us know that in reference to the historical debate?

But these things are not in the report, so where is the concern for truth? When both sides can affirm a proposition on its face as evidence of their alleged unity when, in fact, a frank evaluation of that proposition from both sides would prove that there is no unity, that is not truth. Further, what is the value of instituting a political compromise if all it does in the end is promote equivocation and confusion?

Evangelical leaders should not have signed this document since the very gospel is at stake. This is not a "minor issue" for the church to deal with; it is the most monumental issue of all—the nature of how a person is saved and how a person goes to heaven. For anyone who has ever lived, what is more crucial than this?

What should Evangelicals do who have signed this document and now have come to realize that they have made a mistake? We certainly understand and empathize with the difficulty this imposes on them.

Whether the signer would wish to simply have his name removed from this document in private or publicly confess the mistake is a personal decision. The important thing is for Evangelicals who love the gospel of Jesus Christ to distance themselves from a document that compromises what they truly love.

It may indeed be somewhat embarrassing to remove one's name from a document one has already signed, but the consequences of this act will be less than the consequences of allowing one's name to remain on a document that calls into question before the world one's commitment to the gospel.

One of the truly wonderful realities of the Christian life is forgiveness. None of us stands blameless, and all of us have made decisions that we later regretted—decisions that may have been consequential. Therefore, we think that Christians everywhere are more than willing to forgive any signing of this document that was done in haste, ignorance, or without full reflection upon the consequences.

Perhaps we could not better end this chapter than by quoting the words of Martin Luther himself who advised Christian leaders:

> If I declare with loudest voice and clearest exposition every portion of God's Truth except for the one little bit which the world and the devil are at the moment attacking, I am not confessing Christ no matter how boldly I may be professing Christ.
>
> For the soldier to be steady on all the battlefields besides is mere flight and disgrace if he flinches at that single point.

.14.

What Should Be Agreed Upon?

*T*rue friendship is a wonderful thing. It offers unexpected pleasures and in diverse ways makes life worth living. Friendship is something so powerful that even people who strongly disagree about certain things can become fast friends for a lifetime. As the Proverbs tell us, "A friend loves at all times" and "Wounds from a friend can be trusted" (Proverbs 17:17; 27:6).

Unfortunately, in a world like ours, the wrong kind of friendship can also become a snare: "Do not be misled: 'Bad company corrupts good character'" (1 Corinthians 15:33). And sometimes even wholesome friendships can be found to compromise biblical truth when the proper relationship between friendship and truth is not maintained. As Aristotle wrote, "It would be wrong to put friendship before truth."

In order to avoid the problems that can arise when such a situation exists, it is necessary to preserve one's friendships and one's truth as the delicate riches they are. Many Evangelicals have Catholics as friends, and this is all to the good. But such friendships must never be allowed to compromise biblical truths about salvation. Indeed, a friend who "loves at all times" will honor spiritual truth within his friendships.

Social Versus Spiritual Fellowship

God values the gospel. It is His message provided at the cost of the life of His own dear Son. In relationship to the gospel certain issues need to be kept in mind for Evangelicals who are pondering at what points interaction with Catholics may occur, and when is it biblically inappropriate to give recognition of spiritual unity and fellowship.

People who agree on social matters are obviously drawn to each other. Those motivated by biblical values can work with those motivated by other authorities. This happened under the Moral Majority and other movements started by Christians. At the same time, the people in those groups did not acknowledge each other as fellow believers. Thus, agreement to work toward a common goal in society for moral issues is one thing; spiritual fellowship based on the gospel within the church is something else entirely.

Everyone who has ever been involved in developing friendships outside of his group knows that new friendships can sometimes blur and let slip important distinctions in the area of spiritual fellowship. For example, when Evangelicals get together with Catholics on social issues, a bond of fellowship and friendship is established. And indeed, Catholic "Evangelicals" who sound Evangelical and use the right words can certainly *seem* to be saved. But they really are not if they deny the one gospel and "the simplicity and purity of devotion to Christ" (2 Corinthians 11:3 NASB).

Now the motivation of many Catholics who claim to be Evangelical is characteristically to unite the Protestant church with Rome. Knowing this, Protestants who wish to have fellowship with Catholics on social issues must not compromise the crucial dividing line of the gospel that separates believer and unbeliever. Merely because one's Catholic friends sound Evangelical and are committed to working on difficult social issues does not mean that spiritual fellowship with them is permitted.

Biblically, if the commitment of Catholics who claim to be Evangelical is to salvation by faith-works, God still classifies them as unbelievers. This is logical since even Catholic and Protestant scholars agree that if a person seeks to be forgiven of his sins in a way that God says he won't be forgiven, then that person, however sincere, is not forgiven.

For all true believers, the gospel is the watershed issue. If God clearly tells us there is only one way in which we can be saved—and that is to trust entirely upon His Son and not our own works—then anyone who does not come to God on His terms simply is not saved. God says so.

Unequally Yoked?

We must remember that the apostle Paul has already dealt with the issue of spiritual fellowship between the saved and the unsaved. He warns,

Do not be yoked together with unbelievers. For what do
righteousness and wickedness have in common? Or
what fellowship can light have with darkness? What harmony is there between Christ and Belial? What does a
believer have in common with an unbeliever? What
agreement is there between the temple of God and idols?
For we are the temple of the living God. As God has said:
"I will live with them and walk among them, and I will be
their God, and they will be my people. Therefore, come
out from them and be separate," says the Lord. "Touch
no unclean thing, and I will receive you. I will be a father
to you and you will be my sons and daughters," says the
Lord Almighty (2 Corinthians 6:14-18).

The seemingly stern teaching of Scripture is that the gospel is the
dividing line. Those who accept the gospel are Christians. Those
who mix works with the gospel are not Christians.

Now the argument is made by some Catholics who claim to be
Evangelical that because they believe that all of their works and
merit are grace-inspired and because they are sincerely thankful to
God for His work in their lives—that even if certain disagreements
exist on the gospel, spiritual fellowship should still be permitted.
After all, Catholics agree with Evangelicals that God is the One who
should receive all the glory for the works we do.

But this misses the point. In one of his lectures on Roman Catholicism, theologian R.C. Sproul provides an interesting application of
Jesus' parable of the Pharisee and the tax collector in Luke 18. Tax
collectors, of course, were despised by Jews because they collected
taxes for the Roman government. Jesus' parable then, would have
been surprising to His hearers because it was not the righteous
Pharisee, the religious leader, whom God pronounced justified, but
the despised tax collector.

Sproul argues that the righteous Pharisee can be interpreted to
represent the Catholic view of justification while the tax collector
represents the Reformed or biblical view of justification.

Here is the story:

The Pharisee stood up and prayed about himself: "God, I
thank you that I am not like other men—robbers, evil
doers, adulterers—or even like this tax collector. I fast
twice a week and give a tenth of all I get."

> But the tax collector stood at a distance. He would not even look up to heaven, but beat his breast and said, "God, have mercy on me, a sinner."

> I tell you that this man, rather than the other, went home justified before God. For everyone who exalts himself will be humbled, and he who humbles himself will be exalted (Luke 18:11-14).

Both of these men were religious; they had gone to the temple to pray; they believed in God; they trusted God. But each man had a very different approach to God.

Remember, Roman Catholicism is careful to maintain that the religious works done by the Catholic believer (works of penance, satisfaction, etc.) are not done by the believer entirely in his or her own strength—they are also the work of Christ through him or her.

In a similar manner, the Pharisee did not necessarily claim that he was intrinsically virtuous and righteous in and of himself or that God should reward him because he deserved reward from God. As a religious leader of the Jews, the Pharisee should have recognized God's work within him.

When he said, "I thank you, God, that I am not like other men," in part, he thanked God for the way God had made him and for how God had worked in his life. As a devout follower of Jewish law, he also understood that apart from God working in his life, he could have ended up just like the tax gatherer, adulterer, etc.

So the Pharisee is aware of God having been gracious in his life and having given him power to be a righteous man and religious leader. As Sproul argues, he would probably have conceded that whatever righteousness he had within himself was something that he ultimately owed to God.[1] This does indeed represent the Catholic view of justification.

On the other hand, notice the reaction of the tax collector. He said nothing about his own righteousness at all—not even about God's work within him. He is unable even to lift his eyes up to heaven. With head bowed, he humbly says, "God, be merciful to me, a sinner."

A Crucial Difference

Listen to the further comments of Dr. Sproul:

> Doesn't the prayer of the Pharisee sound on the surface like a very Christian prayer? He says, "I thank you, God,

that I am who I am and that any righteousness I have in myself I owe to you ultimately. I thank you for that."

Isn't that a Christian prayer? Why would Jesus be upset with that kind of prayer? Why would Jesus see that as a false way of justification? Isn't the man being grateful to God and giving thanks to him?

I'll tell you why. Because that man was resting a case for his salvation on the righteousness that he had through the gift of God within himself. The tax gatherer rested his case solely upon the mercy of God. No merit at all! Only the merit of Jesus Christ. Not the merit of Jesus Christ in him but the merit of Jesus Christ in Jesus Christ—this is the basis of biblical justification! Not a goodness that someone may attain through the help of Jesus Christ which they will then thank God for—but the righteousness of Christ alone.[2]

Isn't it true that the Pharisee could be seen as making an argument like the following: "Thank you, God. I owe you all the praise and thanks, but isn't it nice that I cooperated and assented so that now that righteousness is, in part, my righteousness as well? I contribute to the righteousness that you have so graciously helped me to achieve. I contribute to my own atonement, but I realize that I could not do it apart from Jesus Christ who has assisted me. He has given me the grace and strength necessary to achieve that righteousness."[3]

Sproul continues,

"No," says Jesus. As humble as that prayer is—it isn't humble enough. We don't add the tiniest, slightest particle of merit to the merit of Jesus Christ. We don't add a sliver of satisfaction to the cross of Jesus Christ. We are justified on His merits, not His merits in us. We are justified by His merits within Him, which then become ours through God's declaration of forensic justification when we are linked to Christ through faith.[4]

In essence, then, the Pharisee and tax collector had no agreement on the basis of their standing before God. In similar fashion, Evangelicals and Catholics simply cannot call each other brothers and sisters in Christ when they disagree about the gospel. Thus, there is no basis for Evangelical/Catholic recognition, and there is no acceptance based on the doctrine of salvation.

No matter how "righteous and spiritual" orthodox Catholicism may sound, it is still teaching salvation by merit. Cooperation can be based on personal friendship, agreement on moral issues, or social concerns, but it should not be said to be based on the gospel when two parties do not agree.

Remember, in Galatians, those who wanted to teach a "gospel" of faith plus works were condemned by the apostle as teaching a false gospel and were not recognized and welcomed as fellow believers (Galatians 1:6-9; 5:10).

Because of his love for Christ and the truth, Paul also told the Corinthian believers not to cooperate with false teachers. He said they were not really servants of God—in spite of their persuasive ways and spiritual commitment. To become yoked with them was to destroy the harmony and fellowship that unites true believers in Christ.

In conclusion, friendship and social activism are one thing; declaring that we are united as "brothers and sisters in Christ" with those who do not affirm the gospel of justification by faith alone is entirely something else. It is biblically wrong.

.15.

What Does the Bible Say?

*T*ruth may make the devil blush, but the devil sometimes speaks the truth—just not all of it. As Tyon Edwards observed, "Errors of theory or doctrine are not so much false statements as partial statements. Half a truth received, while the corresponding half is unknown or rejected, is a practical falsehood." Further:

> In its influence on the soul, error has been compared to a magnet concealed near the ship's compass. . . . As in the latter case, the more favorable the winds, and the greater the diligence and the skill in working the ship, the more rapidly will it be speeded on in a wrong course . . . and so in the former case, the greater the struggle for safety, the more speedy the progress to ruin.

Thus by accepting half a truth (justification by faith in a Catholic sense) while the other half is unknown or rejected (justification by faith *alone*), one can indeed speedily abandon the truth of the gospel. By proclaiming a gospel of faith-works, the soul's progress to ruin is indeed inevitable.

Discerning the Issue

There is an enormous difference between Catholics who say they are Evangelical and Evangelical "Catholics." The former claim to be Evangelical and yet are committed to Rome, seeking to bring Evangelicals back to the Mother Church. In the latter category are genuine believers in Christ who may still have some association with the Catholic Church in order to minister to their Catholic friends.

With those individuals in the Catholic Church who have truly experienced salvation in Christ and yet remain in the Catholic Church we can have spiritual fellowship, since they are indeed our brothers and sisters in Christ.

But we do not have God's permission biblically to seek agreement and spiritual unity with those who disagree on the gospel merely in order to break down centuries-old barriers which some claim are causing "unnecessary" divisions. Sentimentalism and the desire for unity alone will only compromise the truth, but real love, even "tough love" will safeguard the truth.

Now let's pursue in more detail this crucial issue of Catholics who claim to be Evangelical but are committed to Rome.

Ancient and Modern Judaizers

Many people may not understand how closely the issue of spiritual fellowship between Evangelicals and unsaved Catholics parallels the situation in the New Testament between the Christians and the Judaizers.

The Judaizers accepted a lot of truth—they believed in God, accepted Scripture as God's Word, and claimed Christ as their Savior. They even claimed to understand God's grace and mercy. But they insisted that a person had to be saved by both faith and works.

As Philip Schaff points out in *History of the Christian Church*, "They held circumcision and the whole moral and ceremonial law of Moses to be still binding and the observance of them necessary to salvation."[1] In other words, insofar as they taught a "gospel" of faith-works, they presented a similar situation in Paul's day to the situation we face in our own.

How did the apostle Paul respond to these people? If we understand Paul here, perhaps this will bring more clarity to the issues faced by Catholics who only *claim* to be Evangelical, and true Evangelicals as far as spiritual fellowship is concerned. We will concentrate on Galatians 1:6-9 and 5:10.

The Gospel Is the Major Issue

First, the apostle Paul realizes the tremendous significance of the issue he is writing about; this is evident from the manner in which he writes, as well as the particular words he uses. In Galatians chapter 1, Paul is setting the stage for his emphasis in Galatians chapters 2–4 that salvation comes *entirely* by faith in Christ apart from works. The essence of his argument is distilled in a relatively few verses—Galatians 2:14–3:14—and we would encourage readers to examine this passage of Scripture carefully.

In Galatians 2:5, Paul says that he did not yield to the Judaizers for a minute so that "the truth of the *gospel* might remain with you" (emphasis added). And in verse 14 he says, "When I saw that they were not straightforward about the truth of the *gospel*" (NASB, emphasis added), he opposed them directly. In chapter 3, verse 8, Paul says, "And the Scripture, foreseeing that God would justify the Gentiles by faith, preached the *gospel* beforehand to Abraham" (emphasis added).

In other words, it is very clear that Paul is dealing with one primary issue here—the gospel!

And what is the gospel? Paul makes it clear. It is the good news of salvation by grace through faith alone:

> Nevertheless, knowing that a man is not justified by the works of the Law but through faith in Christ Jesus, even we have believed in Christ Jesus, that we may be justified by faith in Christ, and not by the works of the Law; since by the works of the Law shall no flesh be justified. . . .
>
> I do not nullify the grace of God; for if righteousness comes through the Law, then Christ died needlessly.
>
> For as many as are of the works of the Law are under a curse (Galatians 2:16,21; 3:10 NASB).

The above verses set the stage for the verses we now wish to consider.

Abandoning Christ

Here is how Paul begins his letter to the Galatians:

> I am astonished that you are so quickly deserting the one who called you by the grace of Christ and are turning to a different gospel—which is really no gospel at all. Evidently some people are throwing you into confusion and are trying to pervert the gospel of Christ. But even if we or an angel from heaven should preach a gospel other than the one we preached to you, let him be eternally condemned! As we have already said, so now I say again:

If anybody is preaching to you a gospel other than what you accepted, let him be eternally condemned! (Galatians 1:6-9).

Paul calls the Galatians "foolish" and as having been "bewitched" because they are listening to the Judaizers (Galatians 3:1). As commentator William Hendriksen points out, Paul is stupefied and expresses "painful perplexity" and "overwhelming amazement" that the Galatians should have abandoned not just the gospel but the very One who called them to that gospel.

Hendriksen continues:

> In Galatians *the very essence of the Gospel is at stake.* Had this not been the case, Paul would have been very tolerant, as Philippians 1:15-18 proves. But when the issue is momentous—God's glory and man's salvation—tolerance has its limits. . . . The Apostle is amazed or astonished to hear that the [Galatians] are in the process of changing their position. . . . And it is they themselves who are turning (themselves) away; they are not just being turned away. Neither is it merely a theological position from which they are swerving. On the contrary, they are in the process of transferring their loyalty from the One who in his grace and mercy had called them—that is, God—to a different gospel.[2]

What was this "new gospel" the Galatians were turning to? It was "one which proclaimed faith plus law-works as the way to salvation. It stands to reason that the substitute to which the [Galatians] were turning was a gospel only in name, not in reality. It was really no gospel at all, exactly as Paul here declares."[3]

In fact, it was a "gospel" so terrible that Paul himself places a curse upon those associated with it—"upon him who might—and also upon him who actually does—proclaim it."[4]

What is obvious here is that the Galatians were being confused by the Judaizers who, despite their goodwill, belief in similar doctrines, and persuasive and zealous ways (Galatians 4:17) were actually turning the gospel upside down. They had rejected the gospel that centers in Christ and glories in Him alone. Thus, "Surely, a teaching according to which men are saved through faith plus law-works is a perversion of the true Gospel which proclaims the glad tidings of salvation (grace) by faith alone."[5]

The Galatians are actually in the process of "deserting" *(meta-tithesthe)* the very One who had called them to faith in Jesus Christ. It is not just that they were accepting an:

> . . . errant, though partially valid expression of the Christian faith, as the KJV translation might suggest. The problem was that they were "deserting" the Christian camp altogether. . . .
>
> It is not merely that they have deserted an idea or a movement; rather, they have deserted the very one who had called them to faith. This one is God the Father. . . . It is significant that once again even in the space of a few words ("who called you by the grace of Christ") Paul reiterates the true nature of the gospel: 1) it is of God, for God does the calling, and 2) it is of grace rather than of merit.[6]

As Bible scholar James Montgomery Boice points out, the gospel is one; thus, "any system of salvation that varies from it is counterfeit."[7]

In essence, Paul is objecting to two aspects of the conduct of the false teachers or Judaizers. First, they were perverting the gospel, and, second, they were troubling the church, which is the same:

> To tamper with the Gospel is to trouble the Church. . . . Indeed, the Church's greatest troublemakers (now as then) are not those outside who oppose, ridicule and persecute it, but those inside who try to change the Gospel. . . . Conversely, the only way to be a good Churchman is to be a good Gospel-man. The best way to serve the Church is to believe and to preach the Gospel.[8]

Troubles in the Church

In the material below, we have selected our citations and ask the reader to ponder all of them carefully. Consider the comments of Dr. Ridderbos in *The New International Commentary on the New Testament*:

> To trouble means, in this connection, to bring about spiritual schism and an obscuration of the insight of faith. . . . Their intent was nothing less than to overturn

the gospel that had Christ as its content and to live out an opposing principle. This happens when the cross of Christ is no longer recognized in its all-sufficiency. . . . Then the gospel is turned upside-down and robbed of its strength.[9]

Now consider the comments of the great reformer John Calvin, one well acquainted with Rome and its popes:

Paul charges the Galatians with defection, not only from his own teaching, but from Christ. . . . Thus they were removed from Christ, not in that they entirely rejected Christianity but because in such a corruption only a fictitious Christ was left to them. So today the Papists choose to have a half Christ and a mangled Christ and so none at all and are therefore removed from Christ. They are full of superstitions which are directly opposed to the nature of Christ. Let it be carefully observed that we are removed from Christ when we accept that which is inconsistent with His mediatorial office; for light cannot be mixed with darkness.

For the same reason he calls it another gospel, that is, another gospel than the true one. And yet the false apostles claim to preach the Gospel of Christ; but by mingling with it their own inventions, they destroyed the main force of the Gospel and so held to a false, corrupt and spurious gospel. . . . To desert the Son of God is in itself dishonorable and disgraceful; but to desert Him when He has called us freely to salvation is far more terrible.[10]

Consider another Calvin comment on what the false teachers were actually accomplishing:

He charges them with the second crime of doing an injury to Christ by wanting to destroy His Gospel. And this is a very dreadful crime; for destruction is worse than corruption. And with good reason does he accuse them. When the glory of justifying man is transferred to another and a snare is set for consciences, the Saviour no longer stands firm and the teaching of the Gospel is

ruined. For we must always take care of the main articles
of the Gospel. He who attacks them is a destroyer of the
Gospel.[11]

The Apostle's Response

Now, what does Paul do with those who are teaching a gospel of
faith-works? Paul's argument is both clear and forceful. Paul argues
first from a theoretical or hypothetical situation and second to
actual reality.

> But even if we or an angel from heaven should preach a
> gospel other than the one we preached to you, let him be
> eternally condemned! As we have already said, so now I
> say again, if anybody is preaching to you a gospel other
> than what you accepted, let him be eternally condemned!
> (Galatians 1:8,9).

In other words, Paul first argues from a hypothetical situation.
Even if one of God's good angels, those who live in heaven in
unspeakable holiness, should actually begin to preach a different
gospel, then let *him* be anathema, or eternally condemned.

If even Paul himself should change his mind and begin to preach
another gospel, let him be eternally condemned as well. This is the
hypothetical; now comes the reality.

If anyone *at all* is preaching to the Galatians another gospel, let
them be cursed. Certainly, if Paul argues that the curse of God must
come even upon a holy angel or the apostle himself for preaching a
false gospel, then it must come upon those troublemakers (Galatians 1:7; 5:10) who are attempting to lead the Galatians astray by
their faith-works "gospel."

Calvin proceeds to show why Paul's argument concerning the
angels, though an impossibility, is essential:

> To cast down the false apostles more violently, he rises up
> even to the angels. Nor does he simply say that they
> should not be heard if they brought forward something
> different, but declares that they ought to be held ac-
> cursed. Some might think that it was all wrong to involve
> angels in a controversy about his teaching; but anyone
> who considers it properly will see that he had to do this.
> It is certainly impossible for angels from heaven to teach

anything other than the sure truth of God. But when there was controversy over faith in the doctrine which God had revealed concerning the salvation of men, he did not reckon it enough to refuse the judgment of men without also claiming the higher judgment of the angels.

And thus when he pronounces a judgment of anathema on angels if they should teach anything else, though he argues from an impossibility, it is not superfluous. For this exaggeration helped to increase the authority of Paul's preaching. He saw that he and his teaching were attacked by the use of famous names. He replies that not even angels have the way to overwhelm it.[12]

Concerning the Roman Catholic hierarchy, Calvin points out that they are directly involved in that for which Paul is condemning the Judaizers. "For the teaching of the false apostles was not entirely contrary to . . . that of Paul, but was corrupted by false additions. . . . Of this gospel it is plain that the whole Papacy is a dreadful subversion."[13]

In other words, if even angels or Paul himself were to preach a contrary gospel, then

all the more the divine wrath must be poured out on the self-appointed nobodies who are now making themselves guilty of this crime. Here the storm is unleashed in all its fury. Paul's "let them be anathema" is not a mere wish, but an effective invocation. The Apostle, as Christ's fully authorized representative, is pronouncing the curse upon the Judaizers, who are committing the terrible crime of calling the true Gospel false, and of substituting the false and ruinously dangerous gospel for the true and saving one.[14]

Thus:

To this extent the truth of the gospel transcends all else in importance, and to this extent that man is culpable who, in preaching it, modifies it on his own authority.

On the one hand, this gives expression to how deeply conscious the Apostle was of the divine truth of the gospel. . . . And not only is the truth more [important] than the highest ranking minister of God, but as the gospel—which constitutes the norm of the divine redemption of the world—it is so holy that anyone who independently modifies it brings the curse of God down upon his head.

This, then, is something the Galatians can pause to consider, now that they have given place in their midst to "another" gospel, preached not by Paul, nor by an angel, but by a number of unauthorized persons.[15]

The Meaning of Anathema

For a moment let us pause and consider the word "anathema" that is used here by Paul. Literally the word means "let them be damned" or "let them be eternally condemned." It is generally used of items or "something yielded up to the wrath of God, surrendered to the curse of God."[16] The Greek usage here makes it certain that this is not merely a wish "but a solemn affirmation of what certainly shall be"[17] God's condemnation.

While these are clearly strong words, can anyone logically argue that the gospel is not of sufficient importance to require such a condemnation? As Boice testifies:

The vehemence with which Paul denounces those who teach another gospel (literally, he says, "Let them be damned") has bothered some commentators, as well as other readers of the letter. But this shows how little the gospel of God's grace is understood and appreciated and how little many Christians are concerned for the advance of biblical truth. The word translated "eternally condemned" ("anathema") is related to the Hebrew word *herem* and is used of that which is devoted to God, usually for destruction. In spiritual terms it means damnation. . . . Moreover, he is universal in his judgment. His words include "anybody" who should so teach. How can it be otherwise? If the gospel Paul preaches is true, then both the glory of Jesus Christ and the salvation of men are at stake. If men can be saved by works, Christ has died in vain (Galatians 2:21); the cross is emptied of meaning. If men are taught a false gospel, they are being led from the one thing that can save them and are being turned to destruction (cf. Matthew 18:6).[18]

Now listen carefully again to what John Calvin says. He points out that Paul has said that the doctrine he had preached is the only gospel and that it was something evil to attempt to distort and overthrow it.

> Otherwise the false apostles might object, "We also wish to maintain the Gospel unimpaired, nor do we feel less reverence for it than you." Just as today the Papists proclaim how holy the Gospel is for them and kiss the very name with the deepest reverence. But when it comes to the proof, they fiercely persecute the pure and simple doctrine of the Gospel.[19]

Hence the anathemas at Trent *against* the gospel. Similarly, the Judaizers were not happy about the conclusions the Jerusalem council had reached concerning the gospel message (Acts 15:7-11), and they were doing their best to insert their own gospel of salvation by faith-works (Acts 15:1).

The Leaven of Half-Truths

We must emphasize again that the Judaizers did not teach entirely false doctrine; they taught many things that would have been accepted by Paul:

> The question might be asked, "But was not Paul too severe in his denunciation and in his rebuke? Is it not true that even now the Judaizers believed in Jesus Christ for salvation, the only difference between Paul and those who differed with him being that to this required faith the latter added strict obedience to certain Mosaic regulations?"
>
> The answer is that the "addition" is in the nature of a complete repudiation of the all-sufficiency of Christ's redemption. Read Galatians 5:2. A beverage may be very healthful and refreshing, but when a drop of poison is added to it, it becomes deadly.
>
> Christ, too, used severe language in condemning the hypocrites of His day (Matthew 23, especially verses 15 and 33). Pharisees and Judaizers had much in common, were in fact closely related (Acts 15:5; Luke 11:46; cf. Galatians 6:12,13).[20]

If we turn to Galatians 5:9, we learn what the bottom line was for Paul. He argues that even the smallest amount of leaven (i.e., false doctrine about salvation) leavens the whole lump of dough. Further, those who are teaching false doctrine will bear their judgment, of this we can be sure. When Paul says a little leaven leavens the whole dough,

> [He] warns them how mischievous is the corrupt doctrine, so that they may not overlook it (as is common) as something of little or no danger. Satan goes to work with cunning and does not obviously destroy the whole Gospel but taints its purity with false and corrupt opinions. Many do not consider the seriousness of the evil and therefore make a less determined resistance.

> The Apostle therefore protests that once the truth of God is corrupted, nothing remains sound. He uses the metaphor of leaven, which, however small in quantity, transmits its sourness to the whole mass. We must be very careful not to allow anything to be added to the pure doctrine of the Gospel.[21]

But now Paul proceeds to express his full confidence that the Galatians, having already been regenerated, will adopt no other "gospel." His rebuke is directed almost entirely at the false apostles.

> He almost exempts the Galatians from the vengeance he declares against these others. Moreover, let all who introduce causes of trouble into Churches, who break the unity of faith, who destroy harmony, listen to this, and if they have any right feeling, let them tremble at this word. For God declares by the mouth of Paul that no authors of such scandals will escape unpunished.[22]

It does not matter how famous a person is who has brought a false gospel, nor how influential he may be in the church—or in the whole world:

> Irrespective of how important and esteemed the person may be or may act, the thing that he (or they) have brought about is trouble, that is, spiritual unrest and confusion in the church concerning the way of salvation.

This is the result of the effort to combine Christ and the works of the law. The judgment upon this will not fail to come, however, and the party which has caused the confusion will have to bear his penalty as a heavy burden.[23]

In conclusion, this biblical example of the apostle Paul's stance toward those teaching a mixed gospel instructs us that tampering with the gospel is a very serious matter. The gospel is a message with eternal consequences. No Evangelical should ever accept the false gospel of Rome. To do so would be to unite at the expense of forfeiting the true gospel in favor of a false faith-works gospel which stands eternally condemned by God.

In doing so we would not only be abandoning the gospel, but we would also be abandoning the One who gave us the gospel.

.16.

Results of
Catholic Doctrine

A bad beginning makes a bad ending.

—Euripides

*R*ome has not changed its doctrines, nor have Evangelicals changed. If a group of people holding to biblical authority alone will not move from that position, and another group of people who add to that authority will not budge, the issue will simply not be resolved. Four hundred years of conflict over the gospel cannot be brushed aside, nor should they be. Only when we realize how important the conflict over the gospel is, will clarity be brought to this entire issue.

The Consequences of Catholic Doctrine

We noted earlier that despite recent changes in Catholicism, the majority of priests remain loyal to Rome. We cited one of the most thorough polls of American clergy ever made to the effect that over three-quarters of Roman Catholic priests denied and rejected that our only hope for heaven is through personal faith in Jesus Christ as Lord and Savior. Instead, they believe that "heaven is a divine reward for those who earn it by their good life." Further, "four-fifths of all priests reject the Bible as the first place to turn in deciding religious questions; rather, they test their religious beliefs by what the Church says."[1]

As we will see in our next chapter, this is also illustrated in the fact that a number of former Evangelicals—who have somehow lost their way to Rome—have noted that nine out of ten Catholics don't even understand the basic *Catholic* concept of salvation by grace and works—which itself is not biblical—let alone the *biblical* concept of salvation by grace alone.

The following admission by former Evangelical Peter Kreeft, who has been in the Catholic Church for over 25 years, is important enough to emphasize:

> Incredibly, nine out of ten Catholics do not know . . . the absolutely central, core, essential dogma of Christianity. Protestants are right: most Catholics do, in fact, believe a whole other religion. Well over ninety percent of students I have polled who have 12 years of catechism classes, even Catholic high schools, say they expect to go to Heaven because they tried, or did their best, or had compassionate feelings for everyone, or were sincere. *They hardly ever mentioned Jesus.* Asked why they hoped to be saved, they mention almost everything except the Savior.[2]

A well-known Evangelical author agrees:

> I have been in contact with thousands of Catholics who were saved and left that church. Not one ever heard the true Gospel preached there. Not one was saved by being a Catholic, but by believing a Gospel which is anathema to Catholics. In a recent survey of 2,000 homes in Spain 1,998 Catholics thought that good works, church attendance, etc. would get them to heaven. In their 15 years of evangelizing in Spain, missionaries with whom I spoke had never met one Catholic who was saved or who knew how to be saved.[3]

This same author wrote the following to one of the signers of the 1994 declaration:

> I challenge you to take a representative poll of Catholics, at random, coming out of Catholic churches after Mass across the country. If you can find even one percent who know the Gospel and are trusting Christ without the works and rituals of Roman Catholicism, I will publicly apologize [for my criticism].[4]

A friend of John Weldon's has a tremendous love for the Mexican people; so much so that after his salvation he changed his name and nationality and moved to Mexico as a missionary. He has been there more than 20 years and during that time has had daily contact with thousands of Mexican Catholics. He told us the following:

> Catholics do not know the Gospel; in fact, Catholic teachings become a great hindrance to the Gospel. In twenty years, I have never met a single devout Catholic that I was certain was saved while the vast majority clearly weren't saved. But I have led many Catholics to salvation through Jesus Christ for which the local Catholics have persecuted me and my churches.[5]

The Cause of Catholic Doctrine

What explains this almost universal lack of knowledge concerning the biblical message of salvation—the gospel? The reason would appear to be simple. How do most Catholic laymen, theologians, and priests read the Bible? Unfortunately, they read it through their own unsaved eyes and through the eyes of a non-biblically based tradition. Therefore, they interpret the Bible in a "natural" manner rather than in a spiritual manner illuminated by the Holy Spirit of God.

As 1 Corinthians 2:14 teaches us, "The man without the Spirit does not accept the things that come from the Spirit of God, for they are foolishness to him, and he *cannot understand them*, because they are spiritually discerned" (cf. Romans 8:6-8, emphasis added). So it is not surprising that many Catholics cannot understand the central message of the Bible: salvation by Christ alone through faith alone by grace alone.

The desire for self-justification is, after all, the natural bent and disposition of the unsaved heart and mind. Therefore, Rome's theologians and priests and popes naturally find it easy to erroneously read into the Bible salvation by faith/works—as does every non-Christian religion, cult, and sect which splits its allegiance between Scripture and some other authority.

Regrettably, Rome's allegiance to authorities other than *sola scriptura* has in turn led to a tainted interpretation of the Bible which has led to a false gospel—a fact which has itself been largely ignored by those seeking agreement with Catholics. This false gospel and interpretation of the Bible has all filtered down to the laity in parishes around the world—and to the consequences just cited.

So will Rome's lack of knowledge concerning biblical salvation ever give way to a true reconciliation and agreement with Protestants? Here is the analysis of Gerrit C. Berkouwer, professor of dogmatic theology at the Free University of Amsterdam, in his masterful analysis *The Conflict with Rome*. We believe his comments are worth reproducing at some length:

> Serious reflection on the foundations of the Roman Catholic Church will impress on our minds with increasing force the radical difference between Rome and the Reformation, a difference tangible in every detail of doctrine and practice.... The difference in experience and practice between Rome and the Reformation is felt to be so basic that reconciliation and the hope of reunion are despaired of.... Rome still lives in the atmosphere of Trent and of the doctrinal pronouncements of the nineteenth century. Moreover, Rome still brands the Reformation as heresy.... In the study of Roman doctrine and practice we may suddenly feel hampered by a sense of strangeness, of which Pribilla speaks, and to which Newman gave expression, after his conversion to the Roman Church, in the words: "It is another religion." ... For it is not only a different doctrine that causes the separation, but a different practice, and a fundamentally different sense of life....
>
> Meanwhile we realize that Rome unhesitatingly maintains its anathema. Brom emphatically asserts that the Protestants must relinquish all hope of the "Mother church ever giving up some of the tenets of its doctrine for the sake of reunion!" They had better quickly abandon this idea, "for a pope is not entitled to the least alteration in the faith entrusted to the church." ... [As a result] we shall characterize the age-long conflict as a struggle for ... the gospel of ... free sovereign grace.... This gospel cannot be rendered and summarized in a better way than by the words of Calvin: "The name of Christ excludes all merit." Once we have realized how important the conflict about the gospel is, we shall sympathize with Paul's sense of responsibility when he bent his knees to the Father of our Lord Jesus Christ ... [and said] "that ye may be able to comprehend with all saints what is the breadth, and length, and depth, and height; and to know the love of Christ, which passeth knowledge, that ye might be filled with all the fullness of God."[6]

Berkouwer did not intend to imply that a unity between Protestantism and Roman Catholicism was utterly impossible—for in

God's wisdom and power, all things are possible. But if and until that day of unity comes, no one must underestimate that this is over no less an issue than the gospel itself.

Rejecting the Truth

In conclusion, the reason Rome rejects the gospel and offers the unbiblical doctrines it does is because of the spiritual condition in which it exists: It is unregenerated and therefore rejects the truth. Jesus Himself pointed out that there was a logical connection between abiding in His Word and knowing the truth: "If you abide in My word, then you are truly disciples of Mine; and you shall know the truth, and the truth shall make you free" (John 8:31,32 NASB). To neglect what the Word of God says about salvation, then, is to not know the truth and to not know spiritual freedom.

The apostle John approached this same issue in a different manner. He wrote of those truly saved: "We are from God; he who knows God listens to us; he who is not from God does not listen to us. By this we know the spirit of truth and the spirit of error" (1 John 4:6 NASB).

Those who know and love God will always accept what God has revealed is true concerning salvation, and only this can explain why they have the full assurance of eternal salvation now:

> The one who believes in the Son of God has the witness in himself; the one who does not believe God has made Him a liar, because he has not believed in the witness that God has borne concerning His Son. And the witness is this, that God has given us eternal life, and this life is in His Son. He who has the Son has the life; he who does not have the Son of God does not have the life. These things I have written to you who believe in the name of the Son of God in order that you may know that you have eternal life (1 John 5:10-13 NASB).

In essence, to abide with what Rome teaches about salvation is to abide with the opposite of truth and spiritual life—error and spiritual death. But to abide with what the Bible teaches about salvation is to find the truth and spiritual life that leads both to salvation and genuine freedom.

.17.

Evangelical Catholics

Precious in the sight of the LORD *is the death of his saints.*
—Psalm 116:15

A kind man benefits himself.
—Proverbs 11:17

He who serves two masters has to lie to one.
—Portuguese proverb

*I*n *Beyond Good and Evil*, Nietzsche correctly observed that "The consequences of our actions take hold of us quite indifferent to our claim that meanwhile we have 'improved.'" In *Pensees* Blaise Pascal said wisely, "In each action we must look beyond the action at our past, present, and future state, and at others whom it affects, and see the relations of all those things. And then we shall be very cautious."

As we have seen, there are many voices attempting to bring Evangelicals and Catholics together as common brethren of a common faith. Apparently, thousands of Evangelicals see Catholics as regenerated Christians. And many Catholics who call themselves Evangelical are seeking to bring these Christians into the Catholic fold. One of the more prominent examples of this is Keith Fournier in his book *Evangelical Catholics*. This contains an endorsing foreword by leading Evangelical Charles Colson who says:

> But at root, those who are called of God, whether Catholic or Protestant, are part of the same Body. What they

189

share is a belief in the basics: the virgin birth, the deity of Christ, His bodily resurrection, His imminent return, and the authority of His infallible word. They also share the same mission: presenting Christ as Savior and Lord to a needy world. Those who hold to these truths and act on this commission are Evangelical Christians. . . .

It's high time that all of us who are Christians come together regardless of the difference of our confessions and our traditions and make common cause to bring Christian values to bear in our society. When the [secular] barbarians are scaling the walls, there is no time for petty quarreling in the camp.

Keith Fournier stands in the breech—truly orthodox in his adherence to Catholic doctrine and fully Evangelical in his relationship to Christ and His creation. Keith's ministry is one of healing. Without compromising or diluting his faith, without any false ecumenicism, he calls all of us as Christians to our common heritage and mission. He is building alliances against our mutual enemy. This book is going to make an immense contribution to that cause.[1]

As we have said, Catholics and Evangelicals may indeed work together in support of promoting Christian values in the larger society. What bothers us about Fournier's book is that it is an encouragement for Evangelicals to return to Rome, the "one true Church."

Fournier may claim to be Evangelical but, in fact, he is a Roman Catholic attempting to be committed to both Rome and Scripture— which in the end has caused him to reject Scripture alone as the authority. He earnestly desires those who are not Roman Catholic to see that there is only one true Church and thus, in many ways, his book is a form of "pre-evangelism" to liberal, Evangelical, and charismatic Protestants seeking their conversion to Rome. Despite good motives, Fournier's placing of unity above truth ends ultimately in a betrayal of truth.

Evangelical Catholics?

First, Fournier claims that Catholicism does not teach salvation by works:

Many Christians misunderstand the Catholic theology of
salvation as one of salvation by good works. . . . They
believe that Catholics have rejected the true gospel of
salvation by faith alone and accepted the false gospel of
salvation by faith plus good works. . . . This view does
not represent Catholic theology.[2]

But Fournier never establishes this claim. If you have any doubts,
reread our earlier chapters.

Second, in harmony with Rome, he provides a false definition of
the doctrine of justification:

I will use justification to refer to a part of a fuller understanding of God's grace at work within us in the whole
process of salvation [e.g., sanctification].[3]

Third, in harmony with Catholic teaching, he believes that it is
not possible to have the assurance of salvation in this life:

But the race belongs to those who persevere to the end,
not to those who never start, not to those who begin but
never finish. . . . Catholics say that "I hope to be saved."
We must persevere in our faith in God, love for God, and
obedience to his will, until the end of our lives. . . . We
need to be careful of presumption.[4]

Fourth, he believes that unity in Christianity is more important
than doctrinal truth:

But in relationship to maintaining our unity and love as
members of the Family of families, these issues [e.g.,
right doctrine] pale in significance. We must maintain a
focus on our family relationship. After all, it is the heart-
throb of Jesus for us all. . . . Catholics and Protestants
oppose one another . . . and the devil laughs. . . . We have
cooperated with him well.[5]

And,

We are family. We have the same Head, the same Savior,
the same Elder Brother, and the same Bridegroom—Our
common enemy, Satan, is subtle and dangerous. He

192 • *Evangelical Catholics*

wants us divorced. He knows that as long as we are separated, our effectiveness as witnesses for Christ suffers.[6]

But Fournier also confesses, "I know full well that our bedrock differences in doctrine and practice are serious and must be discussed and worked through."[7]

Yet he is also willing to accept the truth of *Catholic* doctrine over *unity* with Protestants—and therefore rejects partaking in communion with non-Roman Catholics. Thus, Catholic doctrine *is* paramount:

> As a Catholic Christian, I embrace the warning of the Second Vatican Council document on ecumenism: "Nothing is so foreign to the spirit of ecumenism as a false irenicism which harms the purity of Catholic doctrine and obscures its genuine and certain meaning."[8]

And therefore,

> I embrace my church's position that I cannot participate in the Eucharist with Christians of other traditions. We are not one [i.e., we are not all Roman Catholic]. We must long to be one, and it should grieve our hearts that we cannot go to a common table.[9]

Fifth, Fournier wrongly claims that Evangelicals and Catholics share "a common book, a common history, a common creed, a common savior, and a common mission."[10]

In essence, despite his claim to be Evangelical, Fournier's commitment is fully to Rome: "I am a Roman Catholic, not by accident or mistake but by heartfelt conviction."[11] "I have submitted myself to the teaching-office of the Church and its leadership."[12] "[I have] rooted myself in a sacramental and incarnational Catholic/Christian world view."[13]

And this is the problem. Fournier's "Evangelical/Catholic" faith is merely a Roman Catholicism that he has falsely claimed as Evangelical faith. Thus, when he refers to Evangelicals and Catholics cooperating in evangelism, his goal in evangelism is to lead converts into the Catholic Church. Thus:

> The challenge I have as a Catholic Christian is . . . to bring people to Jesus Christ. . . . But . . . that is only the beginning. That salvation must be sustained, nourished, and

deepened...through implantation into Christ's Body, the [Catholic] Church.[14]

To belong to Christ I must be a part of His people, not just in theory and theology, but in fact.[15]

The Catholic Church is...at least in my opinion, the Mother Church.[16]

I believe the Bible is the Book of the Church, not that the Church is the Church of the Book....I believe it would be ingenuine for believers who do not agree on the real presence of Christ in the Eucharist to join this sacrament of unity....I am a sacramentalist.[17]

All this is why E. Calvin Beisner says the following in a review of Fournier's book:

The equivocation at the heart of Fournier's book...is clear from the inconsistency in his use of the key terms. ...The truth is that there is much more to the terms *Evangelical* and *(Roman) Catholic* than Fournier really deals with in his book....The distinctions between Catholicism and Protestantism are real, and they are important. Despite Fournier's good intentions in attempting to bypass them for the outward unity of the body of Christ, he really will do both Catholics and Evangelicals only a disservice if he successfully persuades them that one can be Evangelical and Catholic in the proper sense of those words.[18]

Again, all this is certainly not to say that the Catholic Church is devoid of genuine Christians—there are many of them. Catholics may indeed have experienced true regenerating faith. But the real question is one of commitment to biblical truth and the importance of spiritual growth based on it. The issue then becomes, "Can Christians remain in the Catholic Church without compromising their faith and/or their spiritual growth?"

Where Is Spiritual Nourishment?

We cannot say that God would never allow Christians to remain in the Catholic Church for a time in order to lead others to personal faith in Christ. But in order to do so, they should be thoroughly informed on the issues, weigh them carefully, and resolve not to partake in practices or to accept doctrines that are not biblical. Further, we would suspect that, for the vast majority of Christians in the Catholic Church, acquiring spiritual growth would necessitate a new environment.

Consider a typical example of what Roman Catholic beliefs do to Christian commitment. The following is a statement given to John Weldon by a former roommate (a subsequent youth pastor with whom he roomed for four years):

> Growing up in the Catholic Church definitely made an impact on my life. I attended Church faithfully every Sunday. As a result, on the positive side, I did know something about Jesus and His death on the cross. But beyond that my time in the Catholic Church made the first few years of my Christian life very difficult to enjoy as I had no assurance of salvation at all.
>
> Catholic doctrine taught me that if you are a Catholic and leave the Church, you are damned forever. I was taught that the Catholic Church was the only true Church and that every other Church was wrong. As a young boy, I grew up being told about relatives that had "fallen away" and how evil this was. Those who went to the Baptist Church or other Protestant churches were almost as bad as those who had fallen away from the Catholic Church.
>
> With this background, it was very difficult to believe that Jesus really loved me and that all my sins were fully paid for. I believed my sins were only absolved through confession to a priest. As a result, I never truly felt forgiven nor was I at all sure I would make it to heaven. I was left only with the sobering "hope" that I would at least make it to purgatory and that there I could somehow work my way out.
>
> Further, even for three years after I was saved, I felt incredible guilt and condemnation because I was attending churches that taught the Bible. I would go to various churches with friends, but then go to Mass on Sunday evening to make sure I was covering all the bases.
>
> As my relationship with Christ grew, I finally realized that if God was real and did love me, then He wanted me to grow closer to Him. He wanted me to worship and obey Him and to study the Bible on my own.

In the past, my Catholic teaching had never brought me closer to the love of God, or to God as One whom I wanted to obey. It had only left me with the fear that I would never make it to heaven. Unfortunately, the teaching of the Catholic Church never gave me anything that would motivate me to holiness and a desire to be sanctified in the Lord. As a result, as a Catholic, I fell into all kinds of sexual immorality and drunkenness and I hardly even felt convicted. I knew nothing about what the Bible taught about these subjects and had no motivation from the love of God in order to change my lifestyle.

In the end, it was a slow process of spiritual growth that led me to see clearly how different Roman Catholicism is from biblical faith. Until I really knew the Bible and had grown in my relationship to the Lord, I found it difficult to forsake the Catholic Church. But the more I seriously studied the Bible, the more clearly I saw that my Catholic upbringing had actually hindered both my salvation and my commitment to God and Jesus.

I think that more than anything else, Christians in the Catholic Church need to resolve to be committed to Christ alone and the biblical authority alone. Unfortunately, even after leaving the Church it was difficult to grow as a Christian because of the Catholic teaching I had adopted and believed. I can't imagine what would have happened if I had stayed in the Catholic Church and never learned the Bible.

It is the author's own experience that such stories are anything but uncommon. But if so, the Catholic Church must be seen as a genuine hindrance to the cause of Christ.

No Christian needs to feel guilty over leaving a Church that is not biblical. One's commitment is to Christ first, not a church. Second, no one should feel guilty about an association with the Catholic Church in order to reach unsaved friends or loved ones. But if the consequences involve the sapping of their own spiritual growth, the cost is too high. Again, this would be a compromise of their personal commitment to God. And, in fact, reaching Catholic friends and family can be done just as easily outside the Church.

So we think that when it comes to the crucial issue of spiritual growth, to retain attendance at a Catholic Church is unwise. Most Catholic churches do not teach the Bible to those in attendance. They teach Roman Catholic beliefs. If so, how can new Christians

ever grow in the faith when all they are taught are doctrines which
undermine the faith?

We think it is better for those who become Christians in the
Catholic Church to leave the Church and find a place where they can
receive biblical teaching and Christian fellowship that will encourage their commitment to Christ and His Word alone. Once mature
spiritually, then a program of closer contact with the Roman Catholic community might begin.

Today, far too many Christians and Evangelical Christian organizations are accepting Roman Catholicism as a fully Christian religion and individual Catholics as true Christians. Perhaps what is
needed is a much closer look at Catholicism—and perhaps also a
much closer look at Evangelicalism. Why? Because, as our next
section documents, even Evangelicals are now turning to Rome.
The Evangelical church needs to understand the reasons given for
such a conversion, and whether or not they are legitimate.

There are many reasons why a given individual may convert to
the Roman Catholic Church. Among these are frustration with the
barrenness of secular philosophies and the desire for finding spiritual reality; an attraction to the formal, high style of worship offered
in Catholicism (i.e., a response to the emotional content generated
by Catholic liturgy and worship); exposure to liberal Protestantism
and a resulting confusion over biblical authority/teaching—and the
corollary belief that one must have an authoritarian head (pope) or
teaching office (magisterium) in order to properly interpret the
Bible (in other words, the need for an infallible external authority
to counteract the alleged theological "uncertainty" of "sectarian"
Protestantism). Other reasons include the desire for Christian "unity"
regardless of the cost doctrinally and the belief that Jesus Himself
instituted the papal office under the headship of Peter—and that
therefore the Catholic Church is the one true Church. (We analyzed
this claim in our previous edition of this book.)

In fact, there are perhaps 100 different reasons why any given
individual may join the Catholic Church. Today, no one can deny
that among such individuals are some former Evangelical Christians. Given the kinds of things some Evangelicals get themselves
into these days, this is not necessarily an unexpected turn of events.

Why Do Evangelicals Convert?

Many interesting stories of conversions to Catholicism are illustrated in *Spiritual Journeys: Toward the Fullness of Faith*. In this book, 27

people recount their personal pilgrimage to Catholicism. Our interest concerns three individuals in particular who are well-known in the Evangelical camp: Thomas Howard, Paul Vitz, and Peter Kreeft. Then we will examine the reasons given by Scott Hahn, a popular lecturer in Catholic Churches. Why did these men convert to Roman Catholicism? Let's examine their responses.

Thomas Howard, author of *Evangelical Is Not Enough*, observes: "My recent conversion to Roman Catholicism has puzzled and troubled most of the Evangelicals who know me."[19] Howard left Evangelicalism for several reasons. First, he believed in the authority of Church tradition. He increasingly desired a centralized teaching authority and was troubled by the lack of pastoral accountability which seemed evident in many Protestant churches. He also came to believe in the efficacy of the Catholic sacraments.[20] For example, he recalls the following:

> There are so many hundreds of very small Evangelical denominations and congregations. Some of the "cardinal" parishes in Evangelicalism are totally independent: the minister is accountable to no bishop or synod or superior of any description. This tendency began to trouble me, as the years went by. . . . If the Church is anything at all other than a mere clutter, it is apostolic. There has got to be a Magisterium [authoritative teaching office], and not just a clamor of voices. Christianity is not analogous to Islam—a religion of the Book alone. [In the early Fathers] we find indeed one, holy, catholic, and apostolic Church, and not a clutter of privately launched enterprises, no matter how earnest or laudable those enterprises might be. . . .

> It is the old question of catholicity and apostolicity. What is the Church? Where is the Church? Also, it entails the question of teaching authority. All the heresiarchs [starters of heresy] believed in the inspiration of the Bible. But who has the warrant to *teach* the Scriptures? Anyone? Everyone? If we consult the early Church, we find that it was the bishops in council who said to the faithful, *"This* is the apostolic faith. That which you hear being taught over there is heresy." Christ never doomed his Church to a perennial, *ad hoc* caucus of the whole, with all matters of morals and dogma forever on the table, forever up for grabs. But alas, this turns out to be the case where there is no Magisterium.

> I eventually found myself crowded along to the place where I either had to say, "But none of this matters: all God wants is for

us to be earnest and fervent," or I had to say, "Hum. Independence won't do. That is not the apostolic pattern." Who am I to disassociate myself from this 2000-year-old train of apostles, fathers, bishops, martyrs, confessors, doctors, widows, virgins, and infants, who testify to what Christ's Church is?[21]

In response to the above, we might ask the following questions: First, does the lack of pastoral accountability in some churches require the conclusion that Protestantism as a whole maintains no legitimate mechanisms of accountability? We don't think so. And second, has the Catholic Church escaped similar problems? We don't think so.

Second, we grant that no Christian would deny that if the church should be anything, it should be apostolic. The apostles were inspired to record the very words of God Himself and the teachings they gave for Christian belief and action are our standard. But from this fact, does it necessarily follow that the post-apostolic fathers got their doctrine right in all particulars—or that early and later Church tradition has equal weight with Scripture? Christianity may not be entirely a religion of the Book—but it is primarily so. And it must be so; in earlier pages, we have already seen the tragedy of granting Church tradition equal authority with Scripture.

Third, we don't think that the phrase "a clutter of privately launched enterprises," does justice to the Protestant tradition, especially when it is implied that matters of morals and dogma are "forever on the table." The thousands of Christian churches who accept the inerrancy of Scripture do, in fact, have an infallible authority for determining correct doctrine: Scripture itself. This means that even though these churches reject the Catholic magisterium, their morals and doctrines are not "forever up for grabs." Biblical doctrine and morality are clearly laid out in Scripture, and all genuine Christian churches who accept biblical authority have found general agreement on these issues without the assistance of the Catholic Church.

Fourth, do we have to present ourselves with a faulty dilemma which claims that either 1) we must entirely disregard apostolic and post-apostolic teaching, or 2) we must convert to Roman Catholicism? Isn't the wiser course to accept the Word of God alone as the authority, to grant that the early Church Fathers, being fallible men, wrote both truth and error, and to therefore evaluate their teachings and Church tradition as a whole in light of God's Word? Certainly, the apostles never taught the doctrines unique to Roman Catholic theology, whether or not some in the Church's history have.

Fifth, Scripture itself declares that all believers are at least teachers of the gospel and it never grants exclusive teaching authority to a magisterium or pope.

All in all, we don't think that the specific reasons Thomas Howard gave for converting to Catholicism really justify his decision biblically, however sincere it may have been.

Crisis of Faith

Former atheistic psychologist Paul C. Vitz became a Catholic because his allegiance to secularism had encountered an irresolvable "crisis of faith." The truth of Vitz's evaluation is something any fair-minded academic would have to concede today, given the influence of such liberal pastimes as multiculturalism (affirming all cultures but our own), "political correctness" (intimidation as "education"), and other half-witted campus ideologies:

> In particular, the university, the community of scholars, showed itself so without standards, so without the courage of convictions, as to be a kind of joke. The last vestiges of my respect for academia collapsed as I watched the university leadership cave in to various social and political pressures. By the end of the 60's and the start of the 70's my secular ideals were in shreds.

> One of my concerns was my deepening disillusionment with the field of [experimental and cognitive] psychology itself.

> Even more disturbing was my growing understanding of how other parts of psychology, for example, personality theory and counseling practice, had contributed to the secular madness of what was going on. . . . Modernism is in its *essential* nature subjective, arbitrary and nihilistic.[22]

But in addition, Dr. Vitz's Episcopal church was far too liberal—and apparently provided him with little or no spiritual sustenance whatever.

> Meanwhile, as my understanding of Christian theology deepened, I quickly came into conflict with liberal Christian theology, most of which was Protestant in origin. It was obvious to me that liberal theology was at best a

compromise with anti-Christian modernist thought, and
at worst a thinly disguised denial of Christ. . . . Unfortunately, the Episcopal Church was dominated by liberal
thought, indeed so dominated by it that many couldn't
even see it. As far as they were concerned, liberal theology was the only possible way of understanding things.
It was then that I first experienced the rigid, narrow-
minded character of liberal thought and of so many lib-
erals. I still remember the remark made to me by a young
Episcopal priest—his voice dripping with condescen-
sion—"You mean you believe in the *bodily* resurrection of
Christ?"[23]

Vitz also encountered a series of dramatic "visions" and various
aesthetic or psychological bonds to Catholicism itself. For example:

These dramatic, unexpected experiences were really something like visions. . . . Along with prayer, reading, and
Catholic friends . . . especially many wonderful priests—
these experiences solidified my commitment to the Catholic faith.[24]

Finally,

One of the great liberations in becoming a Catholic was
to be part of the universal character of the Church. . . . I
sensed a new kinship with people in countries as diverse
as Argentina, Poland, and Zanzibar. . . . I was linked to
millions of people of all nations, races and cultures.[25]

While we can certainly sympathize with the frustration of Paul
Vitz over secularism, the tragedy of his experience under liberal
theology, and the dramatic nature of his personal experiences, we
would ask whether or not any of these things justify conversion to
Catholicism—if indeed it is not a religion upholding biblical truth?
If Scripture is the authoritative Word of God, and Roman Catholicism overall denies what Scripture teaches in key areas, then, as a
whole, the Roman Catholic Church cannot be the one true Church.
So we would hope that neither frustrating experiences in the past
nor dramatic encounters in the present would cause us to neglect
adherence to the truth of God's Word. And finally, if by chance we
have failed to become a member of God's true church, then what is
the value of our spiritual fellowship before God?

The Church's Claim

Peter Kreeft converted to Roman Catholicism because of his rather rigid Calvinist and anti-Catholic background—which allegedly contained many "sincere mistakes" about Catholicism. In the end, this apparently rubbed him the wrong way. He also had several unanswered questions, as well as the need for visible objects (e.g., images) to love and worship God.

> "Why don't Protestants pray to saints? Saints pray for one another here." [But saints here pray *for* one another, not *to* one another.] "Was only Calvinism correct among all branches of Christendom? How could God leave the rest of the world in error?" Since no good answer[s] seemed forthcoming, I then came to the explosive conclusion that the truth about God was more mysterious—more wonderfully and uncomfortably mysterious—than anything any of us could fully comprehend.[26]

Other reasons for conversion to Catholicism included "a strong intellectual and aesthetic love for things medieval" and the influence of reading the Catholic mystics. He found that the "richness and mystery of Catholicism fascinated me."[27]

But the central reason for his conversion was the Church's claim to be the only true Church: "There were many strands in the rope that hauled me aboard the ark, though this one—the Church's claim to be the one Church historically founded by Christ—was the central and deciding one."[28]

But again, our only response can be, "If the Roman Catholic Church were indeed the one true Church, it could not possibly deny and oppose what the Bible plainly teaches in the area of salvation!"

All three of these men have had strong contacts with Evangelicalism, appreciate it greatly and, if they were personally associated with it before, still miss aspects of it which they see as tremendous strengths.[29]

Regardless, let us take Peter Kreeft as an illustration of the important issues involved here and the possible mistakes an Evangelical Christian might make when evaluating the Catholic Church for possible membership. Again, he says that it was the Church's claim to be the "one Church historically founded by Christ" that was the deciding factor in his decision to join the Roman Catholic Church:

So the Catholic Church's claim to be the one true Church, the Church Christ founded, forces us to say either that this is the most arrogant, blasphemous and wicked claim imaginable, if it is not true, or else that she is just what she claims to be. Just as Jesus stood out as the absolute exception to all other human teachers in claiming to be more than human and more than a teacher, so the Catholic Church stood out above all other denominations in claiming to be not merely a denomination, but the Body of Christ incarnate, infallible, one, and holy, presenting the really present Christ in her Eucharist. I could never rest in a comfortable, respectable ecumenical halfway house of measured admiration from a distance. I had to shout either "Crucify her!" or "Hosanna!" If I could not love and believe her, honesty forced me to despise and fight her.

But I could not despise her. The beauty and sanctity and wisdom of her, like that of Christ, prevented me from calling her liar or lunatic, just as it prevented me from calling Christ that. But simple logic offered the one and only one other option: this must be the Church my Lord provided for me—*my* Lord, for *me*. So she had better become my Church if He is my Lord.[30]

Although Kierkegaard "almost kept me Protestant," he found himself "surrounded" by reasons to become a Catholic. But he was also aware of the scriptural dilemma he faced. It is here that the issue really *should* have been resolved: Why it wasn't is anyone's guess:

But if Catholic dogma contradicted Scripture or itself at any point, I could not believe it. I explored all the cases of claimed contradiction and found each to be a Protestant misunderstanding. No matter how morally bad the Church had gotten in the Renaissance, it never taught heresy.[31]

Unfortunately, we emphatically disagree that no contradictions between Catholicism and itself exist or between Catholicism and Scripture. They are everywhere and can hardly be brushed aside as "Protestant misunderstandings." And put simply, the Catholic Church does teach heresy (Galatians 1:6-8). It is there in black and white, has been for hundreds of years, and will not go away.

Who Wrote the Bible?

Nevertheless, Kreeft was also impressed by the argument that "the Church wrote the Bible," and therefore the Church allegedly has equality with or priority over the Bible:

> I knew, from logic and common sense, that a cause can never be less than its effect. You can't give what you don't have. If the Church has no divine inspiration and no infallibility, no divine authority, then neither can the New Testament. Protestantism logically entails Modernism. I had to be either a Catholic or a Modernist. That decided it; that was like saying I had to be either a patriot or a traitor.[32]

But this argument itself constitutes a logical fallacy. Why? First of all, it is more correct to say that specific individuals inspired by the Holy Spirit wrote the Bible, not that the Church wrote the Bible—as if to give the Church per se an infallible authority it has never had and can never demonstrate. If the New Testament is divinely inspired, word for word, there is no necessary reason for the Church to have divine infallibility or authority because God's Word, which gives us "everything pertaining to life and godliness" (2 Peter 1:3 NASB), is already present.

Second, to say one must either become a Catholic or a modernist constitutes a limitation on choices that is unnecessary. Here is another example of a faulty dilemma. Certainly another choice would be to be a simple believer in the primary authority of the inerrant Word of God. This is hardly a modernist position. Conservative Protestants cannot be religious modernists in any sense of the term because their fidelity to *sola scriptura* prohibits this.

Regardless, after a time of prayer by himself for God's guidance in his decision, he felt confirmed that he was to join the Catholic Church.[33]

We may note here that the number of individuals who have prayed about whether or not they should join the Catholic Church and then found "divine confirmation" to do so seems legion. But at this point, we are reminded of the Mormon evangelist's prayer that potential Mormon converts pray to God concerning the "truth" of the *Book of Mormon*—with the assurance that the Holy Spirit will reveal this truth to them supernaturally.[34] Millions have found "confirmation."

Perhaps we should remember that prayer can never confirm something God has already declared is false. Kreeft himself seems to have encountered a dilemma at this point:

> One crucial issue remained to be resolved: Justification by Faith, the central bone of contention of the Reformation. Luther was obviously right here: the doctrine is clearly taught in *Romans* and *Galatians*. If the Catholic Church teaches "another gospel" of salvation by works, then it teaches fundamental heresy. I found here however another case of misunderstanding. I read in Aquinas' *Summa* on grace and the decrees of the Council of Trent, and found them just as strong on grace as Luther or Calvin. I was overjoyed to find that the Catholic Church had read the Bible too![35]

But as we saw in chapter 4, it is entirely wrong to say that the Council of Trent was expressing biblical teaching on either grace or justification. Nor do we think the Catholic Church has really read the Bible—at least on the Bible's own terms. If it had, Luther would never have penned his commentary on Galatians and many other works in which he opposed the teaching of Rome on such issues. As we saw earlier, what Catholics and Protestants mean by the terms "grace," "justification," and "faith" are entirely different.

Which Gospel?

Kreeft goes on to discuss what was apparently a problem all along in his personal views about the nature of justification—even calling it a "legal fiction"—perhaps revealing his preexisting bias in favor of the views of Rome:

> I was also dissatisfied with Luther's teaching that justification was a legal fiction on God's part rather than a real event in us; that God looks on the Christian and Christ, sees only Christ's righteousness, and legally counts or imputes Christ's righteousness as ours. I thought it had to be as Catholicism says, that God actually imparts Christ to us, in baptism and through faith.[36]

Of course, this is the key issue: the real nature of justification. If it is an imputed righteousness, then Kreeft and Catholicism are incorrect (see chapters 2–6).

But what is perhaps most relevant is Kreeft's confession that even his own Catholics really don't understand the basic biblical gospel at all. Instead they accept a "gospel" of salvation by works—which is what the Catholic concept has been all along—despite the Church's claimed allegiance to grace. Only this can explain why Catholics so thoroughly believe in works salvation.

It would seem that this would place Kreeft and other former Evangelicals like him in something of a quandary. If the Catholic Church really is the one true Church that God has established, and if the pope is the vicar of Christ on earth, then again, how did the basic gospel of salvation ever get so lost in the first place?

Consider the following crucial admission—one based on Kreeft's own long-standing experience within the Catholic Church:

> At Heaven's gate our entrance ticket, according to Scripture and Church dogma, is *not* [solely] our good works or our sincerity, but our faith, which glues us to Jesus. *He* saves us; we do not save ourselves. But I find, incredibly, that 9 out of 10 Catholics do not know this, the absolutely central, core, essential dogma of Christianity. Protestants are right: most Catholics do, in fact, believe a whole other religion. Well over 90% of students I have polled who have 12 years of catechism classes, even Catholic high schools, say they expect to go to Heaven because they tried, or did their best, or had compassionate feelings to everyone, or were sincere. They hardly ever mention Jesus. Asked why they hope to be saved, they mention almost everything *except* the Savior.[37]

Kreeft has not repudiated his prior statement. He is saying that most Catholics believe good works per se will get them to heaven, and therefore they do not even understand Catholic doctrine about the necessity of prevenient grace. Here he has simply outlined the Catholic view that infused grace and faith may result in salvation and contrasted it with what nine out of 10 Catholics actually believe: that good works apart from grace/faith result in salvation.

And this is precisely our point. If the Catholic Church really were the one true Church, teaching the one true gospel, the above highly distressing situation could not possibly be the final result. We think the real explanation for this unfortunate situation is what we have argued all along—that the Catholic Church is *not* the one true Church and therefore does not teach the one true gospel of salvation by grace through faith alone, but rather a false "gospel" of salvation by works. All its talk of grace is cheap.

Although Kreeft has been "happy as a Catholic for 26 years now" and says, "I am happy as a child to follow Christ's vicar on earth everywhere he leads. What he loves, I love; what he leaves, I leave; where he leads, I follow,"[38] the central problem remains.

Lost Allegiance

So in light of all the above, what do former Evangelicals who are now Catholics do with their allegiance to biblical teaching? Even Kreeft admits that the "serious concern for truth" that he was raised with as a young Evangelical is something that "to this day I find sadly missing in many Catholic circles."[39]

This is also the issue—the importance of "a serious concern for truth." People may indeed convert to Catholicism for an almost endless number of reasons. But there is one reason that no one ever gives for joining the Catholic Church. And this is the heart of the matter. It takes us back to the nature of authority and its importance for deciding the issue of religious truth. To our knowledge, no one has ever joined the Catholic Church who honestly accepted biblical inerrancy and has studied the Bible systematically and interpreted it in light of its own teachings consistently rather than by Catholic tradition. Again, no one has ever logically converted to Catholicism who has consistently maintained an allegiance to the Bible alone as their sole authority.

People have joined the Church either because they don't understand the issues involved (they are either uninformed or confused), or because they are really not committed to biblical inerrancy and authority, or because they simply prefer what the Roman Church has to offer. Some will indeed claim that they "met Jesus and are propelled to the Roman Church in obedience to Him."[40]

Perhaps they did meet Jesus, but they were certainly not propelled to join the Catholic Church out of obedience to Him. The reason is simple: In His own teachings He never taught Catholicism. In fact, He rejected most of the major doctrines of the Catholic Church. As noted authority Dr. Walter Martin once commented, "The Lord Jesus Christ many times used language which the Roman Catholic Church has adopted. The interesting thing, however, is that Christ's usage of the terms is frequently the direct opposite of what the Catholic Church claims for them."[41]

Partial Understanding?

A final illustration should reveal the seriousness of this issue. Yet another story of conversion to Rome is found in the person of Scott Hahn, author of *Rome, Sweet Home*. In a lecture to a parish in Riverside, California (tape on file), he begins by claiming that few people really understand what the Roman Church actually teaches. They only know falsehoods that they have adopted from erroneous sources. Thus, Evangelicals "simply don't understand" Roman Catholicism; "they [only] think they do."

This, unfortunately, is the standard response of Catholics who claim to be Evangelical: No one really understands Catholicism except a Roman Catholic.

Scott Hahn grew up in a nominal Protestant family with little if any church attendance. Later in high school he claims he accepted Christ as his personal Lord and Savior through the ministry of Young Life.

But as a result of his own spiritual journey, Hahn has today thoroughly rejected his Evangelical upbringing and does his best to confirm Roman Catholics in their own beliefs and to convert Evangelicals to Roman Catholicism.

Hahn calls the standard Evangelical gospel view of salvation—accepting Jesus Christ as your personal Lord and Savior from sin—"inadequate from a Catholic perspective." He told his Catholic listeners, "If you're ever asked by a Protestant, 'Are you born again?' you should say, 'Of course, I am. What do you mean by it?' 'Have you accepted Jesus Christ as your personal Lord and Savior?' You should say, 'Yes, of course I have. . . . But that's not why I was born again. I was born again because I was baptized.'"

Hahn makes it clear that, for him, Evangelicals have only "partial truths and insights" and need Rome to correct their errors on salvation and other important matters.

How did Scott Hahn become a Catholic? In many cases like this we suspect that the real reasons are hidden and that the public telling may portray only a small part of the real story.

Regardless, Hahn did have a lot of Catholic friends. His best friends in high school were all Catholic—"the ones who drank the most and swore the most." After he was saved he dated a Catholic girl "very seriously" in spite of his intense dislike for Catholicism.

Nevertheless, after graduation from high school he went to Gordon-Conwell Seminary where he received his M.Div. degree in 1982 and where he also refined his anti-Catholic views, at least initially. But this is also where he began his transformation to Catholicism.

In his second year in seminary, his wife did a study on birth control for one of her own seminary classes. She concluded it was immoral, bringing her and eventually her husband to agreement with the Catholic Church on this topic.

At the same time a professor at Westminster Seminary, whom Hahn was thinking of studying with, was being booted out for rejecting the doctrine of salvation by faith alone. Hahn landed smack in the middle of the debate and concluded that the professor, Shepherd, was correct and that therefore Luther was wrong—and that salvation *was* by both faith and works. This began a very traumatic period of reevaluation for him.

After graduation he took a job as a pastor and also taught a seminary class at night. He began intensive studies into the issues separating Catholicism and Evangelicalism. In his studies of both Old and New Testaments he kept "seeing" that what Catholic scholars had already said was true. By now he had "given up on salvation by faith alone." But he soon discovered that nowhere does the Bible teach *sola scriptura* either, so he threw that out also. That Hahn could not even answer the question of a student (a former Catholic)—"Where does the Bible teach Scripture alone is authoritative and *not* Church tradition?"—indicates there was a serious problem somewhere.

Hahn claims to have called several of the "top [Evangelical] theologians in the country" and found that none of them had an answer in defense of *sola scriptura* either. Goodness, what *have* we Protestants been doing for 400 years, anyway? Nevertheless, he concluded that the doctrine "wasn't scriptural."

All this had occurred by age 26, and now he was asked to become dean of the seminary where he was teaching. In good conscience he had to decline because he realized he was now becoming a Catholic. He also stepped down from his pastorate and teaching job in a further attempt to resolve the issue.

He next read some 200 books by Roman Catholic scholars; he also sought help from Catholics—first from a priest who apparently did nothing but use swear words and was anything but a Christian; second, from the Newman Center staff who apparently told him he would be better staying within Protestantism attempting to influence them with Catholic ideas rather than converting to Roman Catholicism.

Hahn now enrolled in a doctoral program in Roman Catholic systematic theology. This apparently cemented his commitment to Roman Catholicism, and he officially converted.

To illustrate the impact of his many studies in Catholicism, he includes statements such as the following: "I had worked literally through I would guess a hundred different doctrines that the Catholic Church taught that the Protestant Church rejected and I came out Catholic on every one of them."

Given the fact that he had read some 200 books by Roman Catholic scholars, perhaps this is not surprising.

Neither is it surprising that Hahn eventually fell "head over heels in love with the Virgin Mary," although this was the most difficult of Catholic doctrines for him to accept. He now prays the Rosary to Mary every day, and he is convinced that she supernaturally and regularly answers his prayer. Indeed, he argues that prayer to Mary is one of the most powerful tools and weapons a Christian can have. "The real, supernatural proof of [the truth of Roman Catholicism] is Marian devotion." He tells the parish that the Rosary will "supernaturalize" a Catholic's faith.

At the end of his lecture he tells his Catholic audience, "Pray about what you can do to be a witness to the glory and the truth of the Catholic faith."

What Kind of Proof?

But the tragedy of Scott Hahn is not only with Scott Hahn; it is with the many other uninformed Evangelicals he has converted to Roman Catholicism. His tapes and books have been greatly used by "Evangelical" Catholics and other Roman Catholics in the attempt to convert Evangelicals to their faith. Even his own wife, who he describes as "the daughter of one of the most noted Evangelical leaders in America," is "very, very close" to being converted to Catholicism. "On point after point without a single exception, she has come to see how biblical the Roman Catholic faith is on everything."

In a letter to us, one Catholic spoke of the "wonderful and dramatic evidences" that Scott Hahn presented on this tape to confirm Roman Catholicism against Protestantism.

But the truth lies elsewhere. In fact, Mr. Hahn did not present a single convincing argument in defense of Roman faith.

The nature of his arguments are illustrated in his discussion with a Protestant friend about Mary, where Mr. Hahn said, "If you can answer these two points about Mary, I'll grant you the Protestant view." Here were Mr. Hahn's questions:

1. Christ obeyed the law perfectly, right?
   (Friend answers, "Of course.")

2. The Ten Commandments sum up that law, right?
   (Friend answers, "Right.")

3. One commandment reads, "Honor your father and mother,"
   right?
   (Friend answers, "Right.")

4. When Christ fulfills the law He fulfills that commandment,
   right?
   (Friend answers, "Right.")

5. So Christ bestows honor and glory upon His mother, right?
   (Friend answers, "Right.")

The above is the first point that Mr. Hahn makes. What is the second? "We imitate Christ."

Scott Hahn then says, "The Catholic Church isn't exalting Mary, Jesus Christ beat her to it." (To which the audience laughs.) "We are just echoing and imitating our Lord." His friend replies, "I never thought of that before." Scott Hahn replies, "I didn't either until I prayed about three or four hundred rosaries and it dawned upon me in my meditation that all we're doing is what Christ is doing as a perfectly faithful, obedient, loving Son."

That was the essence of his proof for Roman Catholic Mariology! But, of course, this isn't the truth at all. Nowhere can Mr. Hahn or any Roman Catholic show that Jesus honored Mary in Scripture the way Catholic Church tradition venerates and worships her. An examination of chapter 10 on Mary in the first edition of this book will reveal this beyond doubt.

In conclusion, all that we have covered in this chapter reveals that unless the Evangelical Church is prepared to accept more and more of its members converting to Roman Catholicism, perhaps it should begin now to alter its course.

.18.

The One True Church?

[People] need to know which of these churches or communities [Protestant or Catholic] is that of Christ, since He founded only one Church—the only one capable of speaking in His name.[1]

—Pope John Paul II

The fundamental protestant idea is that the Church is not above judgment, inerrant and "self-authenticating" as though she were God Himself; she is the servant of God's Word, and must perpetually be judged by her degree of conformity to the Word.

—Walter M. Horton
Christian Theology (1955)

Rome claims that the true church of Christ is the visible organization of the Roman Catholic Church and its people. But is this claim really valid?

To "discern" is to perceive clearly with the mind or senses. How can we perceive clearly where the true church lies? Only with the truth—by what the Scriptures tell us. Coleridge once wrote of the dangers of loving a false concept of Christianity above truth itself: "He who begins by loving Christianity better than truth will proceed by loving his own sect or church better than Christianity and end in loving himself better than all."

Jesus was correct when He said the gates of hell would never prevail against His church (Matthew 16:18). But His church is not an institution, Protestant or Catholic. It is the company of all those people who truly believe in Him. It is the essence of new life with Christ and in Christ. The Greek word *ekklesia* refers to "those which

211

are called out"—people who, by God's grace, are called out of the world to become believers in Jesus Christ. This is the true church.

When the Scripture declares that "Christ loved the church and gave himself up for her" (Ephesians 5:25), it is referring to all the people who believe in Christ and know Him personally—whether or not they are in a church or part of its liturgy and rituals.

As Harold C. Phillips remarked, "This coming to know Christ is what makes Christian truth redemptive truth, the truth that transforms not just the truth that informs." "For no one can lay any foundation other than the one already laid, which is Jesus Christ" (1 Corinthians 3:11). But as someone else once said, "Christianity is like electricity; it can't enter into a person unless it can pass through them." Thus the faith that enters must be a genuine faith in Christ alone, not faith in a church (1 Corinthians 3:16,17).

All this is why the church of Jesus Christ must be considered "invisible"—because "faith in the heart is invisible for men and known only to God" (Frances Pieper). The old German proverb is true: "In the visible Church, the true Christians are invisible."

Thus, to emphasize the redemptive value of any visible church as being equal to or above that of mere personal trust in Christ Himself does not honor Christ. Even Augustine once said, "Christ is not valued at all unless He will be valued above all"—even above the church.

So how do we finally assess Roman Catholicism? We can only evaluate it by the Bible and Rome's own claims. In such light then should Roman Catholicism really be classified as the one true Church? Should it even be classified as Christian?

No. Roman Catholicism is not the true Church and it is not even a Christian religion. In this chapter we will explain why. To begin, we will add to and summarize our previous arguments and examine what the Roman Catholic Church itself claims in order to show why we believe our conclusions are true.

Many Evangelical Christians today have positive feelings about both the pope in particular and Roman Catholicism in general. Others are uncertain as to how Roman Catholicism should properly be classified in light of biblical teaching. That such support and/or perplexity is undergirded even by many Christian organizations can be seen in the following response sent out to those inquiring about Catholicism by a leading Christian apologetics ministry. This standard reply was given by a group which specializes in the analysis of comparative religion and cult theology. In answer to the question "Is Roman Catholicism Biblical?" the verbatim response was as follows (copy on file):

1. Does the Catholic Church teach orthodox Christianity? Answer: Yes.

2. Does the Catholic Church teach salvation by good works or by faith? Answer: They teach it is by faith.

3. Does the Catholic Church teach another gospel? Answer: No.

This reply would certainly lead many to conclude that Roman Catholicism should be classified as a legitimate Christian faith.

The Claims of Rome

Of course, Roman Catholicism claims it alone is the only true Christian Church on earth. *The Catholic Encyclopedia* argues, "The term Roman Catholic has come to be the accepted designation of the one true Church."[2] It also teaches that God has indeed revealed Himself "and that the Catholic faith is that revelation."[3] In addition, it describes the Catholic Church as "the Church founded by Jesus Christ,"[4] and defines the Church in the following manner,

> When the Church is spoken of, it means that visible religious society, founded by Jesus Christ, under one head, St. Peter, and continuing under the governance of his successors, the popes. . . . It is thus the role of the Church to present the means of salvation given by Christ [e.g., the sacraments].[5]

Under the heading of "Doctrine of the Catholic Church" we read, "It is through Christ's Catholic Church alone, which is the all-embracing means of salvation, that the fullness of the means of salvation can be obtained."[6] The new *Catechism* (1994) says that "The Church . . . is necessary for salvation."[7] Pope Pius IV referred to "this true Catholic faith without which no one can be saved."[8]

Under "Church Membership," we find Pope Pius XII cited in his *On the Mystical Body of Christ* (1943). He teaches that only Catholics are to be considered members of the one true Church. "Actually, only those are to be included as members of the Church who have been baptized, and who profess the true faith [Roman Catholicism], and who have not been so unfortunate as to separate themselves from the unity of the Body" [i.e., Protestants].[9] Finally, under the heading "Protestantism," we find that the official position "of the

Catholic Church was set forth in the twenty-five sessions of the Council of Trent"[10] which, as we saw, thoroughly anathematized Protestantism.

All this proves that Roman Catholicism claims that it alone is the one true Church on earth, and that Protestant churches are false.

Rome's Own Requirements

It is a fact that the Catholic Church itself has officially defined the identifying marks of the one true Church. But what if it fails to meet its own qualifications and requirements? In *The Catholic Encyclopedia* we are told there are four criteria endorsed by the Council of Trent: 1) oneness of doctrine, 2) the generation of true personal holiness dispensed through the Church's means of sanctification (e.g., sacraments), 3) catholicity (universality of mission), and 4) apostolicity—teachings and practices derived from Christ and the apostles.[11]

First, can it logically be maintained that the Catholic Church has a "oneness of doctrine"? In the sense of doctrine, the term "catholicity" was classically defined in the "Vincentian Canon" (fifth century) as "what has been believed everywhere, always, by all."[12] Individual Catholics aside, have even the popes always maintained unity of doctrine? How is this possible with the doctrinal contradictions and controversies in Catholic history, tradition, and Scripture (e.g., the Apocrypha)? What about the serious differences found in the various competing forms of modern Roman Catholicism such as liberal, moderate, conservative, mystical, and charismatic branches? Does Vatican II agree entirely with Trent? No. (For more details on this, see Appendix E.)

Second, on what *biblical* basis can true holiness be said to be dispensed through the Roman Catholic Church and its beliefs and practices? Biblically, it is clear that sanctification, or growth in holiness, comes principally through the work of the Holy Spirit applied individually to true believers in Christ through the renewing power of both learning Scripture and obeying it. If so, of what value are the Roman Catholic sacraments and other practices for the process of sanctification?

Biblically, if individual Catholics are attempting to earn their own salvation by good works, are they even saved? The answer is no. In fact, by inhibiting personal salvation through unbiblical doctrine and practices, Roman Catholicism inhibits true sanctification because sanctification is not possible without regeneration (cf. John 6:63; Colossians 2:23).

Thus, millions of Catholics today think they are Christians when, in fact, they are Catholics. Of course, the same may be said of Protestants who reject the gospel. Nevertheless, perhaps it is the fact of a largely unregenerate Church which explains the strong comments of former Franciscan priest Emmett McLoughlin. In his *Crime and Immorality in the Catholic Church* he argues as follows:

> The purpose of this book is to show that the Roman Catholic Church in its most important work [sanctification] is a failure. Among its members crime and immorality are greater than the unchurched or the members of other churches. Whatever else the Roman Catholic Church may be able to do . . . it cannot, it has not, and it does not make the majority of its members better and holier. . . .

> That the Roman Catholic Church has been one of the most powerful influences in the history of all civilization cannot be seriously denied. . . .

> [Nevertheless] it is my contention and my sincere conviction, from my experience in the Catholic educational system, my life of fifteen years in the priesthood, and thirteen years of constant observation and intense study since leaving the Church, that its influence on all civilization has been far more of evil than of good. . . .

> Morally, this book will show the high rate of crime and sin among Roman Catholics everywhere, and particularly in the United States. It will also demonstrate that this immorality is not in spite of Catholic education and training, but directly because of it.[13]

As an illustration, consider the priestly ban on marriage and Rome's "imposing an unnatural burden upon her clergy that very few could bear":

> The doctrine of celibacy has been broken repeatedly by millions of priests and nuns, bishops, archbishops, cardinals and many popes such as Sergius III, John X, John XII, Benedict V, Innocent VIII, Urban VIII, Innocent X, et al. Celibacy has made sinners of the clergy and harlots out of those with whom they secretly cohabit. The Catholic Church has paid about one billion in out-of-court settlements in the last few years for sexual sins of its clergy in the USA alone.

Even Catholic historians admit that among the popes were some of the most degenerate and unconscionable orgies in all history.[14]

Today, some have even claimed that up to one-third of the 57,000 Roman Catholic priests could be HIV infected. And now several books exist on priestly pedophilia—with up to 3,000 priests apparently involved.[15]

Unfortunately, the Catholic religious system of works/merit not only hinders true righteousness, it actually *increases* sin and pride—as any legalistic, works-oriented religion is destined to do, whether it be Protestant, Hindu, Buddhist, or Catholic.

For example, the Bible records the deeds of the Sadducees and Pharisees of Christ's day, which illustrate how attempts to keep the law only perverted salvation and increased their sin and pride. Look at Jesus' response to them in Matthew 23 to see this:

> They do not practice what they preach. . . . Everything they do is done for men to see. . . . Woe to you, teachers of the law and Pharisees, you hypocrites! You shut the kingdom of heaven in men's faces. You yourselves do not enter, nor will you let those enter who are trying to. . . . You travel over land and sea to win a single convert, and when he becomes one, you make him twice as much a son of hell as you are. . . . Inside [you] are full of greed and self-indulgence. . . . Inside you are full of hypocrisy and wickedness (Matthew 23:3,5,13-15,25,28; see also Acts 15:10,11; Romans 5:20; 6:14; 7:5,8; 8:6-8; Galatians 5:16-18).

Nor should we forget other things:

> Most of Rome's wealth has been acquired through the sale of salvation. Untold billions of dollars have been paid to her by those who thought they were purchasing heaven on the installment plan for themselves or loved ones. The practice continues to this day—blatantly where Catholicism is in control, less obviously here in the United States where (for example) one pays the Church to have a Mass Card placed on the altar in the name of the deceased during Mass to reduce time in purgatory. The wealthy often leave a fortune for masses to be said for their salvation after their death.

In addition to such perversions of the Gospel, there are the further abominations (fully documented in police and court records) of corrupt banking practices, laundering of drug money, trading in counterfeit securities and dealings with the Mafia, which the Vatican and her representatives around the world have long employed. Former *Business Week* correspondent in Rome, Nino Lo Bello, who because of its incredible wealth calls Rome "the tycoon on the Tiber," says the Vatican is so closely allied with the Mafia in Italy that "many people . . . believe that Sicily . . . is nothing more than a Vatican holding."[16]

The third Catholic test for identifying the one true Church is catholicity or universality of mission. But do Roman Catholics really have unity of mission? Aren't there competing factions within the Church, each having their own agenda and definition/outworking of mission? In Appendix A we have briefly discussed the following different "categories" of modern Roman Catholicism: 1) nominal or social Catholicism; 2) syncretistic/eclectic Catholicism; 3) traditional or orthodox Catholicism; 4) "moderate" Catholicism; 5) modernist, liberal Catholicism; 6) ethnic or cultural Catholicism; 7) lapsed or apostate Catholicism; 8) charismatic Catholicism (includes related category of mystical Catholicism); 9) "evangelical" Catholicism; 10) evangelical "Catholicism" (which is truly Christian doctrinally and spiritually but remains in the membership of the Roman Catholic Church). Can it logically be argued that these categories of modern Roman Catholicism constitute a "unity of mission"?

The fourth Catholic test for identifying the one true Church is apostolicity. But if the Roman Catholic Church rejects the teachings of the apostles, how can it logically be considered apostolic? Thus, the Catholic Church fails in all of its four criteria for evaluation of its own authenticity as the one true Christian Church.

What Makes a Religion Christian?

Merely having some degree of doctrinal orthodoxy does not, by definition, prove a religion is Christian.

For example, in church history certain unorthodox or heretical sects have accepted the doctrine of the Trinity and yet denied other cardinal doctrines of the faith. Today, Jehovah's Witnesses believe in the inerrancy of the Bible far more consistently than Catholics. Yet, no one argues they are Christian (except themselves).

Mormonism provisionally accepts the Bible as the Word of God and in certain ways believes in the atonement of Christ. Yet no religion is more anti-Christian.[17] The Way International teaches "salvation by grace" and other biblical doctrines, yet denies the Trinity and the deity of Christ. They cannot be properly classified as Christian either. Even Muslims are devout monotheists having many moral views in harmony with the Bible. But none of these religions can be classified as Christian because what makes a religion Christian is both a) a fundamental body of correct doctrinal belief that true Christians have always believed in without compromise, and b) religious practices and life-style among its members that conform to biblical standards.

Even the orthodox doctrines in Catholicism have a tendency to become compromised in various ways. For example, the deity of Christ is impacted by Rome's false teaching that Christ is incarnated in the Catholic Church.[18]

All this underscores a simple fact. Claims to be Christian need to be thoroughly evaluated with proper attention to 1) word meanings, 2) doctrine as a whole, and 3) life-style and practices. If we look at Roman Catholic doctrine comprehensively as well as its word meanings and practices, this requires the categorization of Roman Catholicism as a whole as not being Christian (see Appendix D).

Even if we must reduce the issue to a single doctrine, what primarily determines whether a religious body is Christian or not is the basic gospel message of salvation, not how close a given religion can come to the historic doctrines of Christianity. Let's take an example. Say there is a very powerful and influential worldwide religion with a billion members. It's called "The Church of Christianity."

Let us first assume this world religion is orthodox on every major teaching of historic Christianity, such as the deity of Christ; salvation by grace through faith in Christ alone; the personality and deity of the Holy Spirit; biblical inerrancy; the fall of man; the incarnation, atonement, and second coming of Christ; the virgin birth; the Trinity; etc.

But now let's change one thing. Let's say this religion is only 99 percent orthodox. There is one historic doctrine it refuses to accept. It absolutely rejects salvation by grace through faith alone and teaches that, in the end, a person is ultimately to recognize that they are saved by their faith *and* their good works.

Is it still a Christian religion? After all, it's 99 percent Christian. It's as orthodox as can be in every area but one. In 99 Christian doctrines its teachings are biblical; there is only one doctrine it opposes.

Biblically, such a religion cannot possibly be classified as Christian. Again, how *close* one gets to Christianity isn't the issue. The issue is, Does one accept the gospel or not?

Now consider Roman Catholicism. The fact that it accepts many Christian doctrines is irrelevant. That it teaches salvation by works proves that it is not a Christian religion. The fact that some people are saved within the Roman Catholic Church only means that some individuals, like Luther, have found salvation by God's grace because they studied the Bible—or because Christians witnessed to them and they were saved by hearing the gospel.

Luther also said this, "If I declare with the loudest voice and clearest exposition every portion of God's Truth except for that one little bit which the world and the devil are at the moment attacking, I am not confessing Christ no matter how boldly I may be professing Christ."

The gospel—anything but minuscule—is what the world, the flesh, and the devil have always opposed. And it continues to be opposed today in the Catholic Church. Therefore, Christians who think Roman Catholicism is Christian, "Evangelical Catholics" who seek to bring their "separated brethren" back to Rome, and Evangelicals who have converted to Rome need to ask where their commitment is to the *gospel*—that doctrine of salvation by grace alone, that the world and the devil are at this moment attacking. And if their commitment isn't to taking a strong stand in defense of the gospel, is their commitment really to Christ and His church? It cannot be.

Salvation Denied

On this key issue alone Catholicism fails the test of being Christian. Roman Catholicism teaches the following doctrines that negatively impact or deny the biblical teaching on salvation:

- Justification as the infusing of righteousness based on good works, not the imputation of righteousness as a judicial decree of God.

- The Mass "as truly propitiatory" and, in some sense, truly resacrificing Christ.

- The seven Catholic sacraments as infusing grace for purposes of sanctification and salvation. (But if the sacrament of

Holy Orders confers supernatural power on Roman Catholic bishops, priests, and deacons to "serve as a teacher as Christ Himself,"[19] how is it that Roman Catholic bishops, priests, and deacons can so consistently oppose the key teachings of Scripture?)

- Baptism, penance, suffering in purgatory, indulgences, etc., as having the power to remit or forgive sin or its punishment.

- Catholicism alone as the one true Church that is necessary for salvation.

No one can deny that, given the above teachings relating to salvation, Catholicism offers a different gospel than the one clearly stated in the Bible.

Biblical Authority Denied

But Catholicism also teaches doctrines which undermine the authority of the Bible itself:

- The pope as infallible in matters of doctrine and morals. Further, Peter was the first pope, and Christ instituted the office of the papacy. Yet all the popes have ever done is to uphold Catholic doctrines that deny what the Bible teaches.

- Catholic tradition has divine authority and is to be equated with the Word of God. Yet Catholic tradition also denies what the Bible teaches.

- The Apocrypha as the Word of God, even though the Apocrypha is full of errors and it, too, denies biblical teaching.

- The teaching authority of the Church as the final and only correct interpreter of the Bible to its people. This means that individual Christians cannot properly interpret the Bible on their own. This is why the Protestant view of individual interpretation is referred to as a product of "theological rationalism" and condemned by Rome.[20] As we saw earlier, *The Documents of Vatican II* teach, "The task of authentically interpreting the Word of God, whether written or handed on, has been entrusted *exclusively* to the living/teaching office of the Church."[21] Yet all this teaching authority has done historically is to pervert what the Bible teaches.

The above proves that the Catholic Church has also undermined the authority and inerrancy of the Scriptures. But further, the Catholic Church also teaches the following items listed below—again, none of which are biblical:

- Mary was born without sin, is sinless, ascended bodily into heaven and is a "co-redemptrix," "mediatrix," and "Queen of Heaven" in God's plan of salvation. She is to be venerated and "worshiped," and offers all the graces of Christ to men who adore her, whether in the Church or at thousands of her shrines and altars throughout the world. She is necessary for the salvation of the world.[22]

- Faith is an intellectual assent to the doctrines of the Church. In fact, true faith "demands that we believe" in Roman Catholic doctrines without which we cannot be sanctified or saved.[23] (Apparently then, Christians whose faith in the Bible alone compels them in their conscience to reject Catholic belief are without true saving faith.)

- Catholic saints are to be venerated. Further, true "saints" and "priests" are comprised of an extremely minuscule portion of the body of Christ, rejecting the biblical teaching that *all* believers are saints and priests.

- Sin is to be compartmentalized into false moral/venial categories.

In conclusion, perhaps it would do well to remind Evangelicals that historically the greatest enemy of Christianity has been religion. It is the growth of false religions throughout the world that has remained the most serious threat to the health of the church and will continue to do so far into the twenty-first century.

Is Roman Catholicism Christian? In a nutshell, there are so many ways in which Catholicism is not biblical that it is logically impossible to classify it as a Christian religion.

All this is why the obstacles between Catholicism and Evangelicalism are insurmountable—at least until there is fundamental biblical reformation in Rome.

.19.

Problems of Dialogue

There is not a fiercer hell than the failure in a great object.
—John Keats

The road to unity is the road to repentance.
—H. Richard Niebuhr

*I*n his *Ecclesiam Suam* (1964) Pope Paul VI commented that "The desire to come together as brothers must not lead to a watering-down or subtracting from the truth. Our dialogue must not weaken our attachment to our faith."

The pope was correct that the desire for unity should never compromise truth and that dialogue must not compromise doctrinal faith. This is why we believe biblical truth must prevail for the sake of Jesus Christ and His glory.

This leads us to ask some questions about many of the kinds of dialogues and declarations we have seen in recent years. While we will concentrate on the 1983 "Lutheran/Roman Catholic Dialogue Group," we will also mention others. For example, in their desire for unity, do these dialogues compromise biblical truth? Do they meet their stated goals? What kind of fruit do they bear? Are the time and resources spent in these dialogues well invested?

The Lutheran Church-Missouri Synod position on dialogue asserts the following:

> The Lutheran Church-Missouri Synod participates in ecumenical dialogues because it regards confession of the biblical Gospel and the effort to achieve agreement in the confession of the apostolic and catholic faith not as an

optional matter but as a scriptural mandate. For the sake of the truth of the Gospel, the Synod therefore remains committed to doctrinal discussions that provide an occasion for identifying points of agreement and disagreement that exist between the partners in dialogue.[1]

From the Evangelical viewpoint we think the dialogue itself must be prioritized from the perspective of the gospel. In other words, the more important necessities for both church and society (such as effective discipleship in doctrinal teachings for Christians, evangelization, etc.) should not be compromised in light of limited time, funds, and other resources. Participation in a dialogue should offer promise of real fruit from a biblical perspective. Dialogue to help clarify positions and defend the biblical gospel is good; dialogue that muddies the water or compromises the gospel is not.

While we have hardly examined the majority of dialogues that have taken place, we have examined several and would like to begin with a few general comments and then cite illustrations from the 1994 and 1983 agreements—declarations which seem to have made an important impact in Evangelical and Catholic discussions.

Three Major Concerns

Our concerns can be gauged in at least three areas. First, dialogues that take years to conclude but never accomplish their theological objective are questionable. When the goal is not met to achieve a "consensus" or significant agreement on key issues such as the gospel and the nature of salvation, justification, etc., this would not be a prudent use of resources.

Second, we object to dialogues which mislead people by making false claims about having achieved genuine consensus when this is not true. To claim that Roman Catholics and Evangelicals are both Christians and part of the same spiritual family without defining clearly how either party relates to the primary biblical passages on salvation or how they have resolved the classic historic points of disagreement is dishonest. It causes confusion. From the Evangelical viewpoint it only serves to misguide uninstructed Christians and make them assume that Catholics are already saved and do not need to hear the gospel or be evangelized. From the Roman Catholic view, it serves to reinforce what instructed Catholics have been taught all along: that Rome is the one true Church and Evangelicals are the ones—the "separated brethren"—who must return to their Mother Church.

Third, bad dialogues dishonor Christ and His cause in at least four ways:

1. *By compromising truth.*

Jesus said, "Sanctify them [set them apart to serve God] in the truth; Thy word is truth" (John 17:17). In light of Jesus' concern that His people be sanctified in biblical truth, how can we safeguard truth in a pluralistic culture like ours? Consider one assessment:

It may be that in an environment which is tolerant of any religious expression, that men naturally begin to invest a degree of absolute value and validity in all religious expressions. . . . Carelessness and complacency are greater enemies of truth than heresy and hell. In the face of absolute religious freedom, the integrity of truth is protected only by men and women submitting absolutely to God's revelation in the Bible.[2]

Further,

In the Word of God, the basis of "unity" and the imperative for "love" are truth. Truth is not the enemy of "unity" and "love," but "unity" and "love" wrongly conceived and/or incorrectly defined are the enemies of truth.[3]

Ecumenical dialogues can easily compromise the gospel by equivocation—that is, carelessness in the use of terminology. The 1994 declaration "Evangelicals and Catholics Together" is an example of this kind of equivocation. It never defined such crucial terms as "faith," "Christian mission," "church," "unity," "love," "accepting Christ," etc., even though participants had two years to do so. If these terms are not defined, how can anyone claim there is agreement? Anyone knowledgeable knows that the historical arguments which have divided us center on these very words.

2. *By spending years on fruitless efforts.*

At least from the Evangelical side, such efforts could more profitably have been spent in evangelism and building up the body of Christ itself.

3. *By confusing priorities—the eternal for the temporal, the political/social for the spiritual, etc.*

If Evangelicals and Catholics are going to work together for moral change in society, this is fine. Our culture and nation *are* in the process of dying, and this cannot be ignored. Worldwide, the church does face a tremendous threat from Islam, as the 1994 document hints at. But at the same time, let's not bring the gospel into the discussion unless we are going to clearly define it and not compromise it, or confuse others into thinking wrongly that real agreement has been reached. A person can be involved in social activism apart from regeneration. But we should not forget the priority and greater power of the gospel in bringing change. Dialogue can sometimes reduce the emphasis of this Evangelical viewpoint that we are commanded to preserve and elevate.

4. *By accepting unrealistic premises and expectations.*

Anyone who understands the biblical doctrines of depravity, regeneration, and election should realize that the Roman Catholic Church does not intend to change its theology, or its necessary rejection of (and even hostility to) the biblical gospel.

Why is this so? Because it can't. Jeremiah asks if "a leopard can change its spots" (Jeremiah 13:23).

The only thing that will change the theology of individual unregenerated Catholics (or Protestants) is regeneration by God so that their spiritual eyes are opened, they are made alive to God, and they have the ability to understand the gospel. Apart from this, no Catholic (or Protestant) and no church will ever accept the gospel because the unregenerate heart and mind find it impossible to do so (John 3:27; 6:44,65; Romans 8:7; 9:18; 1 Corinthians 2:14).

Be Realistic

We should be realistic and not be fooled into thinking that concessions made by a very small group of Catholic theologians to Evangelical belief will have any effect on Rome. Rome is the head of the Church, and until Rome changes, the Church will remain the same doctrinally.

Therefore, in light of the power of Rome, these dialogues would hardly seem to institute a minuscule amount of change. Of course, one impact of these dialogues may be to "break the ice," so to speak, among individual Catholic theologians and laymen in such a manner that they become more open to consideration of the biblical gospel. This is all to the good as a form of pre-evangelism. But one could also argue this might be more efficiently achieved by private individual witness which does not send confusing messages and false hopes.

In essence, Evangelicals are bound by their loyalty to Scripture, Catholics by their loyalty to tradition. When Protestants and Catholics try to join hands to find a consensus on specific matters relating to the gospel—matters that Scripture and tradition are opposed in—what can be achieved? We can only question the wisdom of the approach. Was it all worth it?

Again, this is not to say that dialogue with the Roman Catholic Church per se has no value. We believe only that it should be carried out in a manner that is truly conducive to the kingdom of God and the clear presentation and advancement of the gospel. If this cannot be done, then perhaps we should ask what the point is.

Our criticism, of course, does not at all seek to question the faith, motives, or integrity of those who are or have been involved in these dialogues. It only questions the wisdom and effectiveness of dialogues when "most Christian leaders would argue that the state of the Evangelical Church in America is more anemic than the Church in almost any other part of the world. The state of the Church in North America gives occasion for repentance and mourning, not glorifying."[4] If so, the church in North America should perhaps spend more of its time building up its own deteriorating house rather than attempting to help another completely rebuild theirs.

The "Evangelicals and Catholics Together" Declaration

In terms of the effectiveness of the 1994 declaration "Evangelicals and Catholics Together":

> The signers of this document have found nothing more, it seems, as one reads their document, than the pragmatism of a quasi-political alliance through which to prosecute a social and political agenda. Certainly, the evidence from this 25-page document is that no substantive progress has been made in reconciling the irreconcilable differences between Roman Catholicism and

biblical Christianity. Indeed, reconciliation would require capitulation by one or the other, as the doctrine, ecclesiology, authority and spirit of Roman Catholicism [and Evangelicalism] are mutually exclusive.[5]

We believe this assessment correctly states the case. But those who signed the agreement apparently believe it is part of the "way to the great visible unity for which we hope."[6] But can this unity be achieved apart from a great spiritual revival?

Further, as far as the unity that this declaration seeks to attain:

Non-believers often cannot differentiate between petty squabbling between men, and the righteous conflict which arises from principles which must not be compromised. The only safe way Christians can engage in activities which give the appearance of disunity in the body of Christ is to have a clear doctrine of biblical, God-ordained unity. . . . Unity will never be achieved by concordants, doctrinal agreements, synods or councils. Christian unity will only be achieved by the worship, praise and glory of Jesus Christ. Christian unity is the product of faith in Jesus Christ; it is maintained through continuing fellowship with Jesus Christ in and through the Word of God.[7]

In addition, "Lip service is repeatedly given to biblical doctrine, while political pragmatism [actually] drives this document."[8] For example,

It is noteworthy that the very people who would condemn liberation theology as a Marxist's corruption of the Gospel are now embracing a quasi-politicization of the Gospel which has as its purpose the liberating of secular society from the inevitable decay which results when society operates without moral constraints. While the goals of the signers of the document may be noble and while their motives may be pure, their methodology is antithetical to biblical Christianity.[9]

The "Evangelicals and Catholics Together" document, of course, speaks of the importance of not compromising the love of Christ; however, it gives no definition of "love."

> Love does not excuse heresy, and love does not reassure those in error that it "doesn't make any difference what you believe." . . . Southwestern Baptist Theological Seminary professor, Dr. Jack MacGormon asked the question, "Is admonition in the face of danger as clear an evidence of love as reassurance in the presence of danger?"
>
> He answered, "Yes, but the tone of admonition is such that it is seldom received as love." He continued, "[False] reassurance in the face of danger is not love, it is treacherous." . . . It is treachery to say, "We love you," when we know that those to whom it is said are on their way to destruction (see Proverbs 24:11,12).[10]

In conclusion, by blurring spiritual truths and then using those blurred spiritual truths as a basis for a united political/social action, the 1994 document has failed in generating what could otherwise have been a laudable declaration and blueprint for attempting to deal with the moral crisis in America, and for explaining what is really needed if Evangelicals are to reconcile with Catholics on historical points of difference. If nothing else, such an explanation would have been a clear rather than a confusing presentation of the gospel to unsaved Catholics and Protestants.

The U.S. Lutheran-Roman Catholic Dialogue Group on Justification by Faith

In 1983 a group of Lutheran and Catholic theologians made the newsworthy announcement that they had come to agreement (a "fundamental consensus") on the meaning of the gospel.[11] This alleged consensus has been cited by many Evangelicals as justification for their own acceptance of Catholics as their brothers and sisters in Christ. Books have also been written arguing that Evangelicals and Catholics are now so close together doctrinally that, for all practical purposes, division among them is no longer necessary.

Although this widely publicized statement of consensus on the gospel has now caused many people to conclude that Catholics and Protestants are in agreement concerning the nature of salvation, this, of course, is not the case. The "common statement" and "material convergencies" paragraphs which we cite below (in paragraphs 4, 155-60 in the document) sound evangelical. But upon closer reading one finds what was actually upheld was the traditional Catholic doctrine of justification as infused righteousness based on personal merit.

For example, in paragraph 4 this report clearly equates justification with the Catholic view that the gospel and God's merciful action in Christ includes God working through merit by grace what He makes possible for us to do:

> ...both Catholics and Lutherans can wholeheartedly accept: Our entire hope of justification and salvation rests on Christ Jesus and on the Gospel whereby the good news of God's merciful action in Christ is made known; we do not place our ultimate trust in anything other than God's promise and saving work in Christ. This excludes ultimate reliance on our faith, virtues, or merits, even though we acknowledge God working in these by grace alone *(sola gratia)*.... Agreement on this Christological affirmation does not necessarily involve full agreement between Catholics and Lutherans on justification by faith, but it does raise a question, as we shall see, whether the remaining differences on this doctrine need be church dividing.[12]

The report also clearly equates justification and sanctification, conforming to the Catholic view: "By justification we are both declared and made righteous. Justification, therefore, is not a legal fiction [a reference to the supposed Protestant view]. God, in justifying, effects what He promises; He forgives sin and makes us truly righteous."[13]

In response to statements like this, W. Robert Godfrey, professor of church history at Westminster Theological Seminary in California, observes, "The report yields to the Roman Catholics on the doctrine of justification, and compromises too much that is essential to the Gospel."[14]

Thus, the report never did unite Protestants and Catholics on the nature of justification; it largely upheld the Catholic view while some Protestants and Catholics concluded they had agreed.[15] Yet, incredibly, many knowledgeable "Evangelical" leaders have told us that "strong agreement" was, in fact, reached on this issue.

In fact, some Evangelical signers of the 1994 "Evangelicals and Catholics Together" statement have cited this very paragraph in defense of their signatures to that agreement.

Despite any alleged or actual agreements that may have been reached in this joint declaration in other areas, the fact is that actual agreement was not reached in any areas relating to salvation and specifically to the New Testament doctrine of justification by faith.

Sadly, although this 24,000-word document was the product of five years' work, we cannot possibly agree with this document when it says, "A fundamental consensus on the Gospel is necessary. . . . We believe that we have reached such a consensus."[16]

Additional Claims

The declaration also makes the following claims:

> Lutherans and Catholics are at home with each other and in each other's churches as never before in their divided histories. It is scarcely surprising that they are now closer on the doctrine of justification than at any time since the collapse of their last extended official discussion of the topic at Regensburg in 1541.[17]

Further, "Our intent in presenting this statement is to help our [Protestant and Catholic] churches to see how and why they can and should increasingly proclaim together the one undivided Gospel of God's saving mercy in Jesus Christ."[18]

But from an Evangelical point of view, among the best that can be concluded from this joint effort are some statements like the following:

> Catholics have come to acknowledge that "righteousness/justification" is more prevalent in New Testament teaching than has normally been suspected in earlier centuries.[19]

> "Merit" is a technical Western theological term for a concept that has no single terminological equivalent in the original texts of the Bible.[20]

While the document further claims that its common convictions "constitute a very significant agreement," we cannot see this in the document we have read. Why? Because as the document confesses, these convictions "remain subject to different interpretations and formulations in each tradition."[21]

What else stood out in this supposed consensus?[22] The report starts by noting that the Malta Report of the International Lutheran-Catholic Study Commission stated that "today . . . a far reaching consensus is developing in the interpretation of justification."[23] Yet in the very next paragraph it declares, "Justification is above all a reality to be proclaimed in word and sacrament," conceding the Catholic view.[24]

The declaration agrees that at the time of the Reformation, the doctrine of justification by faith had largely been obscured by Catholic teaching:

> The two chief problems which occasioned the Reformer's appeal to St. Paul's teaching that human beings are "justified by faith apart from works of law" (Romans 3:28 RSV) were, from their point of view, rampant Pelagianism or "works righteousness," on the one hand, and the need to "console terrified consciences" on the other. . . .
>
> Salvation was widely viewed as something to be earned by good works, which included not only fulfillment of the moral and the monastic counsels of perfection, but also observance of a vast panoply of penitential disciplines in ecclesiastical rules and regulations.
>
> Moreover, money paid for Masses and indulgences was often thought of as automatically obtaining the remission of purgatorial penalties. . . . Indulgences were a major source of papal revenues, and Masses for the dead and for other purposes provided the main support for a large proportion of priests. This system of "buying" salvation, furthermore, was administered by a frequently venal hierarchy. . . .
>
> Thus the Reformation emphasis on justification "apart from works of law" was a challenge not simply to transient theology and religious practice, but also to powerful special interest groups.[25]

In addition, contrary to the claims of certain Catholic apologists who have made statements about this document, the declaration itself concedes that the Council of Trent *did* teach the doctrine of justification as infused righteousness, a progressive event, and as capable of being lost.[26]

Disagreements Remaining

The sections on satisfactions include the following statements which underscore the tremendous gaps that remain between Catholics and conservative Lutherans:

Catholics, however, held that the sufferings of the saints, united in a mysterious way with those of Christ himself, could "fill up" what was lacking in Christ's sufferings.... Catholics generally continue to hold that the sufferings of penitent sinners and of the innocent can be prayerfully applied, in union with the immeasurable satisfaction given to Christ, to beseech God's mercy and pardon.... Further study will be needed to determine whether and how far Lutherans and Catholics can agree on these points, which have far-reaching ramifications for traditionally disputed doctrines such as the sacrament of penance, masses for special intentions, indulgences and purgatory.[27]

Is it any wonder that this document confesses, "Some of the consequences of the different outlooks seem irreconcilable"?[28]

Interpretation and Doctrine

What is most telling about the nature and substance of the alleged agreement is the interpretative aspects (see endnote 28). For example, after conceding that their supposed common affirmation "is not fully equivalent to the Reformation teaching on justification according to which God accepts sinners as righteous for Christ's sake on the basis of faith alone,"[29] it proceeds, for all practical intents and purposes, to wholly undermine any claimed agreement delineated:

It must be emphasized that our common affirmation that it is God in Christ alone whom believers ultimately trust does not *necessitate any one particular way* of conceptualizing or picturing God's saving work. That work can be expressed... in a transformist view which emphasizes the change wrought in sinners by infused grace.... [Therefore] wherever this [common] affirmation is maintained, it is possible to allow *great variety* in describing salvation and in interpreting God's justifying declaration.[30]

Although it is maintained that this is possible "without destroying unity" between Catholics and Lutherans, we would simply ask, "How?" Certainly it destroys unity with those who hold to *sola scriptura*—those, that is, who are Evangelical.

The Official Lutheran Response

We are not the only ones to declare there was no fundamental agreement on key doctrine found in the 1983 dialogue report between Lutherans and Catholics. The official Lutheran Church-Missouri Synod response a decade later (1992) also noted that any encouraging aspects of the "Common Statement," "should not and, in fact, cannot, hide the fact that fundamental doctrinal differences still exist between Roman Catholicism and Lutheranism on the doctrine of justification."[31]

Thus, even the official Lutheran response itself does not conclude that agreement on the gospel was reached—in clear contradiction of widely asserted claims to the contrary.

The Lutheran denomination's analysis points out that the use of particular words (e.g., "ultimate trust") and the classification of faith as being recognized as requiring both trust in Christ "and loving obedience to him" are problematic at best.[32] If so, faith is a work in addition to trust. In essence:

> To imply in any way that the sanctified life of the sinner must somehow "intrinsically qualify" justifying faith to accomplish justification before God is not only to misunderstand the nature of faith, but also to call into question the all-sufficient work of Christ itself.[33]

In quoting the 1983 statement which claimed that Roman Catholics and Lutherans had "greatly narrowed the [terminological] differences" between them, the 1992 Lutheran church responded:

> We question, however, whether the dialogue in coming to this conclusion has really advanced much beyond the historic impasse between the churches on the role of faith alone in the justification of the sinner before God.[34]

Below we cite the essence of the final conclusion of the Lutheran Missouri-Synod Church which, after careful evaluation of the 1983 report, argued as follows:

> It is with these significant points of continuing disagreement in mind that the claims for "convergence" on the doctrine of justification between Lutherans and Roman Catholics must be heard. Convergence is not consensus.

234 • *Problems of Dialogue*

Consensus on the doctrine of justification by grace alone, through faith alone, in Christ alone, the article on which the Church stands or falls, is still the absolutely necessary requirement for the resolution of disagreements between Roman Catholics and Lutherans.

In this connection we note that the dialogue participants began their "Common Statement" by stating with reference to the "Christological affirmation" agreed upon by both sides . . . that this affirmation "does not necessarily involve full agreement between Catholics and Lutherans on justification by faith." They further raise the question "whether the remaining differences on this doctrine need be church-dividing." . . . The answer to this question is given in the concluding section of the "Common Statement." . . .

Having reviewed carefully the "Common Statement" we have come to the conclusion that beneath the "differences on theological formulations" often noted, there remains *substantive differences* between the Churches that go to *the very heart of the Gospel* itself and are therefore divisive.[35]

In conclusion, neither the 1983 Lutheran-Catholic Dialogue Group nor the 1994 "Evangelicals and Catholics Together" statement ever achieved what was so boldly claimed for them.

.20.

A Personal Word to Catholics

*I*f you have stayed with us this far, we want you to know we appreciate your perseverance and integrity in examining a critique of the faith you hold dear.

We have written this book because we believe there is one vital issue that all Catholics (and many Protestants) need to think through. In essence, this is the issue of one's personal salvation.

As a Catholic, you, more than anyone else, are aware that it is not possible in this life to have assurance of salvation—except perhaps in very rare circumstances. Catholic literature emphasizes that a belief in the assurance of salvation is a "presumption upon the mercy of God."[1] It also tells us that mortal sin results in "eternal separation from God" and requires penance for restoration.[2] It emphasizes the personal hazards of so-called "triumphalism." Triumphalism is said to be something that "arises out of" an "assurance of having been saved," and which "is a dangerous position" to hold.[3]

Because Catholicism teaches that Christians may lose their salvation, it argues, "Not even faith . . . or conversion . . . or reception of baptism . . . or constancy throughout life . . . can gain for one the right to salvation."[4] All these are held to be only "the forerunners of attainment" toward salvation.[5]

But the good news is that this part of Catholic theology is not biblical teaching. Jesus Himself taught that faith does bring the right to salvation: "As many as received Him, to them He gave *the right* to become children of God" (John 1:12 NASB, emphasis added).

In addition, the Bible clearly teaches that by faith alone people can know that they are eternally saved. The Bible actually teaches in a very clear way that at the moment of saving faith, a person possesses eternal life. As Jesus taught, "Truly, truly, I say to you, he who believes *has eternal life*" (John 6:47 NASB, emphasis added). And,

"These things I have written to you who believe in the name of the Son of God, in order that you may *know* that you have eternal life" (1 John 5:13 NASB, emphasis added).

The Catholic Church does not have the right to tell people that they *cannot* have an assurance of salvation when God clearly teaches they *can*. In fact, any person on earth, no matter how serious his sins, no matter what religion he has been in, or whether he has any religion at all, the moment he fully believes in Jesus Christ as his Savior, he can know that 1) all his sins are forgiven, past, present, and future, 2) he is fully and completely justified (declared righteous) by God, and 3) he now has an eternal salvation that can never be lost under any circumstances (Romans 8:28,29).

Again, anyone can know he is saved by truly trusting in Christ for forgiveness of sins and making Jesus his personal Lord and Savior. This is why the Bible teaches,

> Praise be to the God and Father of our Lord Jesus Christ! In his great mercy he has given us new birth into a living hope through the resurrection of Jesus Christ from the dead, and into an inheritance that can never perish, spoil or fade—kept in heaven for you, who through faith are shielded by God's power (1 Peter 1:3-5).

And,

> For those God foreknew he also predestined to be conformed to the likeness of his Son, that he might be the firstborn among many brothers. And those he predestined, he also called; those he called, he also justified; those he justified, he also glorified.

> What, then, shall we say in response to this? If God is for us, who can be against us? He who did not spare his own Son, but gave him up for us all—how will he not also, along with him, graciously give us all things? Who will bring any charge against those whom God has chosen? ... Who shall separate us from the love of Christ? ...

> For I am convinced that neither death nor life, neither angels nor demons, neither the present nor the future, nor any powers, neither height nor depth, nor anything else in all creation, will be able to separate us from the love of God that is in Christ Jesus our Lord (Romans 8:29-33,35,38,39).

Certainly the above listing of things that cannot separate us from God's love would appear to include such items as mortal sins or lack of penance or confession to a priest. Thus, the biblical truth—the good news for all people—is that they *can* know that they now *have* eternal salvation.

If you are a Catholic and desire to receive Jesus Christ as your personal Lord and Savior, we would urge you to say the following prayer:

> Dear God, it is my desire to enter into a personal relationship with You on the basis of the death of Your Son Jesus on the cross. Although I have believed many things about Jesus, I confess that I have never truly received Him individually as my personal Savior and Lord. I have never understood that the Bible teaches salvation is a free gift that You offer me without cost and good works on my part.
>
> I now receive Your gift of salvation, Your pardon of my sins, as I fully believe that Christ died on the cross for my sins—all of them. I believe that He rose from the dead.
>
> It is my desire, Lord Jesus, that You now become my Lord and Savior. I now invite You into my life. I make You the Lord over all areas of my life, including all personal beliefs or practices that are not biblical—not to get saved, but because I love You and want to serve You for saving me.
>
> Help me to be committed to studying Your Word and to growing as a Christian in ways that honor You. Give me the strength to face difficulty or rejection when it comes to making a stand for You. If it be Your will, and necessary for me to leave the Catholic Church, give me the strength to do this and guide me into a good church and fellowship so that I might know and glorify You the more.
>
> In Jesus' name I pray this, trusting in Your guidance. Amen.

.21.

A Personal Word to Evangelicals

*I*t has become obvious to the reader by now that the concern underlying this book addresses two points: 1) in general, the state of affairs in the Evangelical church and its relationship with the Roman Catholic Church—which for the most part seems increasingly uncertain and not infrequently compromising, and 2) in particular, the 1994 and other declarations which leading Evangelicals have signed, giving approval to things which we believe the Scriptures do not allow.

Since the publication of the first edition of our book, we have received a few responses from Evangelicals who signed this document. We can certainly agree with some of the points they argue, but we must certainly disagree with others. Unfortunately, it still appears that a desire for cooperation on social causes and for a visible unity of the body of Christ carries more weight than concern over a clearly defined gospel.

Let us cite one illustration. This is from a prominent Evangelical who heads up an international evangelistic ministry. His official response states, "I believe the Lord led me to affirm certain carefully worded principles with selected, believing Roman Catholic representatives who love Jesus Christ as I do."[1]

This would be fine if these principles were, in fact, carefully worded; the problem is that they were not carefully worded and this is, in part, what has produced the problem.

He reports that he has received only a "small number of negative reactions to this agreement," most of which have been based on rather inaccurate accounts given in the secular news media. Only a "smaller number" of Evangelicals have expressed disagreement with his signing it.[2]

This would seem to indicate our general concern as noted above— confusion in Evangelicalism over the status of Roman Catholic beliefs, and a cloudiness in thinking concerning the biblical doctrine of justification by faith.

He goes on to state his conviction that there were, in fact, four truths in the document that both Catholics and Evangelicals agreed upon: 1) the lordship of Christ, 2) justification by grace through faith in Christ, 3) all who accept Christ as Lord and Savior are brothers and sisters in Christ, and 4) Christians are to teach and live in obedience to the divinely inspired Scriptures, which are the infallible Word of God.

But if the Catholics who signed the document actually agreed to these four points from an Evangelical perspective, then they could not logically remain Catholics in submission to Rome.

Material which dealt with the official Catholic approach to the inerrancy of Scripture had to be deleted from this book. From our research, we wonder if the Catholic signers of this document accept the Catholic approach to Scripture—which clearly rejects the inerrancy and authority of the Bible alone—or the position of Scripture itself.

This Evangelical leader also referred to the theological discussions on various topics between Protestant and Catholic scholars in the 1980s and to the book published by Augsburg entitled *Justification by Faith* (1985). The author cited the statement of agreement from paragraph 4 of the 1983 Lutheran-Catholic Dialogue which we reviewed earlier.

The paragraph cited can initially seem biblical (see p. 229). But anyone who reads the full 24,000-word document will realize that agreement was not reached on such subjects as the gospel, justification by grace through faith alone, or other subjects relative to salvation.

In fact, as we saw, the agreement itself stated that there were serious problems that remained. The official Lutheran response ten years later also warned that agreement on justification had clearly not been reached. What is worse, even the paragraph cited by our Evangelical friend *conceded* to the Catholic concept of grace as working to produce merit.

Our question is this: After 450 years of division, why did the agreement between Catholics and Evangelicals not deal with the main doctrine that historically has split Catholics and Protestants? If there really is agreement, why not clearly "spell it out"?

We think that the reason God has allowed this document to be signed, even though it compromises and distorts the gospel, is because He intends to raise up a standard and make this point a major issue in the church, just as He did at the Reformation—which will clarify these issues for the church at large.

Those who signed the agreement may want to consider the assessment of the Lausanne Committee for World Evangelization. First, it gratefully acknowledges the recent positive changes in Roman Catholicism:

> Vatican Council II . . . did not alter the central dogma of the sacramental system of salvation, but it did produce a favorable atmosphere for evangelical witness among Roman Catholics. . . . The document on Divine Revelation urges Roman Catholics to own, study, and circulate the Bible as diligently as their "separated brethren," the Protestants. This has generated a growing interest in the word of God among Roman Catholics. . . . The Council statement on ecumenism is a tacit admission that salvation can be found under certain conditions by non-Catholics. This has helped to remove some of the strong religious enmities between Catholics and Protestants. Attendance by Catholics at non-Catholic churches is no longer considered a serious sin by the Roman Catholic Church. This enables Evangelicals to share their faith with Roman Catholics—even in the pulpits of some Catholic churches.[3]

But second, the Committee also expressed the following reservations:

> Historically, the teaching of the Reformers that justification (or acceptance with God) is "by grace alone, in Christ alone, through faith alone" is so central to the Gospel as to be non-negotiable. Therefore, we are convinced that we have an evangelizing responsibility toward every person who, though baptized, does not appear to be trusting in Christ alone for salvation. . . . Although we rejoice in the increase of Christ centered movements within many [Catholic] churches . . . we cannot ignore the fact that the official doctrinal stance of the Roman Catholic Church remains to a great extent "unreformed." Many Evangelicals, therefore, believe it right to encourage members of this church, if they come by God's grace

to justifying faith in Christ, to leave their church and join an evangelical church.[4]

On a personal level, Catholics who look askance at Evangelical missions directed toward them need to understand that Evangelicals are truly attempting to help Catholics come to the fullness of biblical faith. This is something they can prove to themselves through reverent study of the Scripture.

What is needed is for every Evangelical having good opportunity to minister to Catholics to do so, keeping certain safeguards in mind:

- be fully informed on the issues; "honor all men" (1 Peter 2:17 NASB); and be sensitive to the guidance of the Holy Spirit;

- do everything possible to retain the opportunity for witness and ministry in conviction with one's own conscience;

- do all possible to help new Christians grow spiritually in light of the fullness of biblical teaching;

- not compromise on such issues as justification by faith alone through grace alone in Christ alone, with biblical teaching alone as the final authority.

Perhaps we can best close this book with the words of the Lord Jesus Christ Himself:

The harvest is plentiful, but the laborers are few; therefore beseech the Lord of the harvest to send out laborers into His harvest (Luke 10:2 NASB).

Everyone who calls on the name of the Lord will be saved. How, then, can they call on the one they have not believed in? And how can they believe in the one of whom they have not heard? And how can they hear without someone preaching to them? And how can they preach unless they are sent? (Romans 10:13-15).

Appendixes

Notes

APPENDIX A

Categories of Roman Catholicism Today

The issues surrounding Catholic belief and authority are compounded by the fact there are some nine categories of Roman Catholicism around the world. The distinctions between them are often not clear because they may tend to overlap and merge or blur into one another. Nor would individual Catholics necessarily appreciate or agree with such labels. But they will serve as a convenient grouping for purposes of illustration:

1. *Nominal or social Catholicism*—the Roman Catholicism of the largely uncommitted—perhaps those born or married into the Church but who have little knowledge of Rome's theology. In practice, they are principally Catholics in name only, although still Catholics "in Christ" because of baptism.

2. *Syncretistic/eclectic Catholicism*—the Roman Catholicism that is, to varying degrees, combined with and/or absorbed by the pagan religion of the indigenous culture in which it exists (e.g., as in South America and Africa).

3. *Traditional or orthodox Catholicism*—the powerful conservative branch of Roman Catholicism that holds to papal authority and historic Church doctrines such as those reasserted at the Council of Trent in the sixteenth century. Among this group may be classified the ultratraditionalist Catholics who adamantly reject Vatican II and generally distrust modern changes (e.g., abandoning the Latin Mass—something Trent pronounced an anathema upon).[1] Also included are traditionalist Catholics who, while adhering to the entirety of creedal Catholicism and papal authority, more or less accept Vatican II reforms while yet staunchly rejecting liberalism.

245

246 • Categories of Roman Catholicism Today

4. *"Moderate" Catholicism*—the Roman Catholicism of post-Vatican II which is neither entirely traditional nor entirely liberal.

5. *Modernist, liberal Catholicism*—the post-Vatican II "progressive" Roman Catholicism that to varying degrees rejects traditional doctrine.

6. *Ethnic or cultural Catholicism*—often retained by migrants to America who use "their religion to provide a sense of belonging. They feel that not to be Roman Catholic is not to belong and to lose [their] nationality and roots."[2]

7. *Lapsed or apostate Catholicism*—the Roman Catholicism which involves alienated, backslidden, or apostate Catholics who are largely indifferent to the Catholic Church and its God.

8. *Charismatic Catholicism*—the Roman Catholicism which seeks to accept the "baptism of the Holy Spirit" and speaking in tongues and other spiritual gifts as signs of a deeper Catholic spirituality. (This illustrates the related, if largely distinct, category of mystical Catholicism, undergirded by the mystical and not infrequently occult writings of the Catholic mystics.)

9. *"Evangelical" Catholicism*—former Protestant Evangelicals who may retain some of their former beliefs but who now accept Roman Catholicism as the one true Church and its doctrines as authoritative.

10. *Evangelical "Catholicism"*—the branch of former Roman Catholics who are truly Evangelical and who have rejected the unbiblical teachings of Rome, often deciding to remain in the Church as a means to evangelize other Catholics or help reform their Church.

If we consider several of these categories in a bit more detail, we will be better able to understand modern Catholicism. First, it should be noted that for Rome, once a person is baptized a Catholic, they are officially held to remain a Catholic, regardless of their degree of variation from Rome. Thus, even the nominal, syncretistic, and evangelical "Catholics" (point 10 above) may be deemed genuinely Catholic, irrespective of spiritual condition or belief. This is so because of what Catholics maintain happens in baptism and through other Church sacraments. In essence, with few exceptions, once baptized a Catholic, always a Catholic.

Nominal, modernist, and cultural Roman Catholics comprise millions of persons and possibly the majority of American Catholics. In large measure they are born Catholic and have become emotionally attached to the Mother Church. Characteristically, however, they do not understand or reject its authority and are not too concerned with obedience to the ethics or practices of the Church. Like many liberal Protestants, they remain Catholics primarily because of social convenience, religious needs, or perhaps personal guilt, rather than because of personal conviction concerning Rome's authority.

Syncretistic/eclectic Catholics are possibly more representatively described as "pagan" Catholics because, while accepting the Catholic faith to some degree, they have also retained much or most of their indigenous pagan religion. As a result, Catholic beliefs and practices are combined with animistic beliefs and practices so that a blending of the two occurs.

The traditionalists are arguably the most influential segment of the Church because through the pope, bishops, and orthodox priests, they occupy the center of power in Catholicism. Traditionalists believe that by being obedient to the Church they are, in essence, being obedient to God and Christ. Why? Because they have been taught that whatever the Church decrees as orthodox belief and practice through its tradition is, by definition, the will of God.[3] Thus, to obey the Church is equivalent to submitting to what God has revealed as His will for a person's life. As a result, the traditional Catholic feels no need to examine the Bible for himself to determine whether or not what the Church teaches is actually biblical. This is because he has been taught that the Church has been granted divine power to interpret the Bible infallibly. As a result, he completely trusts whatever the Church tells him that the Bible teaches.

The modernist, liberal branch of the Church is "liberal" largely in relationship to the authority of Rome and not necessarily liberal in the Protestant sense of being primarily rationalistic. Liberal Catholics vary widely in the degree to which they have departed from traditional Catholicism. One example would be Catholic theologians who may question the legitimacy of papal infallibility, or the Church's teaching on justification or birth control, but who otherwise seek to remain loyal to Rome. Another example would be the destructive Marxist-oriented "liberation theology" of many Central and South American priests and theologians whose primary concern is more "political liberation" and "social justice" than anything principally biblical or spiritual.

Nevertheless, although the term "liberal" is used specifically in relationship to the authority of Rome, there are also many Catholic leaders who are more or less liberal in a Protestant sense in that they reject biblical authority, apply rationalistic higher critical methods to biblical study, deny Christ's deity, teach universalism, etc.

Charismatic Catholics emphasize faith as a personal commitment to Jesus and loyalty to Scripture. This branch of Catholicism frequently encourages Bible studies, speaking in tongues, and oftentimes a "born-again" or "baptism in the Spirit" experience. But more frequently than not, it remains Roman Catholic, attempting to integrate this newfound faith and experience with traditional doctrines involving Mary, papal authority, and the sacraments. In fact, in practice the Catholic experience of the "baptism in the Holy Spirit" actually seems to lead most often to greater devotion to Catholic beliefs and practice. For example, thousands of Catholics have reported how the "baptism in the Spirit" affected them in terms like the following: "The mother of God has become more special," "I have a deeper devotion to Mary," and "I have taken up the Rosary since baptism in the Spirit."[4]

The Evangelical "Catholic" is truly an Evangelical believer and not a Catholic. In other words, he is not a committed Roman Catholic who merely appropriates the title of Evangelical Christian. He understands the issues doctrinally and spiritually and attempts to walk what can be a very difficult, and to some people's minds inconsistent, line of fidelity to the Bible while remaining a member of the Roman Catholic Church. That this can occasionally be successfully negotiated is known personally to coauthor Weldon. A friend of his in Bible school had such a love for Catholics that he not only found a parish which accepted his Evangelical training as priestly ordination but whose superiors permitted him to teach the Bible in its entirety on the basis of personal conscience (i.e., as an Evangelical Protestant). Not that it was easy: His parish got so much Bible that many of them decided that they were no longer Catholics while others attempted a synthesis of Evangelical Catholicism. Nevertheless, how the situation finally ended, we were unable to determine.

APPENDIX B

How the Roman Catholic Church, the Papacy, and Catholic Tradition Arose

A number of historical factors explain the rise of the Roman Catholic Church, the papacy, and Catholic tradition.[1] Perhaps the single most important element was the Church's failure to abide by scriptural teaching.

This topic can be divided into three basic sections (these are not given in any particular order of importance): 1) historic factors and internal conditions that permitted the rise of the Roman Catholic Church and the papacy—which actually did not occur until the seventh century; 2) key figures historically who guided the church in this direction; and 3) the historical results—the accumulation of authoritative tradition.[2]

We will begin with the historic factors.

The Evolution and Increase in Ecclesiastical Offices

From the simplicity of the biblical deacon and presbyter, which are roughly equivalent, the Church added additional offices including subdeacons, readers, acolytes, and bishops, who became distinguished from presbyters. For example, in A.D. 252, the Roman bishop had 46 presbyters. One Roman bishop, Callistus I, actually said that no presbyter could ever depose a bishop—even if the bishop committed a "mortal" sin. Bishops became subdivided even among themselves. Bishops in the country were held to be inferior to bishops in the city. In capital cities with more than one bishop, one among their number became the head bishop. Thus, in Alexandria 12 bishops convened to elect one superior bishop from among

249

their number. In the fourth century the office of metropolitan was recognized as being superior to the office of bishop.

This growing ecclesiastical hierarchy provided justification for the emerging Roman hierarchical system and for increasing divisions between clergy and laity. The addition of clerical garb also helped to distinguished clergy from laity.

Ironically, the increasing ecclesiastical divisions in the Church undergirded the subsequent Romanization of the Church. Even though the goal itself was laudable (desire for greater visible unity), this demanded an increasing centralization of power that was not biblical.

The historical relationship of this emerging hierarchy to Roman Catholicism can be seen as follows:

Roman Catholicism	Evolving Church
Pope	Patriarch—head over an entire geographical region
Cardinal	Metropolitan—head over several bishops
Bishop	Bishop (subdivision; inferior to metropolitan)
Priest	Presbyter (distinguished from bishop)
The people	The people

The Emergence of a Sacerdotal System

This system was justified from the Old Testament model where the high priest acted as the mediator between God and the people. In essence, the Old Testament high priest, altar, and sacrificial system became replicated in the Roman Church. The priest mediates or officiates between God and the people, the altar separates them, and the elevation and transubstantiation of the host resacrifices (or "re-presents") Christ. Finally, the priest officiates between God and the people through the confessional.

The basis of sacerdotalism is laid in the early Church Fathers. For example, Cyprian (A.D. 200) is considered the "father" of the sacerdotal system. He believed the bishops were the special bearers of the Holy Spirit who, through ordination, was passed on from Christ to the apostles to the bishops. An episcopacy or "rule by bishops" slowly developed through the concept that only those who have had hands laid on them by a bishop are qualified to be in the ministry. Cyprian believed that the Church existed in the bishop and the bishop existed in the Church. Therefore whoever was not with the bishop was not with the Church. Along with other factors, this led to the idea that one had to be within the one true visible Church in order to be saved—to be outside the Church meant to be outside of salvation.

Additional Church Fathers supported similar ideas, including Irenaeus, Tertullian, and Origen. For example, the church was described as being similar to Noah's ark. To be in the ark (the Church) was to be saved from judgment; to be outside was to perish—thus the Church was the safe haven to which the world must flee for salvation.

In the third century the term "priest" was used only for the bishop, not anyone else. But once the idea emerged of a priestly rule (i.e., priests as a special class of people), the biblical teaching of every believer as a priest was eventually undermined (1 Peter 2:5,9, etc.). This had the result of producing further division between clergy and laity. (Something similar occurred with the concept of "saint"; whereas biblically every true believer of every moral or spiritual state is a saint; the term became applied only to certain special people the church recognized for particular reasons; 1 Corinthians 1:2,11; 3:1-3; 6:1,7-8.)

The Concept of Unity

In the second century Irenaeus used the term "Catholic" Church. "Catholic" means "universal." The growing power and influence of the Roman bishop was beginning to be undergirded by a perceived need for visible unity before the world. In other words, the Church believed it should have a united front—and this led increasingly to the acceptance of centralized power.

For example, if Christ actually ruled over the earth, even though He was now in heaven, and if the bishop was the visible symbol of Christ on earth, then on earth the bishop can rule in Christ's place and maintain a position of centralized authority in order to undergird the visible unity of the Church.

Thus, the Church was also coming to be seen as a visible, rather than invisible, entity. While this idea, along with the episcopacy, or government of the Church by bishops, would undergird Church unity, it would also undermine the fact that the true Church is made up of people who are true believers in Jesus Christ, wherever they are—inside or outside a visible church or structure. In other words, the "invisible" church of true believers was starting to be ignored in favor of the visible Church as the true Church.

The Prominence of the Roman Church

The Roman Church had the only patriarch, or bishop of high rank, in the West. All others were in the East—Constantinople, Alexandria, Antioch, etc. This helped Rome to centralize its spiritual power without competition.

Many factors contributed to the prominence of the Roman Church.

1. The city of Rome itself had the prominent position as the capital city, center of trade, etc. It was the most powerful and influential city in the entire Roman empire.

2. The Roman Church, quite in error, claimed Peter as supreme among the apostles. Peter allegedly held a superior position because 1) Jesus Himself supposedly singled him out (Matthew 16:18), 2) Jesus singled out no one besides Peter, and 3) the Roman Church believed that Peter's power and position were transferable to his successors. This is why Roman popes trace their lineage back to the "first" pope, Peter. Just as in the Old Testament the high priest had to be of the tribe of Levi and a descendant of Aaron, so the pope had to be a "descendant" of Peter spiritually by apostolic succession, laying on of hands, etc.

3. Rome claimed it was the only apostolic, ancient Church (actually the Church of Jerusalem was older). Rome also claimed that both the apostle Peter and the apostle Paul were directly associated with it. Since two major apostles were related directly to Rome, Rome was allegedly the superior Church. Paul, at least, was related to the Roman Church—he wrote the book of Romans. But Rome was not perfect: "Rome had a tradition of tolerance for modalist tendencies since the time of Victor [189–98]."[3] But in the midst of persecution she sided with orthodoxy and as such became increasingly respected. Other churches began to acknowledge her superiority—even accepting her rebuke and excommunication for minor issues.

4. The Roman Church was a suffering Church which engaged in good works and had a respectable, caring, orthodox leadership. This also granted the Church favor in the eyes of other churches.

5. The Roman Church so actively shared the gospel that their "faith [was] being reported all over the world" (Romans 1:8).

Many early Church Fathers agreed that Rome was a superior Church. Irenaeus said Rome was among the greatest of churches. There seemed to be a common consensus that Rome was "first among equals," which rather quickly degenerated to simply "first." Roman bishops even claimed supremacy in their own districts. While some like Hippolytus opposed this claim, it was generally accepted.

The Increasing Doubt That Salvation Is by Grace Through Faith Alone

Human nature being what it is, this is not so surprising. That salvation by pure grace is truly revolutionary—and utterly antithetical to fallen human nature—can be seen in two facts: 1) all non-biblical religions in the world, throughout history and today, have taught salvation by works. As Luther once noted, there are really only two religions in the world: the religion of works and the religion of grace; and 2) even the true Church has had to struggle to maintain the gospel of grace. The Catholic Church is proof positive, while Protestantism itself has often accepted forms of salvation by grace/works. For example, many Protestants today—misinformed Evangelicals among them—believe they will get to heaven because they are good people or engage in good works. This is an explicit denial of the gospel of salvation by grace.

Thus, like the ancient Israelites who forgot their God even after their great deliverances through Moses, many of the early Church Fathers quickly forgot that salvation was entirely apart from works. Many came to believe that baptism remits sins and, in logical progression, good works were soon seen as necessary for salvation. Once the biblical teaching of justification by faith alone was increasingly obscured, the door swung open to various views of self-salvation, building brick upon brick for an entire system of salvation by works.

Again, while this evolution was understandable, it was also regrettable in that it laid the foundation for the later complex system of Roman soteriology. As an illustration consider the concept of the martyrs emerging as a special class of people.

The early church was persecuted so heavily that yearly memorials of those martyrs ballooned into an unbiblical system. These commemorations began as mere grave-side services where accounts of their sufferings were read to honor their sacrifice for Christ and to encourage Christians to remain steadfast in their faith. But soon martyrdom itself became 1) a greater Christian virtue, 2) a substitute for baptism, 3) a power to cleanse from sin, and 4) a guarantee of heaven. Origen even ascribed an atoning value to others from a martyr's death. In the end, the clothes, bones, etc., of martyrs became objects of veneration, resulting in another division among the body of Christ: special Christians (martyrs) versus less-special Christians.

The concept of martyrdom became so important that marginal or heretical groups began teaching that backsliders were not permitted into the Church (the Novatians) or that those who gave up their Scriptures in the persecutions committed an unpardonable sin (the Donatists).

Eventually the very idea of ascribing a special status to the martyr meant that there was a certain act one could do which could earn merit before God, thus justifying in part the concepts of penance and indulgences. This was one of many factors which undergirded merit before God on the basis of good works. The veneration of martyrs gave way to veneration of "saints" in general, opposing the biblical teaching that every believer is a saint. Eventually this led to an entire cultic substructure.

The Division of Sin

Another factor was the concept of different categories of sin. This apparently began with the legalistic, ascetic, charismatic Montanists. If some sins were held to cause the loss of salvation and were thus "mortal" or deadly, then less-serious sins were merely "venial" or of secondary importance. If the Church sacraments could also dispense grace, then the sacramental system of Roman Catholicism could be established in which penance was required to forgive mortal sins.

The above constitute some of the historic factors that permitted the rise of the Roman Church to a position of prominence and laid the foundation for the papacy.

Six key figures subsequently built upon that foundation to bring about the concept and reality of the papal office as we find it in the Roman Catholic Church today.

Leo the First (died 461)

Leo was not a pope, but a Roman bishop who served from A.D. 440–461. During the Robber Council (449), Eutychian/monophysite controversy, Leo did everything in his ability to increase the power and control of the Roman bishop in order to more effectively oppose heresy. (The monophysite heresy held that Christ had only a divine nature, downplaying His humanity.)

Thus, Leo was the one who called the great Council of Chalcedon to refute the Eutychian heresy. The result was one of the classic creeds of Christendom which upheld the Nicene Creed (325) and undergirded orthodoxy by declaring that Christ was undiminished deity and full humanity in one Person. Leo's involvement in the council and on the side of orthodoxy increased the power and respect of the Roman bishop. However, it also raised serious questions about the use of political power within the Church.

Gregory the First (540-604)

Also known as Gregory the Great, he served just before and after A.D. 600 (590-604).

Gregory may be considered the first pope. In many respects he was a great man who did many good things. He was a good preacher and teacher and used his gifts in the Church widely. In fact, he sent so many missionaries to England that the country was converted to Christianity. He protected Rome militarily from pagan hordes; he also fed the poor by the thousands.

Although the concept of a universal rule of the Church was repugnant to him when it was first mentioned by an Eastern Constantinople bishop (he called it "antiChrist"), ironically his term and the offices he held greatly undergirded the concept of a papacy. In essence, Gregory was the first to be 1) a bishop of Rome, 2) a metropolitan (over Roman territory), and 3) a patriarch (of Italy, for all the West).

The mere fact that one man held all three offices clearly laid the foundation for the papacy while it also greatly increased Roman power. If the official Roman Catholic Church begins to emerge anywhere, it is here.

Leo the Third (died 816)

Leo the Third served just before and after A.D. 800 (795-816). As evidence of the increasing secular and political power of the

Church, Leo actually crowned Charlemagne as emperor, raising the issue of whether or not any secular ruler or king could be such without the "blessing" of the Church.

Until Hildebrand (Gregory the Seventh) and Henry the Fourth, mutual coronations became the rule, not the exception. Of course, if a king could not be a king without the Church's approval, the ruler of the Church had more power than the state itself. In this respect, Leo the Third was a key ingredient in the union of Church and state.

In between Leo the Third and Gregory the Seventh are found the "Pseudo-isidorian Decretals." These were allegedly written around A.D. 600 and undergirded the primacy of Rome and its papalism. Unfortunately, they were forgeries used for hundreds of years to strengthen papal power, beginning with Nicholas the First around 865. It was not discovered until much later that they were written in the mid ninth century.

Gregory the Seventh (Hildebrand) (1021-1085)

Hildebrand was pope from 1073-85. He reformed the papacy by outlawing corruptions such as simony, and by insisting on the celibacy of the clergy. He also strengthened the Church's power base, which all along had been gathering great influence and wealth from various landholdings, conquests of war, tithings and gifts, etc.

Hildebrand saw the Church as the one visible object with the pope at its head as the "vicar" of Christ. The Church was equivalent to the kingdom of God. To be in the Church was to be saved; to be outside the Church was to be damned. Hildebrand saw the Church as supreme over the state—indeed the Church was the glorious sun while the state was merely the moon which gets its light only from the sun.

Hildebrand instituted what is known as the "Gregorian theocracy." His personal convictions are acted out in his battles with King Henry the Fourth whom he both excommunicated and placed an interdict (a censure of spiritual benefits) on. This meant that Henry could not receive the sacraments and his subjects were no longer duty-bound to obey him. In part, this provided justification for subsequent papal political use of excommunication, and even the use of an interdict against nations.

King Henry did repent—at first. But in 1084 he seized Rome, forcing Gregory to flee, underscoring the problem of Church-state politics.

In between Gregory the Seventh (1025-85) and Innocent the Third (1161-1216), we find the Lateran Council of 1059. This decreed that popes were to be elected by cardinals, from among Roman delegates in Rome. At this point the Church had clearly become the *Roman Catholic Church*.

Innocent the Third (1161-1216)

Innocent the Third ruled as pope from 1198-1216. He represents the height of medieval papal influence and power. Overall, no pope before or after has been more powerful. Innocent believed an interdict could even be placed on nations. He forced King John of England to become his vassal and had Emperor Otto deposed in favor of Frederick II. During his reign we have the Magna Carta battle with King John and the Fourth Lateran Council (1215). This council:

1. Began the Inquisition.
2. Forbade monastic orders.
3. Held that membership in the visible Church was necessary for salvation.
4. Declared the transubstantiation dogma.
5. Declared yearly confessions mandatory.
6. Instituted a crusade against the Turks for the Holy Land.

But the papal office also began degenerating here. The Crusades were ever less popular, indulgences and papal dispensations for money caused endless amounts of corruption and evil, as did the Inquisition. Relatives could be bought out of purgatory, while neighbor turned against neighbor as land could be received as payment for reporting "heretics." Taxes on bishops and churches also became oppressive. From this point on, papal authority was destined to decline.

Boniface the Eighth (1235-1303)

Boniface the Eighth ruled just before and after 1300 (1294-1303). He steadfastly asserted papal authority over European leaders and issued the *Unam Sanctam*, which was the highest expression of papal authority, going so far as to claim temporary papal rule over nations. This led to conflict with Philip IV of France and Boniface's eventual death.

Papal degeneration continued. The rise of separate states and rebellion within the Church, leading to sects and "heretical" pre-Reformation groups such as the Waldensians, eventually culminated in the Reformation wherein Martin Luther not only nailed his historic Ninety-Five Theses on the cathedral door, but he enunciated the doctrine of salvation by grace through faith *alone* declaring it to be the central dogma upon which the Christian Church stands or falls.

In conclusion, the Reformation had begun, but Rome still retained its power. It instituted certain reforms and solidified what remained through the Council of Trent and the Counter-Reformation. From the above discussion the reader can at least see the outlines of how the Catholic Church developed and the process by which unbiblical teachings could be added on the basis of Church authority.

Examples of how such tradition actually works to deny what the Protestant Bible teaches are seen in the following list of Catholic dogmas and practices that have no biblical justification (as even some Catholics confess), and yet most are accepted as having divine authority.

Authoritative Tradition

Collectively these dates are given by several sources, are approximate, and refer to the time such practices were either 1) first introduced, 2) formulated, 3) adopted by council, or 4) proclaimed by a pope.[4]

> 310 — Prayers for the dead began.
>
> 375 — The worship of saints.
>
> 394 — The Mass was adopted.
>
> 431 — The worship of Mary began to develop, although it was not popularized for 350 years.
>
> 593 — The doctrine of purgatory was introduced.
>
> 606 — Claims to papal supremacy took root.
>
> 650 — Feasts in honor of the Virgin Mary started.
>
> 750 — The pope first assumed temporal power.
>
> 787 — The worship of images and relics was introduced.
>
> 819 — The first observance of the Feast of Assumption began.

850 — The invention of holy water.

965 — The blessing of the bells.

983 — The canonization of saints was formulated.

998 — Lent, Advent, and abstinence from meat on Friday.

1003 — Feasts for the dead were introduced.

1074 — The celibacy of the priesthood was asserted.

1076 — The doctrine of papal infallibility was first announced [or suggested].

1090 — The use of prayer beads (cf. the Rosary).

1115 — Confession was instituted.

1140 — The doctrine of seven sacraments was introduced.

1190 — The sale of indulgences started.

1215 — The dogma of transubstantiation was adopted by Pope Innocent III

1216 — The acceptance of auricular confession of sins to a priest.

1220 — Holy water accepted.

1226 — The elevation and adoration of the wafer began.

1274 — Purgatory was declared doctrine at the Second Council of Lyons.

1303 — The Roman Catholic Church was proclaimed as the only true Church where salvation can be found.

1316 — The Ave Maria was introduced.

1414–15 — The declaration that only priests could say the Mass and partake of the wine.

1438–39 — Purgatory and the seven sacraments were officially decreed by the Council of Florence.

1546 — Roman tradition and the Apocrypha were officially placed on the same level as Scripture by the Council of Trent.

1547–62 — Trent officially rejected justification by faith alone and upheld salvation by faith-works.

1562 — The Mass was declared a propitiatory offering.

1854 — The immaculate conception of the Virgin Mary was announced by Pius IX.

1864 — The doctrine of the temporal power of the pope was proclaimed.

1870 — Papal infallibility was proclaimed at Vatican I.

1950 — The bodily assumption and personal corporeal presence of the Virgin in heaven was proclaimed by Pope Pius XII.

Perhaps the above list makes it easier to understand why many of these unbiblical doctrines and practices—for the very reason they were unscriptural—were added to the Church in the midst of debate among Catholic scholars and laymen themselves.

These traditional teachings slowly crept into the Catholic Church over hundreds of years—but again, not infrequently without dissension by Catholic scholars themselves. For example, at the Council of Trent not all participants thought it credible that the Apocrypha was Scripture. Nacchianti and Bonuccio even rejected the idea that tradition held equal weight with Scripture.[5]

At Vatican I not all believed the pope should be considered infallible, nor did all accept the idea of Mary's immaculate conception.[6]

At Vatican II the bodily assumption of Mary was contested and the notion that Scripture and tradition had equal authority as divine revelation also endured great debate.[7]

It would seem that the longer the passage of time, the more difficult it became to adopt a new doctrine that the Church had already somehow failed to recognize for hundreds of years.

In conclusion, the history of the Roman Catholic Church proves that both doctrine and tradition can be corrupted and that only God's Word is an adequate standard to keep them pure. Otherwise, it is perilously easy for sinful human tendencies to undermine either.

APPENDIX C

What Does Rome Think of Evangelicals?

Rome no longer has the power it once had over Protestants. Yet because it still assumes the role of the only true Church on earth, it still hopes to wield its influence. In part, the recent dialogues could seem to be one attempt to secure such effect. The modern Catholic Church views Evangelicals as "separated brethren" who, at best, have been spiritually misled into abandoning the one true Church of Christ. For example, *The Catholic Encyclopedia* teaches that Rome considers Protestants as those who revolt against "discipline and authority."[1]

Because of Rome's assumption that it alone is the one true Church, Catholicism feels bound to reform Protestants so that they will see the error of their ways. In part, this is why Catholicism emphasizes that "All heresies are against the unity of the Church."[2] Thus, although many Catholics attempt to seek reconciliation with Protestants and unite with their alleged brethren, this is often an attempt merely to bring them into the Catholic fold. As indicated earlier, a good example of this is Keith A. Fournier's *Evangelical Catholics*.

Yet while offering the hand of friendship, numerous articles in Catholic magazines have condescendingly ridiculed Evangelicalism, such as "Fundamentalists [Evangelicals] Give the Bible a Bad Name" in *US Catholic* for April 1980 and in "Fundamentalism: A Pastoral Concern" published in *The Bible Today* for January 1983. The latter article by Fr. Eugene LaVerdiere, associate professor of New Testament theology at the Catholic Theological Union in Chicago, states the following about Evangelical faith:

> Fundamentalism has long been associated with a number of Protestant groups . . . some of which are large

evangelical churches. . . . In recent years fundamentalism has been making significant inroads in the Roman
Catholic Church, not that we have ever been altogether
free of it.

[Fundamentalism] is primarily a pastoral problem. . . .
[It is also] a social problem, and we should respond to it
with the same breadth of vision which we bring to other
social problems.

. . . The temptation to raise our voices or to ridicule is
strong. Our best response . . . is not a biblical argument
but the strength of faith.[3]

Increasing Threat?

As hundreds of thousands of Catholics have left the Church for
biblical and not Catholic faith, the Church has felt itself increasingly
threatened. This has resulted in some Catholics engaging in verbal
attacks and even physical persecution of Christians—sometimes,
it would seem, with papal sanction. In fact, the popes have characteristically been pristine examples of those who oppose biblical
faith. For example, when John Paul II prayed before millions on
television for the Polish strikers in August 1980, to whom did he
pray? He did not pray to Jesus; rather, he prayed to Mary. And in a
direct rejection of Christian ethical teaching, when in Guatemala,
Mexico, he apparently did nothing to hinder Catholic attacks on
Evangelicals. He even went further and forcefully rejected biblical
faith publicly when he emphasized that "man is justified by works
and not by faith alone."[4]

In a 1991 visit to Brazil, Pope John Paul II also spoke of "nesting
perils" and warned Catholics about "Evangelical sects."[5]

The 1994 "Evangelicals and Catholics Together" declaration spoke
of the animosity and "violent conflict" (pp. 3, 13) of Evangelicals
and Catholics against one another in various places around the
world. But is it the Evangelical church which is really at fault? Hasn't
Rome persecuted Evangelicals throughout history, while Evangelical sins in this regard have been almost nonexistent by comparison?
Consider some illustrations.

Coauthor John Weldon has missionary friends in Mexico. Here,
Evangelical faith is not only assailed, it is even suppressed by the
Catholic Church. For example, for many years Evangelical radio

programs have not been permitted. Catholic bishops themselves may identify Christian faith as "cultic" and "evil"—even teaching that Evangelical Christians should be expelled from Mexico. The Catholic Church has also attacked Evangelicals in the press referring to them as sects, CIA agents, and destroyers of the natural culture. In 1992, after petitioning the Vatican, a new diocese in Tlapa was established specifically "to counteract the influence of Protestantism" in the southwestern Mexico region. As the apostolic delegate to Mexico, Archbishop Girolamo Prigione, was quoted as saying, "The sects are like flies."[6]

In addition, *Moody Monthly* reports there have been "shameful attacks" by Catholics on Wycliffe Bible Translators.[7]

When Catholic leaders stir up animosity or malign biblical faith as a spiritual and social evil to the laity, perhaps they should not be surprised at the consequences. For example, in 1992 over 50 Christians were wounded as the Catholic majority in San Cristobal, Las Casas, Chiapas, attempted to throw them out of town. Throughout Mexico, every year Evangelicals residing among a Catholic majority are actually killed for their faith in Christ.[8]

In fact, it seems that wherever Catholicism has been the dominant religion in a given nation, Evangelicals seem to have suffered for it: "Evangelical churches have often been oppressed and marginalized in the exercise of their religion and in their civil rights."[9]

In March 1994, Catholic Bishop Sinealo Bohn declared the following at the thirty-first National Conference of Bishops of Brazil: "We will declare a holy war; don't doubt it. . . . The Catholic Church has a ponderous structure, but when we move, we'll smash anyone beneath us."

The article reporting on the priest's comments noted the following,

> According to Bohn, an all-out holy war can't be avoided unless the 13 largest Protestant churches and denominations sign a treaty—similar to treaties signed by nations to end wars. He said it would require Protestants to stop all evangelism efforts in Brazil. In exchange, he said, Catholics would agree to stop all persecution directed toward Protestants. Bohn called his proposal an "ultimatum," and said it would leave no room for discussion [10]

In March 1994 the Associated Press reported on the publication of a 130-page Vatican document, "The Interpretation of the Bible in the Church" and it noted the following:

> A new Vatican document on how to interpret the Bible condemns the fundamentalist approach as distorting, dangerous and possibly leading to racism. . . . The . . . harsh language reflects the challenge that fundamentalism poses to the Church. . . . Fundamentalism actually invites people to a kind of "intellectual suicide," said the document, written by the Pontifical Biblical Commission. . . . The authors save their harshest language for Christian fundamentalist denominations. . . . The fundamentalist approach is dangerous, for it is attractive to people who look to the Bible for ready answers to the problems of life.[11]

In his critique of "Evangelicals and Catholics Together," Larry Holly, M.D., president of the Baptist "Mission and Ministry to Men, Inc.," referred to "the national Catholic Conference of Bishops warning to Roman Catholics that they must beware of fundamentalist Christians who are trying to 'get them born again.' . . . [Further,] there have been increasing efforts on the part of the Roman Catholic hierarchy to limit contact between 'born-again fundamentalists' and Roman Catholic laity."[12]

He then points out what could easily be assumed as one motive for the Catholic participation in the "cooperation" declarations such as that released in 1994: "What the Roman Catholics seem to want from this document is to have evangelicals accept them as Christian so that evangelicals will not feel the imperative for witnessing to Roman Catholics."[13]

All this at least is consistent with the actions of Rome historically. We should never forget that the Catholic Church has frequently kept the Bible out of the hands of the common people:

> Seventy-five years ago, in the United States, the cardinals and bishops who reigned in the Roman Catholic Church declared that it was against the wishes of the Church that the people should have the Bible, and that they should be instructed solely by the priest. The pages of Catholic literature one hundred years ago confirms this beyond dispute.[14]

Persecutions Then and Now

During and since the Reformation, Rome has openly persecuted Christians. (The Spanish Inquisition, although distinct from the papal institution, was not dissolved until 1820.) It is a sad commentary on Catholicism, which claims to be the true Church of Christ, that throughout history hundreds of thousands of Protestants died at the hands of Catholics. The Crusades may have been directed against the Muslims, but the Inquisition was directed against the "heretics"—principally the Protestant Reformers.

Given the power and image of the modern Catholic Church, it is easy to forget the persecutions of the past:

> One thinks immediately of the Inquisitions (Roman, Medieval and Spanish) which for centuries held Europe in their terrible grip. Canon Llorente, who was the Secretary to the Inquisition in Madrid from 1790-92 and had access to the archives of all the tribunals, estimated that in Spain alone the number of condemned exceeded 3 million with about 300,000 burned at the stake....

> Do not forget that the Church has never officially admitted that these practices were evil, nor apologized to the world or to any of the victims or their descendants. Nor could John Paul II apologize today because "the doctrines responsible for those terrible things still underpin his position."

> "Christian" Rome has slaughtered many times the number of both Christians and Jews that pagan Rome did. Beside those victims of the Inquisitions, there were Huguenots, Albigenses, Waldenses and other Christians, massacred, tortured and burned at the stake by the hundreds of thousands simply because they refused to align themselves with the Roman Catholic Church....

> Why should Rome apologize for or even admit this holocaust? No one calls her to account today. Protestants have forgotten and evangelical leaders join Rome to evangelize together. They don't want to hear any "negative" reminders of the millions tortured and slain by the Church to which they now pay homage, or the fact that Rome has a false gospel of sacramental works.[15]

Even today the Catholic Church has never repudiated the curses pronounced on biblical faith by the Council of Trent. Thus, at least officially, Protestantism remains condemned by Catholicism as heresy.[16]

This may explain why, according to *The Catholic Encyclopedia*, the Church forbids Catholics to read certain books that are considered "gravely dangerous to one's faith or morals."[17] This includes certain non-Catholic versions of the Bible, books written by non-Catholics on the subject of religion, and books that "attack Catholic dogma or the hierarchy or defend errors condemned by the Holy See."[18] Keating tells his Catholic readers, "You'll do yourself a disservice if you rely upon any translation not approved by the Church."[19]

If the Catholic Church rejects all "private judgment" of the Bible by its own members, it is at least consistent to reject "private judgment" outside the Church. In other words, Catholics who wish to obey their Church would even be forbidden to read this book, since it "defends errors" condemned by the pope such as salvation by grace through faith alone.

Whether all this is in the best interests of the Church is for individual Catholics to decide.

How Far Has Roman Catholic Doctrine Deviated from Biblical Theology?

Theology is the study of God. Theology begins with God, leads to God, speaks of God, and glorifies God. This majestic discipline teaches us about God, what He is like, what He has revealed, what He has done in history, and what He expects of us. In all the world, there is no greater study for the Christian. Because theology teaches us about God and leads us to understand Him better, it should be loved and honored by every believer in Christ.[1]

Perhaps the single largest tragedy of the modern church, Protestant or Catholic, and the single greatest loss for the individual Christian is the lack of discipline in studying systematic and biblical theology.

How does Roman Catholicism relate to biblical theology? In this section we are going to briefly examine several key doctrines which further document the teaching of the Roman Catholic Church in relation to Scripture. The major broad areas of theology include the following:

Bibliology	The doctrine of the Bible
Theology Proper	The doctrine of God (Theism, Trinitarianism)
Angelology	The doctrine of angels
Anthropology	The doctrine of man
Harmartiology	The doctrine of sin
Ecclesiology	The doctrine of the Church
Christology	The doctrine of Christ

Pneumatology	The doctrine of the Holy Spirit
Eschatology	The doctrine of last things
Soteriology	The doctrine of salvation

In all of the above categories, Roman Catholic teaching histori-cally (to one degree or another) has distorted these key theological doctrines. To the observer having only a general familiarity with Catholic teaching and conservative Protestant theology, this may not at first seem evident. Yet, it would be possible to write an entire text on each one of the above doctrines revealing how Catholicism has distorted what the Bible teaches on these subjects—either through tradition, its approach to biblical interpretation, or other means.

In other words, whatever truths Catholicism may teach in theol-ogy generally, serious errors are also encountered. We can see this, in theology proper (the Catholic Church as the continuing incarna-tion of Christ); in bibliology (tradition as revelation; the Apoc-rypha); in ecclesiology (Catholicism as the only true Church of Christ); in harmartiology (aspects of pelagianism; mortal and venial categories); in Christology (Mariology; the Church as continuing incarnation; the Mass); and in soteriology (Catholic teaching on justification, sanctification, regeneration, and the sacraments).

No single doctrine is more important to each of us personally than the doctrine of salvation. In examining the component parts of the biblical portrait of salvation, we find the following:

1. *Depravity*—the spiritual condition of man before God.

2. *Imputation*—to reckon sin or righteousness to another's account.

3. *Grace*—the fact of God's nature making Him spontaneously favorable in His dealings with man.

4. *Propitiation*—the satisfaction of God's justice and righteous-ness through the atonement of Jesus Christ.

5. *Atonement*—the vicarious (substitutionary), efficacious (pro-ducing the desired effect) death of Christ for human sin.

6. *Reconciliation*—to restore to fellowship with God by remov-ing the barriers preventing this.

7. *Calling (efficacious)*—the work of God drawing men to Him-self.

8. *Regeneration*—the miraculous work of God making the human spirit alive to Himself and the imparting of eternal life to the individual believer.

9. *Union with Christ*—the spiritually living union of the believer and Jesus Christ.

10. *Conversion*—the human side of regeneration; turning to Christ in faith and repentance (leading to a change in both attitude and behavior).

11. *Repentance*—changing one's mind (mental) and turning from sin (behavioral) (i.e., a change of attitude and action).

12. *Faith*—trust in God, leading to right belief about Him, dependence upon Him, and right behavior toward Him.

13. *Justification*—the forensic or legal declaration of God concerning the believer's absolute righteousness before Him as a result of his faith in Jesus Christ.

14. *Adoption*—to be brought into the personal family of God.

15. *Sanctification*—to be set apart to God's purposes (i.e., growth in relationship to and holiness toward God).

16. *Eternal security*—the absolute security of the true believer with respect to his salvation from the point of regeneration.

17. *Perseverance*—the continuation of the saints in faith until death.

18. *Election/predestination*—to be chosen by God for salvation.

19. *Redemption*—to remove one from slavery to sin and Satan by payment of a ransom (i.e., the atonement of Christ).

20. *Death, resurrection, and the final state*—involving the physical/spiritual nature of death, the intermediate state, resurrection of the body, immortality, heaven and hell (the physical resurrection of the believer to eternal glory and the unbeliever to eternal ruin).

21. *The church*—the collective body of true believers called out of the world by God for His glory who are joined together visibly in worship and invisibly in union with Christ and one another.

Again, if we were to examine each of the above doctrines in detail, examining what the Bible teaches about them on the one hand and what Catholic tradition/doctrine teaches about them on the other, we would discover that Roman Catholicism has denied, altered, or confused all but one or two.

It is in light of our study of such theology that we find it most difficult to reconcile the current movement on the part of many Catholics and Evangelicals to join themselves together as spiritual brothers and sisters in Jesus Christ. For their part, Evangelicals characteristically maintain that they are not abandoning or glossing over important differences in doctrine between orthodox Catholicism and conservative Protestantism; they merely want to stress the unity of the true church, whether Catholic or Protestant. The problem, however, is that if we are not going to gloss over important doctrinal differences, then it becomes impossible to maintain that Catholics and Protestants are genuine brothers and sisters in Christ.

Again, this is not to deny that many Catholics, individually speaking, are saved individuals because they have placed true faith in Jesus Christ and trust in Him alone for salvation—not in their good works, the sacraments, or the Church. The problem arises when we say that all those committed to the traditional orthodox doctrines of the Catholic Church are saved individuals just as much as the simple believer in Jesus Christ. If so, it would seem that what an individual believes (i.e., whether it is either Catholic or Protestant teaching), has little or no bearing as to his individual salvation. But to say this is to abandon biblical authority and teaching entirely.

The bottom line is this: It is virtually impossible to claim to maintain important doctrinal distinctions on the one hand and to simultaneously unite Catholic and Protestant believers into a spiritual fellowship on the other.

We can illustrate this by examining the following five doctrines and considering briefly how each doctrine relates to Catholic teaching:

> *Propitiation/atonement.* This doctrine demonstrates that the death of Christ fully propitiated or satisfied God's wrath and paid the full divine penalty for all the believer's sin past, present, and future, thereby proving that neither the sacraments, penance, purgatorial suffering, indulgences, the Mass, priests, nor any other aspect of the Catholic Church is involved in any way in the propitiation or remitting of sin.
>
> *Reconciliation.* This doctrine involves one result of the death of Christ for sin wherein the state of enmity between God and

man is replaced by one of peace and fellowship, proving that final reconciliation between God and man is something accomplished by God on behalf of man, not by the Church on behalf of man.

Regeneration. This doctrine involves the making alive of the human spirit toward God and the imparting of eternal life, proving that true spiritual life is eternal and a miracle of God, not something instituted by the Church through sacraments or good works.

Justification. This doctrine constitutes the legal declaration of the believer's absolute righteousness before God on the basis of his personal faith in Jesus Christ, proving that our perfect standing before God is not dependent upon Church teaching, sacraments, personal character, or good works, but solely upon our faith in Christ.

Sanctification. This doctrine involves being set apart to God for His glory. A correct understanding of its past, present, and future applications proves that sanctification does not lead to justification, nor should it be confused with regeneration, as Catholicism teaches.

A brief evaluation of the above doctrines illustrates our central concern: As a result of its tradition and/or interpretation of Scripture, the Catholic approach to biblical doctrine is characteristically colored in a nonbiblical fashion.

Finally, in brief response to those who argue that the subject of theology/doctrine is either "divisive" (something that divides rather than unites the Church) or that it is something really not taught in the Bible and that Christians should simply unite and "love one another" but not discuss doctrine, we mention the following three points.

First, historically, theology is something that has united the true church in common confession, and not something that has divided it. Theology only becomes divisive when unbelievers or schismatics in the church refuse to accept what the Bible clearly teaches, or when theology itself becomes dry, academic intellectualism, or when theological positions are carved out and made tests of orthodoxy when Scripture itself is not clear on such a position. But none of these are the fault of theology itself—only of the people who are perverting it for their own purposes. In essence, if the church does not identify itself by what it believes (doctrine), it is impossible to identify what it means to be a Christian.

Second, anyone who takes the time to examine all the biblical usages of the word "doctrine" in the New Testament will prove personally that God is very much concerned about correct doctrine. Therefore, His people should be also. For example, "Reprove, rebuke, exhort, with great patience and instruction. For the time will come when they will not endure sound doctrine. . . . Exhort in sound doctrine and . . . refute those who contradict. . . . Speak the things which are fitting for sound doctrine" (2 Timothy 4:2,3; Titus 1:9; 2:1 NASB).

All doctrine is, is biblical truth. Because God is a God of truth who has honored His name by revealing the truths of doctrine to us, God's people should also honor correct doctrine in their own lives.

Third, the following example from the book of Ephesians could be duplicated from most books in the New Testament. This proves that doctrine is a major component of biblical teaching and something that cannot be ignored by any Christian who loves God's Word. Notice how many doctrines are covered in the first chapter of Ephesians alone (additional references from later chapters are sometimes added):

Ephesians

> 1:1 —*union with Christ* (1:3,4,7,10,13,22,23; 2:6,7,13,15,21; 4:5; 5:8,30)
>
> 1:2 —*grace* (1:6,7; 2:5,7,8; 3:2,7,8; 4:7; 6:24)
>
> 1:2 —*reconciliation* (2:14-17; 3:12; 6:15,23)
>
> 1:4 —*election* (1:5,11)
>
> 1:4 —*sanctification* (2:10; 3:17; 4:1-3,12-16,22-25; 5:1; 6:18).
>
> 1:4 —*glorification*
>
> 1:5 —*adoption*
>
> 1:7 —*redemption* (1:14; 4:30)
>
> 1:7 —*propitiation* (2:13,16; 4:32; 5:2,25)
>
> 1:7 —*atonement* (2:13,16; 4:32; 5:2,25)
>
> 1:11 —*eternal security* (1:14)
>
> 1:12 —*glorification* (5:27)
>
> 1:13 —*conversion* (faith and repentance)
>
> 1:13 —*sealing* (4:30)

1:15 — *faith* (1:19; 2:8; 4:5,13; 6:16)

1:18 — *calling*

1:20 — *resurrection* (4:8,10)

1:22 — *the church* (2:14,16,19-22; 3:10; 5:23-29,32)

2:1-3 — *depravity* (2:5; 2:12; 4:17-19; 5:8)

2:5 — *regeneration* (2:10; 3:16; 4:24)

6:14 — *justification*

6:18 — *perseverance*

As the above illustration reveals, it is incorrect for anyone to argue that theology/doctrine is irrelevant to New Testament study and the individual Christian life.

APPENDIX E

Internal Fomentation in the Catholic Church: How Rome Has Changed and Not Changed

All of us have experienced change in our lives. We know from experience that change can be either good or bad depending upon the circumstances and its outcome. But most of us just do not like change. As the American bureaucrat Frederick Hayes once noted in *Fortune* magazine, "There is no way you can make people like change. You can only make them feel less threatened by it."

When the news release concerning the Evangelical/Catholic declaration of cooperation and agreement was broadcast around the world, some commentators implied that Catholics had actually changed their doctrine. But others thought just the opposite—that the Protestants had actually changed theirs. Everyone else wondered what really did happen—and was it really of any significance?

We will here attempt to show how the winds of change are blowing more than ever before and are making some people uncomfortable.

Do We Now Agree on a Common Faith?

As we have seen, a number of recent affirmations by Protestants and Catholics have said that they do agree on key issues and that they have simply agreed to disagree on certain other doctrines, but still to be united as brothers and sisters in Christ. For example, in chapters 12 and 13 we evaluated the recent report which confesses both sides found disagreement on such things as Scripture, Bible interpretation, tradition, and even salvation, but then it concluded that there was still enough agreement to recognize "Catholics and Evangelicals as brothers and sisters in Christ."[1]

Without explanation it declared that both Catholics and Evangelicals share:

> ... the faith that we affirm together;[2]

> ... our unity in the love of Christ;[3] and that

> This is a time of opportunity—and ... of responsibility—for Evangelicals and Catholics to be Christians together.[4]

The statement also recognized:

> Much more important, we thank God for the discovery of one another as brothers and sisters in Christ. Our cooperation as citizens is animated by our convergence as Christians. We promise one another that we will work to deepen, build upon, and expand this pattern of convergence and cooperation.[5]

Other Catholic/Protestant dialogue groups have announced similar agreement. As we saw, "The U.S. Lutheran-Roman Catholic Dialogue Group on Justification by Faith" claimed that a "fundamental consensus on the gospel"[6] had been achieved. In addition, their 24,000-word document "constitute[d] a very significant agreement"[7] and claimed that "today...a far reaching consensus is developing in the interpretation of justification."[8] (We evaluated the claims made by this group in chapter 18.) In its December 16, 1983, issue, *Christianity Today* also referred to "dramatic" agreements between Roman Catholics and Lutherans.

Recently, a third major example of dialogue and/or the search for a common faith is the Anglican-Roman Catholic International Commission which sought to help unify Protestants and Catholics. This was also true of the Baptist/Roman Catholic International Conversation (1988) and the Malta Report of the International Lutheran-Catholic Study Commission.

All of the statements found in these agreements recognized by Catholic scholars might lead one to believe that there must be real change taking place in Catholicism. But is this the case?

How Much Is Rome Willing to Change?

According to the documents of Vatican II, the Catholic Church continues to maintain that it is the only true Church and it alone offers the fullness of salvation:

> Nevertheless, our separated brethren [the Protestants], whether considered as individuals or as Communities and Churches, are not blessed with that unity which Jesus Christ wished to bestow on all those whom He has regenerated and vivified into one body and newness of life—that unity which the holy Scriptures and the revered tradition of the Church proclaim.

> For it is through Christ's Catholic Church alone, which is the all-embracing means of salvation, that the fullness of the means of salvation can be obtained.

> It was to the apostolic college alone, of which Peter is the head, that we believe our Lord entrusted all the blessings of the New Covenant, in order to establish on earth the one Body of Christ into which all those should be fully incorporated who already belong in any way to God's people.[9]

Catholic lay apologist and theologian Karl Keating confesses, "The Catholic Church did not change any of its doctrines at Trent and it did not change any at Vatican II"[10] and "there has been no alteration at all in basic doctrines. . . . The Catholic Church is still the sole true Church."[11]

A recent Evangelical Council on Catholicism likewise concluded, "There are many indications that Rome is fundamentally the same as it has always been."[12]

A former Carmelite priest observed, "Vatican II made no doctrinal changes. . . . There was a change of image, but no change of substance."[13] In 1964 no less an authority than Pope Paul VI himself affirmed that "nothing really changes in the traditional doctrine."[14]

Others have written: "Roman Catholicism does not change. At heart, it is the same as it ever was."[15]

The Internal Fomentation Within Roman Catholicism

Paradoxically, one cannot fully understand modern Roman Catholicism unless one realizes that Rome is not entirely what it used to be. There is an internal fomentation within Catholicism taking place as a result of Vatican II, as well as the influence of modern culture upon the Church. This can be seen everywhere. The February 4, 1985, cover issue of *Time* magazine headlined, "Discord in the Church," while the cover article noted, "Rome must decide what is Catholic and what is not."

Catholic apologists frequently point out that the alleged "Achilles' heel" of Protestantism is its lack of central ecclesiastical teaching authority and resultant splintering into a hundred different denominations based on the "private" interpretation of Scripture.[16] But in many ways Roman Catholicism has now become much like its so-called "separated brethren," the Protestant churches.

In the words of one editorial, it is "a vast Noah's Ark of beasts, clean and unclean."[17] Even the power and authority of the pope is failing to keep unity within Catholicism today:

> This argument [papal infallibility] has boomeranged today as Rome is herself obviously divided. Possession of one who is claimed to be the infallible guide has not led to a condition in which unity in the faith is the hallmark, for the guide himself is assailed by dissident voices who, while claiming to accept his guidance, insist on interpreting his statements even if he himself rejects their interpretation! The debate over the papal encyclical on birth control, *Humanae Vitae*, is a recent illustration of this.[18]

Part of the fomentation seen in Catholicism today is the result of the changes made at Vatican II. For example, salvation is now possible outside the Catholic Church—a teaching Rome had formerly rejected for hundreds of years as heretical.

Vatican II also instituted significant nondoctrinal (ecclesiastical) change, and its overall conclusions implied significant hermeneutical (interpretative) alterations that could call into question even traditional doctrine.

But ironically, a key problem in Catholic interpretation is ascertaining where infallibility can be found. In other words, who infallibly interprets the documents of Vatican II and other official Church pronouncements, and how can such determinations objectively be established as infallible?

In the minds of many, sufficient elasticity now exists to allow fundamental doctrinal change—at least for those who wish it. That is why some Catholic theologians have accommodated Vatican II to traditional orthodoxy while others have used Vatican II to forge new doctrinal perspectives.

The problem is illustrated in the following analysis which, written seven years after Vatican II, points out the continuing evolution of Rome and the difficulty it raises:

> The task of interpreting the Roman Catholic mind is difficult. Cardinal Newman once remarked that "none but the *Scola Theologorum* is competent to determine the force of Papal and Synodal utterances, and the exact interpretation of them is a work of time." But even with the passage of time, nuances and implications still elude the most diligent analysts, especially if they are Protestant. Despite this, at least the main lines of the new Catholic theology seem clear, and they are certainly quite different from those of traditional orthodoxy. Says Gregory Baum:
>
> > A conservative outlook on the magisterium and the conservative claim that church teaching never changes simply cannot explain what happened at Vatican II. After all, at that council, the Catholic Church, formally, solemnly, and after a considerable conflict, changed her mind on a number of significant issues.[19]

This means that Protestant evaluation of Catholic doctrine has been made a bit more difficult by the changes of Vatican II. As Protestant theologian Millard J. Erickson observes in *Christian Theology:*

> [Examining Catholic theology] is difficult because, whereas at one time there was a uniform, official position within Roman Catholicism on most issues, now there appears to be only great diversity. Official doctrinal standards still remain, but they are now supplemented, and in some cases are seemingly contradicted, by later statements. Among these later statements are the conclusions of the Second Vatican Council and the published opinions of individual Catholic scholars.[20]

But in spite of these "winds of change" and the resulting fomentation that is occurring, no one should doubt that official doctrinal standards do remain. To accept the authority of Rome is to accept the official doctrines in spite of any interpretive problems or implications of Vatican II, and whether or not individual Catholics accept them. We might want to say that unity of doctrine is legitimate when considered from a *Roman* perspective, even if not always from a *Catholic* perspective.

Thus, as a result of the complex and disquieting forces operating on Rome today, Roman Catholicism is now evolving more toward subjectivism, mysticism, theological universalism, and ecumenism; more toward concern with people's authority than papal authority; more toward concern with the infallibility of religious experience than the infallibility of Scripture; more toward concern with higher critical methods for evaluating biblical content than biblical content itself. This is clearly seen in John Paul II's book *Crossing the Threshold of Hope* (1994).

Rome's Shift from Objective Facts to Subjective Experience

This shift toward subjectivism explains the degree of confusion and divergence one finds in Roman Catholicism as a whole. We think that the following comments by Church historian Dr. David Wells bear out our analysis. In a paper titled, "The Long Winter of Wreckage,"[21] Dr. Wells points out: "However turbulent the post-conciliar days have been," in effect they are only "the Indian Summer which has preceded a long winter of wreckage."

> When the storms break and the old moorings finally snap, Evangelicals will want to be able to show Christ's compassion to those who have been abandoned and battered. To do so they must have a new apologetic.[22]

What changes does Dr. Wells want Evangelicals to be aware of in their study of modern Catholic thought? We quote from his analysis of Vatican II:

> The Catholic Church . . . has embarked on a process of theological reconstruction. . . . The emphasis is being shifted away from outward and visible ecclesiastical structure to the inward and invisible spiritual experience of its members. . . . The old dictum that salvation cannot be secured outside the Church has been repudiated.

> Sincere religious experience, either inside or outside the Church, is considered to be salvific [*Con. LG*, 9]. . . . Even an atheist may be secretly moved by grace to find salvation. The Council nowhere insisted that this atheist must rescind his atheism in favor of an explicit theism before salvation can take place. . . .

> The Second Vatican Council has deliberately attempted to reverse the last three centuries of its history. . . . As the emphasis has shifted away from outward Church structure to its inward spiritual reality, the people are rapidly replacing the Pope in importance.[23]

The truth of Dr. Wells' assessment can be verified by observing that the constitution on the Church from Vatican I contained four chapters "all of which were concerned with the Pope";[24] however, the corresponding document from Vatican II had eight chapters, but only one dealt with the pope.

Further, there was a strong emphasis placed on "the people's role in the formation of doctrine. The former doctrine of the Pope's infallibility has been matched, in the documents of Vatican II, by a corresponding infallibility which has been ascribed to the people [*Con. LG*, 25, 49]."[25]

This continuing change in emphasis from the objective to the subjective has also resulted in a new approach toward Scripture. For example, it has led to the acceptance of higher criticism:

> The New Catholicism has moved away from the notion of an objective revelation given in Scripture (and tradition) to that of a subjective revelation given in experience [*Con. DV*, 2, 8]. . . . The predominance of the subjective over the objective in this conception is strongly reminiscent of Schleiermacher's theology. Consequently, Catholic biblical scholars are rapidly establishing a new relationship with non-evangelical Protestant scholars. Catholic scholars are freeing themselves from the innumerable commitments which the Church has made on the matter of an inerrant Scripture and are busy immersing themselves in Protestant critical scholarship. . . . The infallibility of the Bible need not be defined in terms of its propositional form. The notion of infallibility properly belongs to the moment of encounter between man and

God's Spirit in which the Bible is instrumental. The Bible, then, is not infallible but religious experience is.[26]

An example of the Church's acceptance of higher criticism can be seen in the Vatican document released March 18, 1994, titled, "The Interpretation of the Bible in the Church," which officially accepts higher critical methods—and castigates Evangelical reliance on a literal approach to Scripture as "naive" and as "a kind of intellectual suicide."[27]

Still, paradoxically, both Scripture and tradition were upheld by Vatican II as "one sacred deposit of the Word of God,"[28] even though the interpreters have become more enmeshed in the subjective. Thus, "Both Scripture and tradition are the outward records of the same inward religious experience. There is no generic difference between them; Scripture is merely the first chapter in a long history of tradition."[29]

In summary, the new emphasis upon the subjective has brought Catholicism more problems than it can solve. First, it "has subjugated the Church, the Pope, the Bible and tradition to the vagaries of a shifting and blurred religious experience."[30]

Second, with the subjective religious experience of God becoming paramount, it is difficult to deny claimed religious experiences with God among the faiths of other people. If one does not have an objective standard by which to appeal, it is easier to conclude salvation can be found not only within Catholicism but also within non-Christian religions as well.[31] All this, of course, implies "the tenets of universalism which are implicit in the stance of the New Catholicism [and] are profoundly antithetical to biblical theology."[32]

As an example of the problem consider *Crossing the Threshold of Hope* by John Paul II. The pope first cites Vatican II (Lumen gentium, 14), which states, "Men cannot be saved who do not want to enter or remain in the Church" and, "Therefore, if someone does not respond to this grace in thought, in word, and in deeds, not only will that person not be saved, he will be even more severely judged."[33] This would certainly seem to teach that the *only* way to be saved is by membership in the Catholic Church. Yet the pope *himself* goes on to state, "It would be difficult to deny that this doctrine is extremely *open*."[34]

In a sense, then, within modern post-Vatican II Catholicism, we have Scripture being subjugated to dual enemies: inward religious experience and the vagaries of religious tradition. Where Catholicism chooses to emphasize the inward experience of "Spirit," "the meaning of Scripture becomes subject to the knowledge derived from religious experience."[35] On the other hand, where Catholic tradition holds sway, "Catholics subjugate the content of the written Scriptures, not to religious experience, but to tradition."[36]

Unfortunately, in neither case is Scripture permitted to speak for itself. Rather, Scripture is allowed to assert its own meaning only insofar as either religious experience or tradition will permit it to do so. In both cases biblical content becomes obscured through the eyes of foreign elements.

> The thrust, then, of the New Catholicism, is in three directions. Firstly, religious experience is being allowed to dissolve the Church structure. Secondly, religious experience is undermining the authenticity of biblical records. Thirdly, religious experience is providing the basis on which the whole human race may be redeemed. This thrust represents a dramatic triumph of the subjective over the objective, of the inward over the outward, and of the experiential over the historical.[37]

Has Rome Officially Changed?

Have the doctrines of Rome changed? Thirty years after Vatican II, it is clear that officially the historic doctrines of Rome which are handed down from its centralized teaching authority have changed little or not at all. Nor is this surprising.

For example, to have instituted major changes in key doctrines relating to the very nature of salvation itself would be tantamount to admitting error and even heresy. Why? Because Rome has historically claimed direct counsel and infallible guidance from God. To change Church doctrine would be tantamount to admitting Rome has actually been teaching falsehoods and leading its own people astray.

What implications does this have for the recent ecumenical statements between Protestants and Catholics?

It can mean only two things: 1) Evangelicals are probably conceding the most in the agreements—not Rome, and 2) the real issue of official Catholic doctrine is probably not being properly addressed.

Notes

Note to reader: Any brief quotations not referenced are taken from *The International Thesaurus of Quotations;* F. Mead, *The Encyclopedia of Religious Quotations;* or R.L. Woods, *The World Treasury of Religious Quotations.*

Chapter 1: The Winds of Change
1. "Evangelicals and Catholics Together: The Christian Mission in the Third Millennium," released March 29, 1994. Available from B.A.S.I.C., Truth Ministries, P.O. Box 504M, Bay Shore, NY 11706, vol. 1, no. 10, April 1994, p. 1.
2. Ibid., pp. 5-6.
3. Ibid., pp. 4, 12.
4. Ibid., p. 11.
5. Ibid., p. 4
6. John A. O'Brien, "The Faith of Millions" (Huntington, IN: *Our Sunday Visitor,* 1974), p. 46.
7. Arthur H. Matthews, "Cooperation, Not Communion," in *World,* April 9, 1994, p. 10.
8. Karl Keating, *What Catholics Really Believe—Setting the Record Straight* (Ann Arbor, MI: Servant, 1992), p. 112.
9. John Paul II, *Crossing the Threshold of Hope* (New York: Alfred A. Knopf, 1994), p. 141 (emphasis added).

Chapter 2: The Dividing Issues
1. Sanctification is God's *purpose* for believers after He has called them to Himself by the gospel. Because sinners have been justified and then sanctified, set aside to serve God in conduct, they are to cleanse themselves from all defilement, forsake sin, and live a holy (or separated) life to God (1 Peter 1:15; 2 Peter 3:11).

   How can the newly justified sinner now serve God and forsake his sin? He can do this because God gives him His Holy Spirit. The Holy Spirit is given both as a result of the sinner's justification and for his sanctification.

   The apostle Paul says, "If anyone does not have the Spirit of Christ, he does not belong to Christ" (Romans 8:9). "So I say, live by the Spirit, and you will not gratify the desires of the sinful nature" (Galatians 5:16).

   As a result of justification, God promises the new believer the inward presence of the Holy Spirit. The Spirit is said to be God's deposit or "down payment" to us, guaranteeing that we have been saved and will be in heaven. "Having believed, you were marked in him with a seal, the promised Holy Spirit, who is a deposit *guaranteeing* our inheritance" (Ephesians 1:13,14, emphasis added).

   God pronounces the verdict of justification concerning the sinner on the basis of Christ's substitutionary work, not on the basis of any work done by the sinner. But in sanctification, God places the Holy Spirit into the sinner's life and the new believer is then expected to cooperate with the Spirit in transforming his sinful self into a Christlike person.

   Thus, sanctification is not for the purpose of attaining justification, as Catholicism maintains; rather, sanctification flows from justification, and it is because God has saved us that we are free to joyfully serve Him and grow in grace.
2. John Paul II, p. 194 (emphasis added).
3. For recommended books on eternal security, see Charles Stanley, *Eternal Security: You Can Be Sure;* J.F. Strombeck, *Shall Never Perish;* H. Barker, *Secure Forever;* Robert Gromacki, *Salvation Is Forever;* R.T. Kendall, *Once Saved, Always Saved.*

   We should point out that although Luther agreed that the merits of Christ were the sole basis of a man's justification, and that it did not depend in any way on a man's deeds, Luther still thought that a man could lose his justification if he totally and finally turned away from Christ.

   Since God's gift of forgiveness of sins and eternal life was appropriated by faith, if a man decided not to rest his eternal destiny in Christ, and totally turned against Him, Luther believed that only then would a man lose his salvation. In other words, the only sin that Luther thought would cause a man to lose his salvation was the sin of unrepentant apostasy.

   On the other hand, Calvin taught the biblical truth that once God justified a man, God would strengthen that man's faith and protect him so that he would never apostatize and turn away from believing in the work of Christ on his behalf. Calvin taught that those whom God has chosen for salvation to be His own will certainly be saved by Him, since it was His purpose to save them from eternity (Ephesians 1).

4. H.J. Schroeder, translator, *The Canons and Decrees of the Council of Trent* (Rockford, IL: Tan Books, 1978), p. 35.

Chapter 3: The Apostle James

1. R.C. Sproul, "Justification by Faith," transcript of lecture, n.d.
2. Henry Alford, *Alford's Greek Testament: An Exegetical and Critical Commentary*, vol. 4, part 2: James-Revelation (Grand Rapids: Guardian Press, 1976), p. 301. Alford goes on to say, "provided that faith includes in it the condition of obedience," but by this he obviously does not mean what Roman Catholicism means.
3. Robert Jamieson, A.R. Fausset, and David Brown, *A Commentary—Critical, Experimental, and Practical on the Old and New Testaments*, vol. 3 (Grand Rapids: Eerdmans, 1984), p. 589 (emphasis added).
4. J.P. Lange and J.J. Van Oosterzee, *The General Epistle of James*, in John Peter Lange, *Commentary on the Holy Scriptures: Critical, Doctrinal, and Homiletical* (Grand Rapids: Zondervan, 1980), p. 87 (emphasis added).
5. R.V.G. Tasker, *The General Epistle of James*, in the *Tyndale New Testament Commentaries* (Grand Rapids: Eerdmans, 1977), vol. 16, pp. 67-68, 70.
6. The entire thrust of James is proving what true faith *does*. In James 1:22-27, James refers to and illustrates those who are doers of the word rather than mere hearers, "who only delude themselves." Thus those of true faith help widows and orphans. In James 2:1-9 he provides another illustration of the outworking of genuine faith, showing what true faith does. In James 2:14-16 he refers to a third illustration of true faith: When a brother or sister appears at your door having literally no clothes or food, true faith in God will certainly cause you to provide for his or her needs. If you merely send them on their way, telling them to "be warmed and filled," you prove that your faith in God is nonexistent. James next cites the illustration of Rahab the harlot. She also proved that her faith was real by what she did, and thus James says her faith was "justified by [her] works" (James 2:25 NASB).

In fact, James says that "just as the body without the spirit is dead, so also faith without works is dead" (James 2:26 NASB). This illustration shows in a powerful manner that living faith *will* produce good works. For example, coauthor John Weldon well remembers when he was present at the death of his brother-in-law. One moment a living person resided within a warm body. The next instant everything was gone: The person was no longer there. When the spirit leaves the body at death, the body is truly dead—cold, vacant, and lifeless. In a similar manner, a "faith" alone—alone without works—is just as cold, lifeless, and dead. (See endnote 4 under Appendix C.)

Chapter 4: The Official Catholic Standard

1. Keith A. Fournier, *A House United?: Evangelicals and Catholics Together: A Winning Alliance for the 21st Century* (Colorado Springs: NavPress, 1994), p. 208.
2. Ludwig Ott, *Fundamentals of Catholic Dogma* (Rockford, IL: Tan Books and Publishers, 1974), p. 264.
3. Peter Toon, *Foundations for Faith: Justification and Sanctification* (Westchester, IL: Crossway, 1983), p. 84, from Norman Geisler, prepublication manuscript.
4. *Catechism of the Catholic Church* (Liguori, MO: Liguori Publications, 1994), p. 3.
5. Ibid., pp. 1, 5-6 (emphasis added).
6. Ibid., p. 6.
7. Ibid., pp. 489-90.
8. As cited in Robert D. Brinsmead, ed., "The Basic Doctrine of Justification by Faith," in *Present Truth: Special Issue—Justification by Faith*, n.d., p. 7. Available from P.O. Box 1311, Fallbrook, CA 92028.
9. *Catechism of the Catholic Church* (1994), p. 487.
10. H.J. Schroeder, translator, 7th Session, Canon 1, 51, cf. pp. 29-46.
11. Cited in Brinsmead, ed., p. 8.
12. Ibid.
13. Karl Barth, "A Letter to the Author" (1981) in Hans Kung, *Justification: The Doctrine of Karl Barth and a Catholic Reflection* (Philadelphia: Westminster, 1964), p. XL.
14. Karl Keating in "The Salvation Debate," conducted at Simon Greenleaf School of Law, Anaheim, CA (March 11, 1989), cassette tape.
15. R.H. Bainton, *Here I Stand: A Life of Martin Luther* (Nashville: Abingdon, 1965), p. 65, from Norman Geisler, prepublication manuscript on Roman Catholicism from chapter 12 on justification.

16. Schroeder, translator, p. 29.
17. Ibid., p. 42.
18. Ibid., p. 45, Canon 24.
19. Geisler, ms., p. 4.
20. Schroeder, translator, p. 36.
21. Ibid., p. 41.
22. Ibid., p. 43, Canon 11.
23. Ibid., Canon 9.
24. Ibid., p. 37.
25. Ibid., p. 44, Canon 14.
26. Ibid., Canon 20.
27. Ibid., p. 53, Canon 7.
28. Ibid., p. 36.
29. Ibid., p. 43, Canon 12.
30. Ibid., p. 39.
31. Ibid., pp. 45-46, Canon 29.
32. Ibid., p. 46, Canon 30.
33. Ibid., p. 46, Canon 32.
34. Ibid., p. 46, Canon 33.
35. Martin Chemnitz, *Examination of the Council of Trent* (St. Louis: Concordia, 1971), part 1, pp. 514-15.
36. Ibid., p. 515.
37. Ibid., pp. 515-18.
38. Robert C. Broderick, ed., *The Catholic Encyclopedia*, revised and updated (New York: Thomas Nelson Publishers, 1978), p. 402.
39. Karl Keating, *What Catholics Really Believe—Setting the Record Straight* (Ann Arbor, MI: Servant, 1992), pp. 66-67.
40. Walter Martin, *The Roman Catholic Church in History* (Livingston, NJ: Christian Research Institute, Inc., 1960), pp. 64-65.
41. Ibid., p. 253.
42. Ott, p. 251.

Chapter 5: The Bible and Justification

1. As cited in Geisler, prepublished manuscript on Roman Catholicism, p. 35.
2. Geisler, p. 34, citing respectively Anthony A. Hoekema, *Saved by Grace* (1989), p. 154, and Millard J. Erickson, *Christian Theology* (1987), 4th printing, p. 955.
3. Kung, *Justification* (Philadelphia: Westminster, 1964), p. 209; Geisler observes, "For an extended treatment of the Old Testament understandings of these terms and the difficulties inherent in translating from the Hebrew into Greek and Latin, see Alister E. McGrath, *Lustitia Dei*, vol. 1, Cambridge University Press, 1986, pp. 4-16," (from Geisler, ms.).
4. E.g., Geisler, p. 29.
5. Broderick, ed., p. 319.
6. Gerhard Kittel, ed., *Theological Dictionary of the New Testament* (Grand Rapids: Eerdmans, 1978), vol. 2, pp. 215-16.
7. Statements by Bruce Metzger cited by Dr. Rod Rosenbladt in "The Salvation Debate." Because of the lexical evidence, if the believer actually possesses the righteousness of Christ by divine decree, it can hardly be called a "legal fiction" as Catholics maintain. Catholics argue that for God to declare a sinful person righteous is inconsistent with His justice. But God says just the opposite. Because of Christ's willing substitutionary death on the cross, God is able to impute Christ's righteous status to the sinner's account and, in turn, to impute the sinner's sin to Christ's account, thereby proving God is just: "He did it to demonstrate His justice at the present time, so as to be just and the one who justifies those who have faith in Jesus" (Romans 3:26).
   Thus, standard Greek dictionaries define the Greek word for justification as an imputed, not actual righteousness: *The Hebrew Greek Study Bible* (1984, p. 23): "to render just or innocent"; Arndt and Gingrich (1967, p. 196): "being acquitted, be pronounced and treated as righteous"; *New Thayers' Greek-English Lexicon* (1977, p. 150): "which never means *to make* worthy, but to judge worthy, to declare worthy, to declare guiltless, to judge, declare, pronounce righteous and therefore acceptable"; Loruv and Nida's *Greek-English Lexicon* (1988, p. 557): "the act of clearing someone of transgression—'to acquit, to set free, to remove guilt, acquittal'"; W.E. Vine, *Expository Dictionary of New Testament Words* (1966, p. 285): "*dikaioo*—to declare to be righteous, to pronounce righteous, being the legal and formal acquittal from guilt by God as Judge, the pronouncement of the sinner as righteous, who believes on the Lord Jesus Christ."

286

8. Statement by J.I. Packer cited by Dr. Rod Rosenbladt in "The Salvation Debate." Sometimes we find the present continuous tense used (e.g., "being justified" in Romans 3:24 NASB). As W.E. Vine points out, this indicates "the constant process of justification in the succession of those who believe and are justified" (*An Expository Dictionary of New Testament Words*, p. 285), or it refers to the results of justification that continue from the point of justification (i.e., sanctification).
9. *Roman Catholicism*—transcript of a series of televised programs prepared by the Ankerberg Theological Research Institute for "The John Ankerberg Show" (Chattanooga: ATRI), 1994, p. 81.
10. W.E. Vine, *An Expository Dictionary of New Testament Words* (Grand Rapids: Revell, 1966), part 2, p. 317.
11. Millard J. Erickson, *Christian Theology*, p. 968.
12. Ibid., 967.
13. Geisler, ms., taken from unnumbered footnote section.
14. *Catechism of the Catholic Church* (1994), p. 291.
15. Schroeder, translator, p. 45.
16. *Catechism of the Catholic Church* (1994), p. 487.
17. Ibid., p. 483.
18. Ibid., p. 482.
19. Ibid.
20. Ibid.
21. Martin, p. 68.
22. Everett F. Hanson, ed., *Baker's Dictionary of Theology* (Grand Rapids: Baker, 1972), p. 305.
23. Bainton, *Here I Stand*, p. 65, from Geisler, ms.
24. John Paul II, p. 194.

Chapter 6: The Catholic Sacraments
1. John Paul II, pp. 74-75.
2. *Catechism of the Catholic Church* (1994), p. 292.
3. H.M. Carson, *Dawn or Twilight? A Study of Contemporary Roman Catholicism* (Leicester, England: InterVarsity Press, 1976), p. 36; cf. James Neher, *A Christian's Guide to Today's Catholic Charismatic Movement* (Hatfield, PA: James Neher, 1977).
4. *Catechism of the Catholic Church* (1994), p. 289.
5. Ibid., p. 292.
6. Schrotenboer, ed., *Roman Catholicism: A Contemporary Evangelical Perspective* (Grand Rapids: Baker, 1980), p. 7, cf. Carson, pp. 89-92.
7. Broderick, ed., p. 65.
8. Ibid., p. 131.
9. Ibid., p. 319.
10. Ibid., pp. 466-68, 319.
11. Ibid., pp. 375-76.
12. Ibid., p. 372.
13. Ibid., pp. 39-40, 208.
14. Ibid., pp. 438-39.
15. Ott, p. 340.
16. Ibid., pp. 340-41.
17. Broderick, ed., pp. 534-35.
18. Ibid., p. 246.
19. Ibid., p. 253.
20. Karl Keating in "The Salvation Debate."
21. Schroeder, translator, p. 51 (7th session, March 3, 1547).
22. Ibid., p. 52, Canon 4.
23. Ibid., p. 53, Canons 3, 5.
24. Ibid., pp. 88, 90 (14th session, November 25, 1551).
25. Ibid., pp. 102-03, Canons 6, 7, 9.
26. Ibid., pp. 149-50.
27. Ibid.
28. Ott, p. 264.
29. John Hardon, *The Catholic Catechism: The Contemporary Catechism of the Teachings of the Catholic Church* (Garden City, NY: Doubleday, 1975), pp. 506-07.
30. *Catechism of the Catholic Church* (1994), p. 320.
31. Ibid., p. 324.
32. Ibid., pp. 321-22.

33. Ibid., p. 322.
34. Ibid., p. 321.
35. Karl Keating in "The Salvation Debate."
36. Ibid.
37. Broderick, ed., p. 65.
38. Leaflet Missal Company, *Outlines of the Catholic Faith* (St. Paul, MN: 1978), p. 33.
39. Keating, *What Catholics Really Believe*, p. 19.
40. *Catechism of the Catholic Church* (1994), pp. 269-70.
41. Ott, p. 356.
42. *Catechism of the Catholic Church* (1994), pp. 334, 336.
43. Ibid., p. 346.
44. Ibid., p. 351.
45. Ibid., p. 347.
46. Ibid., p. 343.
47. Ibid., p. 344 (emphasis added).
48. Ibid.
49. Ibid., p. 345 (emphasis added).
50. Ibid., pp. 351-52 (emphasis added).
51. Ibid., p. 355.
52. Carson, p. 111.
53. Hardon, p. 468.
54. Ott, pp. 407, 412.
55. Schroeder, translator, p. 146 (7th Session, Canon 1).
56. Martin, pp. 74-75.
57. Carson, p. 112, citing part 2, chapter 1, p. 72.
58. Ibid., p. 113.
59. Abbott, ed., *The Documents of Vatican II* (New York: Guild Press, 1966), p. 543.
60. Keating, *Catholicism and Fundamentalism*, p. 248.
61. Ibid., p. 248, quoting Rev. John A. O'Brien.
62. Carson, p. 111.
63. Ibid., p. 112.
64. Broderick, ed., pp. 375-76.
65. Carson, p. 119. See John Paul II, p. 139.
66. Schrotenboer, ed., p. 74.
67. Schroeder, translator, p. 51, citing 7th Session, Council of Trent, Canon 1.
68. Ibid., p. 52, citing 7th Session, Canon 4.
69. Ibid., p. 53, citing 7th Session, Canon 5.
70. *Catechism of the Catholic Church* (1994), p. 315.
71. Ibid., pp. 486-87.
72. Geisler, ms., p. 15.
73. Chemnitz, vol. 1, pp. 654-55.
74. Geisler, ms., from unnumbered footnote section.

Chapter 7: Penance, Confession, and the Rosary

1. Broderick, ed., p. 254.
2. Ibid., p. 476.
3. Ibid., p. 466; cf. Ott, p. 425.
4. Broderick, ed., p. 467.
5. Schroeder, translator, p. 102, citing 14th Session, Canon 2.
6. Ibid., p. 39.
7. *Catechism of the Catholic Church* (1994), p. 363, brackets in original.
8. Ibid., p. 362.
9. Ibid., p. 361.
10. Ibid., p. 357.
11. Ibid., p. 366.
12. Broderick, ed., p. 402; cf. pp. 466-68.
13. Ibid., p. 208.
14. Schroeder, translator, p. 46.
15. Ibid., p. 292.
16. Schrotenboer, ed., pp. 68-69, citing the encyclical *Ad catholic sacerdotii*, 1935, and Pope Paul VI in *Mysterium fidei*, no. 38.
17. Ott, p. 431.
18. Schroeder, pp. 102-03, citing 14th Session, Sacrament of Penance, Canon 6, 7, 9.

19. Martin, p. 63.
20. Cf. S.T. Louis De Montfort, *The Secret of the Rosary*, Mary Barbour, translator (Bay Shore, NY: Montfort Publications, 1976), passim (this text contains the *nihil obstat* and *imprimatur*); cf. *Catechism of the Catholic Church* (1994), pp. 253, 650.
21. Pope Paul VI, *Devotion to the Blessed Virgin Mary [Marialis Cultus]* (Washington, D.C.: United States Catholic Conference, 1974), p. 31.
22. Ibid., p. 37.
23. De Montfort, p. 17.
24. See "Rosary," in *The Catholic Encyclopedia* (New York: The Encyclopedia Press, 1913), vol. 13, pp. 184, 187.
25. De Montfort, pp. 47, 70, 86.
26. Ibid., pp. 120, 123.
27. Ibid., p. 65.
28. Ibid., pp. 78-79.
29. Ibid., p. 12.
30. Keating, *Catholicism and Fundamentalism*, pp. 166-68, 175.
31. Joseph F. Bernard, "My Ticket to Heaven," n.d., pp. 3-10. On p. 24 of this tract, John A. Hardon, S.J., calls it "a straightforward presentation of the cardinal mysteries of the Christian Faith."

Chapter 8: Indulgences
 1. Keating, *What Catholics Really Believe*, p. 91.
 2. Ott, p. 441.
 3. Keating, *What Catholics Really Believe*, p. 95.
 4. Broderick, ed., p. 291.
 5. *Catechism of the Catholic Church* (1994), p. 370.
 6. Ibid., p. 371.
 7. Ibid., p. 370.
 8. Hardon, p. 526; cf. Broderick, ed., p. 513.
 9. *Outlines of Catholic Faith*, p. 43.
10. Keating, *What Catholics Really Believe*, p. 92.
11. Ibid., p. 93.
12. Broderick, ed., p. 553.
13. Ibid., p. 529.
14. Ibid., p. 105.
15. Ibid., p. 291.

Chapter 9: Purgatory
 1. Keating, *What Catholics Really Believe*, p. 86.
 2. Ibid., p. 90.
 3. Broderick, ed., p. 117.
 4. Ott, p. 485.
 5. Schroeder, translator, p. 146.
 6. Ibid., p. 214.
 7. Hardon, p. 273.
 8. Ibid., p. 274.
 9. Ibid., pp. 263-74.
10. Ibid., p. 274.
11. Broderick, ed., p. 502.
12. Martin, pp. 79-80.
13. Hardon, p. 279.
14. Hardon, pp. 278-79.
15. R.H. Charles, *The Apocrypha and Pseudepigrapha of the Old Testament in English* (Oxford: Oxford University Press, 1978), p. 149.
16. Martin, p. 77.
17. John Ankerberg and John Weldon, *Protestants and Catholics: Do They Now Agree? An Evaluation of Modern Protestantism and Roman Catholicism in Light of the Bible*, first edition (Chattanooga: Ankerberg Theological Research Institute, 1994), pp. 194-209.
18. J.P. Arendzen, *Purgatory and Heaven* (Rockford, IL: Tan Books, 1972), p. 47.
19. Broderick, ed., p. 288.
20. F.X. Shouppe, S.J., *Purgatory: Illustrated by the Lives and Legends of the Saints* (Rockford, IL: Tan Books, 1973), pp. 276, 286-87.

21. E.g., Mark Miravalle, *The Heart of the Message of Medjugorje* (Steubenville, OH: Franciscan University Press, 1988), p. 48; Shouppe, pp. 155-59.
22. Shouppe, pp. 185-86, 280-81.
23. Ibid., pp. 194-96.
24. Ibid., pp. 243, 250, 264, 278, 288-89.
25. Ibid., pp. 137-39.
26. Ibid., p. 279; cf. Broderick, ed., pp. 174, 599.
27. E.g., Shouppe, ibid., pp. 289-91; cf. Broderick, ed., pp. 48, 64, 70, 218, 256, 327, 339-40, 359, 392, 442.
28. E.g., Kevin McClue in *The Evidence for Visions of the Virgin Mary* (Wellingborough, Northamptonshire: Aquarian Press, 1985); p. 133 lists between 200 and 300.
29. Ott, p. 323; and Shouppe, p. viii.
30. Shouppe, p. 265.
31. Broderick, ed., p. 539.
32. Ibid., pp. 459, 463.

Chapter 10: Redefining Biblical Words

1. John Warwick Montgomery, *The Shape of the Past* (Minneapolis: Bethany, 1975), p. 6.
2. Cf. John Ankerberg and John Weldon, *Cult Watch: What You Need to Know About Spiritual Deception* (Eugene, OR: Harvest House, 1991).
3. Keating, *Catholicism and Fundamentalism*, p. 103.
4. As cited in the *Los Angeles Times*, March 8, 1983, part 1, p. 10.
5. Keating, *Catholicism and Fundamentalism*, p. 81.
6. Schroeder, translator, p. 42, Canons 1-3.
7. Anne Freemantle, *The Papal Encyclicals in Their Historical Context: The Teachings of the Popes* (New York: New American Library/Mentor, 1956), p. 11.
8. Dom Bernard Orchard et al, *A Catholic Commentary on Holy Scripture* (Nashville: Thomas Nelson, 1953), p. 1049 (from Geisler, ms.).
9. Keating, *Catholicism and Fundamentalism*, p. 316.
10. Ibid., p. 317.
11. R.C. Sproul, "Justification by Faith" lecture.
12. Freemantle, p. 11.
13. Ibid., p. 8.
14. Keating, *What Catholics Really Believe*, p. 29.
15. Abbott, ed., pp. 117-18 (emphasis added).
16. Chemnitz, part 1, p. 213.
17. Broderick, ed., p. 21.
18. Ibid., p. 115.
19. Hardon, p. 36.
20. Freemantle, p. 11.
21. Dom Bernard Orchard et al, *A Catholic Commentary on Holy Scripture* (Nashville: Thomas Nelson, 1953), p. 1049 (from Geisler, ms.).
22. The Lutheran Church-Missouri Synod Convention workbook for July 10-17, 1992, *With Great Boldness... Tell Everyone What He Has Done!* (58th Regular Convention, Pittsburgh), Reports and Overtures, Appendix 1, "Theological Documents": A Response to the U.S. Lutheran-Roman Catholic Dialogue Report VII, "Justification by Faith," p. 314, adopted by the Commission on Theology and Church Relations, the Lutheran Church-Missouri Synod, February 25, 1992.

Chapter 11: Two Ways of Reading the Bible

1. Abbott, ed., p. 117.
2. Editorial, "What Separates Evangelicals and Catholics?" *Christianity Today* (October 23, 1981), pp. 14-15.
3. Garrit C. Berkouwer, *The Conflict with Rome* (Philadelphia: Presbyterian and Reformed, 1958), p. 112.
4. Martin, p. 67.
5. Keating, *What Catholics Really Believe*, pp. 66-67.
6. Keating, *Catholicism and Fundamentalism*, p. 166.
7. Cf. William J. Cogan, *A Catechism for Adults* (Youngtown, AZ: Cogan Productions, 1975), p. 50, from James G. McCarthy, *Catholicism: Crisis of Faith*, video documentary (annotated transcript), Lumen Productions, P.O. Box 595, Cupertino, CA 95015, p. 31.

8. Martin, p. 87.
9. John Paul II, p. viii, 146-51, cf. 153-65.

Chapter 12: Evangelicals and Catholics Together?

1. "Evangelicals and Catholics Together: The Christian Mission in the Third Millennium," published by Truth Ministries, P. O. Box 504M, Bay Shore, NY 11706, vol. 1, no. 10, April 1994, pp. 26-28.

In response to critics, those Evangelicals who have signed the document and/or sided with them have stated that, first, the document is not primarily about theology but about religious liberty—the right of all Christians to share their faith unfettered by church or state. In fact, they argue that the major theme throughout the document is evangelism and world missions because more space is given to these subjects than anything else.

They also argue that at last Catholics are admitting that Evangelicals and other Protestants are legitimate religious groups rather than perverted schisms to be treated as sects and cults.

In response, we agree that the document stresses the subjects of religious liberty, evangelism, and world missions, as well as the threat of Islam and secularism. But none of these can ultimately be divorced from the importance of defending the true message of the gospel itself.

No one denies that there are certainly things that both Catholics and Evangelicals can agree upon; a number of these are cited in the report. For example, one of the most serious threats to the health of Christian religion in our own nation is the increasing secularization of culture and subsequent distortion of the Constitution. Thus Catholics and Evangelicals can both heartily concur with the following statement from the document:

We are deeply concerned by the Court's narrowing of the protections provided by the "free exercise" provision of the First Amendment and by an obsession with "no establishment" that stifles the necessary role of religion in American life. As a consequence of such distortions, it is increasingly the case that wherever government goes, religion must retreat, and government increasingly goes almost everywhere. Religion, which was privileged and foundational in our legal order, has in recent years been penalized and made marginal. . . . The argument, increasingly voiced in sectors of political culture, that religion should be excluded from the public square must be recognized as an assault upon the most elementary principles of democratic governments. That argument needs to be exposed and countered by leaders, religious and other, who care about the integrity of our constitutional order (p. 14).

With this in mind we would advise the following:

First, while Evangelicals and Catholics can work together to improve the moral climate of America, it must never be forgotten that the truly major social change occurs by regeneration, not by social or political action. This is especially so if a political alliance ends up compromising the gospel—where the true source of change originates.

As Dr. Holly comments:

The impact of faith on the affairs of state will be determined by the power of the Gospel, and by the evidence of that power in the lives of those who profess faith, much more than it will be by the attempt by Christians to exert political power and pressure. It is probable that society in general will continue to be skeptical of the benefits of the Christian faith and doctrine for public policy until the society in general sees the benefit of the Christian faith and doctrine of the Christian church (Larry Holly, "Evangelicals and Catholics Together: The Christian Mission in the Third Millennium: A Critique" [Beaumont, TX: Mission and Ministry to Men, Inc., 1994], p. 3).

In essence, while political and social work are good, these must be subject to biblical priorities. Although this document claims that both individual Christians and the church as a whole are responsible "for the right ordering of civil society" (p. 12), the fact is that there is no scriptural mandate for the "right ordering of civil society" by the church. Christ's kingdom is "not of this world"; His people are "aliens and strangers" here (John 18:36; Hebrews 11:13; 1 Peter 2:11). While Christians are to be "salt and light" in the world, their real mandate was stated by Jesus: "Go into all the world and preach the good news to all creation" (Mark 16:15).

If the gospel itself is not to become subordinated to political and social activism, the message of the church must be on its eternal mission—the salvation of souls—which will then impact the temporal situation. An evaluation of the cause and consequences of the liberal "social gospel" or Marxist "liberation theology" shows how easy it is for those in the church to distort the nature and priorities of the true gospel of Christ.

2. Ibid., p. 5.
3. Ibid., p. 4.
4. Ibid., p. 5.
5. Ibid., p. 6.

6. Ibid., p. 11.
7. Ibid., p. 12.
8. Ibid., p. 8.
9. Ibid., pp. 2, 4.
10. Ibid., p. 25.
11. Ibid., pp. 7-8.
12. Ibid., p. 8.
13. Ibid., p. 1
14. Ibid., p. 2.
15. Ibid., p. 4.
16. Ibid., p. 5.
17. Ibid.
18. Ibid., p. 8.
19. Ibid., p. 1.
20. Ibid., p. 2.
21. Ibid., p. 4.
22. Ibid., p. 8.
23. Ibid., p. 4.
24. Ibid., p. 3.
25. Ibid., p. 4.
26. Ibid.
27. Ibid., p. 5.
28. See chapter 10.
29. "Evangelicals and Catholics Together," p. 5.
30. Ibid.
31. Ibid., p. 6.
32. Ibid., p. 25.
33. Ibid., p. 4.
34. Ibid., p. 8.
35. Ibid., p. 10.
36. Ibid., p. 9.
37. Ibid.
38. Ibid.
39. See chapters 2-10.
40. See Luther's commentary on Galatians for a classic exposition of this book.
41. "Evangelicals and Catholics Together," p. 9.
42. See John Ankerberg and John Weldon, *Protestants and Catholics: Do They Now Agree?* first edition, chapters 9 and 10, for information on Mary and the pope.
43. Ibid., p. 10.
44. Ibid.
45. Ibid., pp. 10-11.
46. Ibid., p. 11.
47. Ibid.
48. Ibid., p. 20.
49. Ibid., pp. 20, 22.
50. Ibid., p. 21.
51. Ibid., pp. 21-22.
52. Ibid., p. 21.
53. Ibid.
54. Ibid., p. 22.
55. Ibid., p. 24.
56. Ibid., pp. 23-24.
57. Holly, p. 17.
58. "Evangelicals and Catholics Together," p. 5.
59. Ibid., p. 21.
60. Ibid., p. 9.
61. Pascal once said, "We know the truth not only by reason but also by the heart." Unfortunately, in our world today truth is often compromised—even by the church that should love truth. Compromise, of course, is often necessary in politics and even in life in general. In the words of George Herbert, "A lean compromise is better than a fat lawsuit." But compromise can also be the devil's best business. Indeed, consider the "devil's" own definition of "compromise" in Ambrose Bierce's *The Devil's Dictionary* (1881): "COMPROMISE, n. Such an adjustment of conflicting interests as gives each adversary the satisfaction of thinking he has got what he ought not to have, and is deprived of nothing except what was justly his due."

In *On the Road to Christian Unity* (1961), Samuel N. Cavert said correctly, "If we really believe that our unity in Christ lies at a deeper level than our differences, we will find more and more ways of manifesting it in common action."

Chapter 13: Impact of Ecumenism
1. John Paul II, p. 146.
2. Matthews, p. 10.
3. Editorial, *Christianity Today*, May 16, 1994, p. 16; *Christian American: A Christian Review of the News*, May/June 1994, p. 4.
4. Editorial, *Christianity Today*, May 16, 1994, p. 16.
5. *Christian American: A Christian Review of the News*, May/June 1994, p. 1.
6. Ibid., p. 4.
7. Ibid.
8. Letter of Larry Lewis sent to and published in Dave Hunt's *The Berean Call* (August 1994), P.O. Box 7019, Bend, OR 97702.
9. Matthews, pp. 12-13.
10. Ibid., p. 13.
11. Dave Hunt, "The Gospel Betrayed," *The Berean Call* (May 1994), pp. 1-2.
12. Holly, pp. 7, 13, 17.

Chapter 14: What Should Be Agreed Upon?
1. R.C. Sproul, "Justification by Faith," transcript of lecture, slightly edited and modified for readability.
2. Ibid.
3. Ibid.
4. Ibid.

Chapter 15: What Does the Bible Say?
1. Philip Schaff, *History of the Christian Church* (Grand Rapids: Eerdmans, 1978), vol. 1, p. 567.
2. William Hendriksen, *New Testament Commentary: Exposition of Galatians* (Grand Rapids: Baker, 1974), pp. 37-38 (emphasis added).
3. Ibid., p. 39.
4. Ibid., p. 40.
5. Ibid.
6. James Montgomery Boice, "Galatians," in Frank E. Gaebelein, ed., *The Expositor's Bible Commentary* (Grand Rapids: Zondervan, 1977), p. 428.
7. Ibid.
8. Ibid.
9. Herman N. Ridderbos, *The New International Commentary on the New Testament: The Epistle of Paul to the Churches of Galatia* (Grand Rapids: Eerdmans, 1974), pp. 48-49.
10. John Calvin, *Calvin's Commentaries: The Epistle of Paul the Apostle to the Galatians, Ephesians, Philippians and Colossians*, T.H.L. Parker, translator (Grand Rapids: Eerdmans, 1979), p. 13.
11. Ibid., p. 14.
12. Ibid., p. 15.
13. Ibid., p. 16.
14. Hendriksen, p. 41.
15. Ridderbos, p. 50.
16. Ibid.
17. Ibid.
18. Boice, p. 429.
19. Calvin, p. 14.
20. Hendriksen, p. 42.
21. Calvin, p. 97.
22. Ibid., p. 98.
23. Ridderbos, p. 193.

Chapter 16: Results of Catholic Doctrine
1. Editorial, "What Separates Evangelicals and Catholics?" pp. 14-15.
2. Robert Baram, ed., *Spiritual Journeys: Toward the Fullness of Faith* (Boston: Daughters of St. Paul, 1988), p. 176 (emphasis added).
3. Dave Hunt, "The Gospel Betrayed," in *The Berean Call*, May 1994, p. 2.
4. David Hunt, "Q&A" (response to Larry Lewis, president of the Home Mission Board of the Southern Baptists), in *The Berean Call*, August 1994.

5. Personal conversation.
6. Berkouwer, *The Conflict with Rome*, pp. 3-13.

Chapter 17: Evangelical Catholics
1. Keith A. Fournier, *Evangelical Catholics* (Nashville: Thomas Nelson, 1990), p. vi.
2. Ibid., p. 96; cf. pp. 96-107.
3. Ibid., pp. 100.
4. Ibid., pp. 106-07.
5. Ibid., p. 147.
6. Ibid., p. 167.
7. Ibid., p. 191.
8. Ibid., p. 157.
9. Ibid., p. 161.
10. Ibid., pp. 211-14.
11. Ibid., p. 168.
12. Ibid., p. 18.
13. Ibid., p. 47.
14. Ibid., p. 18.
15. Ibid., p. 47.
16. Ibid., p. 165.
17. Ibid., p. 17.
18. E. Calvin Beisner, "A Summary Critique: Evangelical Catholics," in *Christian Research Journal*, Summer 1991, p. 37.
19. Thomas Howard, "From Evangelism to Rome," in Robert Baram, ed., *Spiritual Journeys: Toward the Fullness of Faith* (Boston: Daughters of St. Paul, 1988), p. 159.
20. Ibid., pp. 160-62.
21. Ibid.
22. Paul C. Vitz, "A Christian Odyssey," in Baram, ed., pp. 383-84, 387 (emphasis added).
23. Ibid., p. 389 (emphasis added).
24. Ibid., pp. 391-92.
25. Ibid., p. 393.
26. Peter Kreeft, "Hauled Aboard the Ark," in Baram, ed., pp. 167-69.
27. Ibid., pp. 167, 170.
28. Ibid., p. 173.
29. Baram, ed., pp. 154-55, 163, 167, etc.
30. Kreeft in Baram, ed., pp. 172-73.
31. Ibid., p. 174.
32. Ibid., p. 175.
33. Ibid.
34. Moroni 10:3,4, *Book of Mormon*.
35. Kreeft in Baram, ed., p. 175.
36. Ibid., p. 177.
37. Ibid., p. 176. At proof stage we did find a statement by Kreeft that is orthodox; the publication date was too close to the current work to determine priority; however, we sincerely hope his views have changed (emphasis added).
38. Ibid., pp. 177-78.
39. Ibid., p. 167.
40. Nancy M. Cross, "The Attraction of Evangelical Christians to Catholicism," in *Homiletic and Pastoral Review*, December 1991, p. 53.
41. Martin, pp. 9-10.

Chapter 18: The One True Church?
1. John Paul II, p. 146.
2. Broderick, ed., p. 528.
3. Ibid., p. 44.
4. Ibid., p. 99.
5. Ibid., p. 115.
6. Ibid., p. 170.
7. *Catechism of the Catholic Church* (1994), p. 224.
8. Pius IV, *Profession of the Tridentine Faith*, article 12, cited in Joseph R. Schonfield, Jr., *Escape from Purgatory* (Albuquerque, NM: Matthew 10:32 Ministries), 1994, p. 167.
9. Broderick, ed., p. 381.

10. Ibid., p. 499.
11. Ibid., p. 371.
12. F.F. Bruce, *The Canon of Scripture* (Downers Grove, IL: InterVarsity Press, 1988), p. 262.
13. Emmett McLoughlin, *Crime and Immorality in the Catholic Church* (New York: Lyle Stuart, 1964), p. 19.
14. Dave Hunt, *The Berean Call*, July 1994.
15. Patrick Dixon, *The Whole Truth About AIDS* (Nashville: Nelson, 1989), p. 22; cf. Jason Berry, "Lead Us Not into Temptation," in *U.S. News and World Report*, October 5, 1992.
16. Dave Hunt, *The Berean Call*, July 1994.
17. John Ankerberg and John Weldon, *Everything You Ever Wanted to Know About Mormonism* (Eugene, OR: Harvest House, 1992).
18. Berkouwer, *The Conflict with Rome*, pp. 192-211; Abbott, ed., p. 141; Schrotenboer, p. 41; Carson, pp. 41-42.
19. Broderick, ed., p. 438.
20. Ibid., p. 514.
21. Abbott, ed., pp. 117-18 (emphasis added).
22. John Ankerberg and John Weldon, *Do Protestants and Catholics Now Agree?* first edition, chapter 10.
23. Broderick, ed., p. 213.

Chapter 19: Problems of Dialogue

1. The Lutheran Church-Missouri Synod Convention workbook for July 10-17, 1992, *With Great Boldness . . . Tell Everyone What He Has Done!* (58th Regular Convention, Pittsburgh), Reports and Overtures, Appendix 1, "Theological Documents": A Response to the U.S. Lutheran-Roman Catholic Dialogue Report VII, "Justification by Faith," p. 313, adopted by the Commission on Theology and Church Relations, the Lutheran Church-Missouri Synod, February 25, 1992.
2. Holly, p. 4.
3. Ibid., p. 11.
4. Ibid., p. 4.
5. Ibid., p. 4.
6. Ibid., p. 8.
7. Ibid., p. 6.
8. Ibid., p. 7.
9. Ibid., p. 7.
10. Ibid., p. 8.
11. U.S. Lutheran-Roman Catholic Dialogue Group in the United States, "Justification by Faith," published in *Origins*, vol. 13, no. 17 (October 6, 1983), a publication of the National Catholic Documentary Service of the National Catholic News Service, Washington D.C., publication No. ISSNOO93-6O9X. In the references below, citations are given by both paragraph and page number; only the paragraph numbers will be accurate in all versions.
12. Paragraph 4, p. 279.
13. Ibid., paragraph 156.5, p. 298; cf. paragraphs 96, 158 (pp. 290, 298).
14. W. Robert Godfrey, "Reversing the Reformation," in *Eternity*, September 1984, p. 28; cf. Roger Wagner, "New Confusions for Old: Rome on Justification," in *Anti Thesis: A Review of Contemporary Christian Thought and Culture*, vol. 1, September/October 1990, pp. 24-33.
15. Personal conversation with several "Evangelical" Catholics who were emphatic in stating that Catholics and Evangelicals had come to "very close" agreement on the doctrine of justification. The report's denial of justification is confirmed by an examination of the final "convergences" statements, especially when read in light of the previous discussions of Catholic views. See paragraphs 96, 99-149 (pp. 290, 291-97).
16. Paragraph 164, p. 299.
17. Paragraph 151, p. 297.
18. Paragraph 4, p. 279.
19. Paragraph 123, p. 293.
20. Paragraph 143, p. 296.
21. Paragraph 155, p. 297.
22. To its benefit, the 1983 declaration does faithfully (technically) describe the historical differences between Catholics and Lutherans on justification and related matters—a careful portrayal absent in the 1994 declaration. For example, paragraph 109 (p. 292) reads as follows: "Catholics, convinced that justification removes whatever is hateful to God in the justified, hold that the good works of the righteous give a title to salvation itself in the sense that God has covenanted to save those who, prompted by grace, obey his will" (cf. paragraphs 94, 121, pp. 290, 293).

23. Paragraph 2, p. 279.
24. Paragraph 3, p. 279.
25. Paragraphs 22-23, p. 281.
26. Paragraphs 53-55, p. 285.
27. Paragraphs 114, 116, pp. 292-93.
28. Paragraph 121, p. 293. This report, for example, concedes the following to Roman Catholic belief and hermeneutics: "Of special importance has been, within general Roman Catholic biblical emphasis, the encouragement given by church authorities to Catholic interpreters in the last 50 years to make use of historical-critical methods" (paragraph 122, p. 293). Illustrations of this in the report include the reference to "all seven of [Paul's] uncontested letters" (paragraph 133, p. 294) and in its classification of Ephesians, Colossians, and other of Paul's epistles and the pastorals as "Deutero-Paulines" (i.e., "Pauline epistles widely conceded [as a result of higher criticism] to be the product of Paul's pupils and the Pauline school," but not the apostle Paul himself) (paragraph 138, p. 295); that among the justified, "of themselves they remain capable of losing justification" (paragraph 156, p. 298).
29. Paragraph 157, p. 298.
30. Paragraphs 157-59, p. 298 (emphasis added).
31. Lutheran Church-Missouri Synod, Appendix One: Theological documents, p. 314.
32. Ibid. In essence, "such formulations allow an intolerable ambiguity to stand about the nature and role of faith. . . . Even granting the primacy of God's grace at work, is not the possibility of human performance as meritorious for salvation, in fact, left open?"
33. Lutheran Church-Missouri Synod, Appendix One: Theological documents, p. 314.
34. Ibid., p. 315; cf. "Part b. Justification as a Critical Principle."
35. Lutheran Church-Missouri Synod, Appendix One: Theological documents, p. 316 (emphasis added). As an illustration, in light of the above, consider the following declaration which both sides claimed agreement on. Biblical justification is first upheld but then qualified as merely a *partial* picture of what the Bible actually teaches about salvation:
    Paul's classic thesis is set forth in Galatians 2:16: "A human being is not justified (*dikaioutai*) because of deeds (i.e., observances) of (the) law, but rather through faith in Jesus Christ" (cf. Romans 3:21). The verb "is justified" is surely used in a declarative, forensic sense; whether there is also an effective sense here (i.e., that the person is made, as well as declared, righteous) is not resolvable by philological analysis alone. . . . It is he [Paul] among biblical authors who most fully and carefully discussed "righteousness" and "faith" and who, in the light of his understanding of these terms, thinks of justification as simply "by grace" and "through faith" without additions or qualifications. . . . In brief, a faith-centered and forensically conceived picture of justification is of major importance for Paul and, in a sense, for the Bible as a whole, although it is by no means the only biblical or Pauline way of representing God's saving work (paragraphs 133, 146, pp. 294, 296).
    Finally, when the document itself confesses that Catholics *insist* that the gospel must be interpreted by, for example, Catholic tradition, who can possibly argue that "agreement" has been reached on the gospel? "Catholics insist that the gospel cannot be rightly interpreted without drawing in the full resources available within the Church. . . . Catholics . . . are on guard against criticism that might erode the Catholic heritage" (paragraphs 118, 120, p. 293)

Chapter 20: A Personal Word to Catholics
 1. Broderick, ed., p. 270.
 2. Ibid., p. 402.
 3. Ibid., p. 585.
 4. Ibid., p. 539.
 5. Ibid.

Chapter 21: A Personal Word to Evangelicals
 1. Letter on file.
 2. Ibid.
 3. Lausanne Committee for World Evangelization, *Christian Witness to Nominal Christians Among Roman Catholics*, no. 10: Thailand Report (Wheaton, IL: Lausanne Committee, 1980), p. 8.
 4. Ibid., p. 7.

Appendix A: Categories of Roman Catholicism Today
 1. Schroeder, translator, p. 150 (Canon 9 on the sacrifice of the Mass).
 2. Lausanne Committee, *Christian Witness to Nominal Christians Among Roman Catholics*, p. 10.
 3. Broderick, ed., p. 372.

4. Carson, p. 36; cf. Broderick, ed., pp. 107, 469, 521-22; James Neher, *A Christian's Guide to Today's Catholic Charismatic Movement* (Hatfield, PA: James Neher, 1977).

Appendix B: How the Roman Catholic Church . . . Arose
1. These and others can be traced in Williston Walker et al, *A History of the Christian Church* (New York: Scribner's), fourth ed., 1985, pp. 75-78, 82-83, 98-101, 125, 135-36, 151-53, 159-60, 167-70, 183-86, 203, 213-17, 235-39, 250, 268, 275-76, 277-79, 290, 368-71, and other historical sources.
2. Most of this material was excerpted from John Weldon's 1987 notes in Dr. Harold Lindsell's class on Church history at Simon Greenleaf University, Anaheim, CA.
3. Harold O.J. Brown, *Heresies* (Garden City, NY: Doubleday, 1984), p. 121.
4. Dates are taken from Martin, pp. 31-33; John Phillips, "Can a Christian Remain a Roman Catholic?" in *Moody Monthly*, April 1992, pp. 31-32; F.C.H. Druyer, E.P. Weller, *Roman Catholicism in the Light of Scripture* (Chicago: Moody, 1960), p. 252; *Catholicism: Crisis of Faith*, pp. 43-44; Broderick, ed., pp. 56, 285, 292, 365, 529.
5. Gerrit C. Berkouwer, *The Second Vatican Council and the New Catholicism* (Grand Rapids: Eerdmans, 1965), p. 93.
6. See encyclopedia articles on Vatican II and August Bernhard Hasler, *How the Pope Became Infallible: Pius IX and the Politics of Persuasion* (Garden City, NY: Doubleday, 1981), pp. 189ff.
7. Berkouwer, *The Second Vatican Council*, pp. 89-93, 241.

Appendix C: What Does Rome Think of Evangelicals?
1. Broderick, ed., p. 140.
2. Ibid., p. 262.
3. Eugene LaVerdiere, "Fundamentalism: A Pastoral Concern," in *The Bible Today*, January 1983, pp. 3-5.
4. As cited in the *Los Angeles Times*, March 8, 1983, part 1, p. 10. The pope may have been quoting James 2:24, although interpreting it in light of Catholic doctrine. James is emphasizing the fruit of a true and living faith and contrasting this with a hypocritical, dead, or intellectual "faith" only—not a true faith at all. This is clear from the context (2:14-20,26). Thus a man may *claim* to have faith (2:14), but if it is dead faith (nonexistent), how can it save anyone (2:17)? Even the demons believe intellectually (2:19), but their actions prove their hatred of God, not their faith in Him. Because true regenerating faith by definition makes a person spiritually alive to God (2 Corinthians 5:17), it will naturally lead to good works (Ephesians 2:8-10). Thus, just as we can prove that a body without a spirit is dead, so we can prove that a faith without works is dead (2:26). James cannot be teaching that a person is justified by lawkeeping (2:24) when he emphasizes that the least transgression of the law is what nullifies *all* the lawkeeping as a means of salvation (2:10).

Finally, in James 2:10 and 3:2, James proves that he cannot be teaching a justification by works, as Catholics maintain. Why? First, because James says that anyone who stumbles in only one point of the law has become guilty of transgressing the entire law. But then he agrees that "we all stumble in many ways." In other words, James is admitting that all believers are guilty of breaking the entire law of God, so how could he expect believers to keep the law of God in order to maintain and gain their salvation through religious performances? As we have stressed throughout this book, Rome argues that we must "keep the commandments" and perform meritorious works in order to attain salvation. But James never even hints at salvation by lawkeeping or salvation by faith and works; he only proves what true faith is and does. Thus James vindicates true faith in the same manner that Paul vindicates true justification. In other words, James proves that true faith results in good works while Paul proves that true faith alone justifies one before God.
5. Holly, p. 1.
6. Schonfield, Jr., *Escape from Purgatory*, p. 166, citing an article in the award-winning Catholic circular *The People of God*, May 1992.
7. *Moody Monthly*, March 1989, p. 82, for this and other examples.
8. Personal conversation with missionaries in Mexico.
9. Schrotenboer, p. 22.
10. Reported in *Charisma* magazine, May 1994, p. 74; cited by Holly, p. 1.
11. Cited in Holly, p. 2.
12. Holly, p. 14.
13. Ibid.
14. Martin, p. 34.
15. Dave Hunt, *The Berean Call*, July 1994.
16. Abbott, ed., pp. 181-82, 261.

17. Ibid., p. 290.
18. Ibid.
19. Keating, *What Catholics Really Believe*, p. 31.

Appendix D: How Far Has Roman Catholic Doctrine Deviated...?
1. Recommended reading includes: Sinclair B. Ferguson, *Know Your Christian Life: A Theological Introduction* (InterVarsity Press); J.I. Packer, *God's Words: Studies of Key Bible Themes* (InterVarsity Press); Bruce Milene, *Know the Truth: A Handbook of Christian Belief* (InterVarsity Press); Mark G. Cambron, *Bible Doctrines: Beliefs That Matter* (Zondervan).

Appendix E: Internal Fomentation in the Catholic Church...
1. "Evangelicals and Catholics Together," p. 4.
2. Ibid., p. 5.
3. Ibid., p. 7.
4. Ibid., p. 25.
5. Ibid., p. 12.
6. The U.S. Lutheran-Roman Catholic Dialogue Group in the United States, "Justification by Faith," in *Origins: NC Documentary Service*, vol. 13, no. 17, October 6, 1983, p. 299, paragraph 164 (Washington D.C.: National Catholic Documentary Service of the National Catholic News Service, 1983, publication no. ISSN0093-609X).
7. Ibid., p. 297, paragraph 155.
8. Ibid., p. 279, paragraph 2.
9. Walter M. Abbot, ed., *The Documents of Vatican II* (New York: Guild Press, 1966), p. 346.
10. Rod Rosenbladt and Karl Keating, "The Salvation Debate," conducted at Simon Greenleaf School of Law, Anaheim, CA (March 11, 1989), cassette tape.
11. Keating, *Catholicism and Fundamentalism*, p. 103.
12. Paul G. Schrotenboer, ed., *Roman Catholicism: A Contemporary Evangelical Perspective* (Grand Rapids: Baker, 1980), p. 7.
13. James G. McCarthy, *Catholicism: Crisis of Faith*, video documentary (annotated transcript), Lumen Productions, P.O. Box 595, Cupertino, CA 95015, p. 37.
14. *L'Osservatore Romano*, no. 22, 1964 (the Vatican's official newspaper), in his constitution *De Ecclesia*, from Schrotenboer, p. 21.
15. John Phillips, "Can a Christian Remain a Roman Catholic?" in *Moody Monthly*, April 1982, p. 31.
16. Keating, *Catholicism and Fundamentalism*, pp. 82, 141.
17. Editorial, "What Separates Evangelicals and Catholics?" in *Christianity Today*, October 23, 1981, p. 13.
18. Ibid.
19. David F. Wells, *Revolution in Rome* (Downers Grove, IL: InterVarsity, 1972), p. 117.
20. Millard J. Erickson, *Christian Theology* (Grand Rapids: Baker, 1986), one-volume ed., p. 901.
21. David Wells, "The Long Winter of Wreckage," photocopy of lecture, n.d.
22. Ibid., p. 6.
23. Ibid., pp. 1, 2
24. Ibid., p. 2.
25. Ibid., p. 3.
26. Ibid.
27. Greg Burke, "Vatican Takes Aim at Fundamentalists," in *World*, April 9, 1994, p. 13.
28. Abbott, ed., p. 117.
29. Wells, "The Long Winter of Wreckage," pp. 3-4.
30. Ibid., p. 4.
31. Ibid., p. 5.
32. Ibid.
33. John Paul II, pp. 139-41.
34. Ibid.
35. Wells, "The Long Winter," p. 4.
36. Ibid.
37. Ibid., p. 6.

Other Good
Harvest House Reading

A WOMAN RIDES THE BEAST
by *Dave Hunt*

Virtually all attention these days is focused on the coming Antichrist—but he is only half the story. Many are amazed to discover in Revelation 17 that there is another mysterious character at the heart of prophecy—a woman who *rides* the beast. Tradition says she is connected with the church of Rome, but is such a view outdated? After all, today's Vatican is eager to join hands with Protestants worldwide. Hunt sifts through biblical truth and global events to present a well-defined portrait of the woman and her powerful place in the Antichrist's future empire.

ONCE A CATHOLIC
by *Tony Coffey*

More and more Catholics are asking, "Who speaks for God today?" "Is the papacy taught in Scripture?" "Is there a need for purgatory?" Whether it is birth control, confession, or the Virgin Mary, Catholics are wondering if the hierarchy of the Church is speaking for God—and should they listen? Tony Coffey, who grew up in the Catholic Church, shares the startling and life-changing answers to these questions and more with a loving, sensitive spirit. *Once a Catholic* offers real answers and great encouragement to people everywhere. Only when you realize who speaks for God can you really know and follow Him.

THE GOSPEL ACCORDING TO ROME
by *Jim McCarthy*

The Catholic Church has put on a new face, and both Catholics and evangelicals are confused: Just what *is* happening in the Catholic Church today? Have any key doctrinal views or beliefs changed? Drawing directly from the new *Catechism of the Catholic Church*, McCarthy answers those questions and more, and pinpoints with clarity and accuracy just where Roman Catholicism stands today in relation to Scripture. Most important of all, he emphasizes how Catholics can know with certainty the life-transforming power of Jesus Christ in their hearts.

THE "FACTS ON" SERIES

by *John Ankerberg* and *John Weldon*

John Ankerberg, host of the award-winning "The John Ankerberg Show," and author John Weldon deal with many controversial issues facing Christians and non-Christians alike. In concise 48-page booklets, Ankerberg and Weldon focus on the most relevant aspects of each subject in a readable, straightforward style. Topics range from astrology to the Masonic Lodge to rock music.